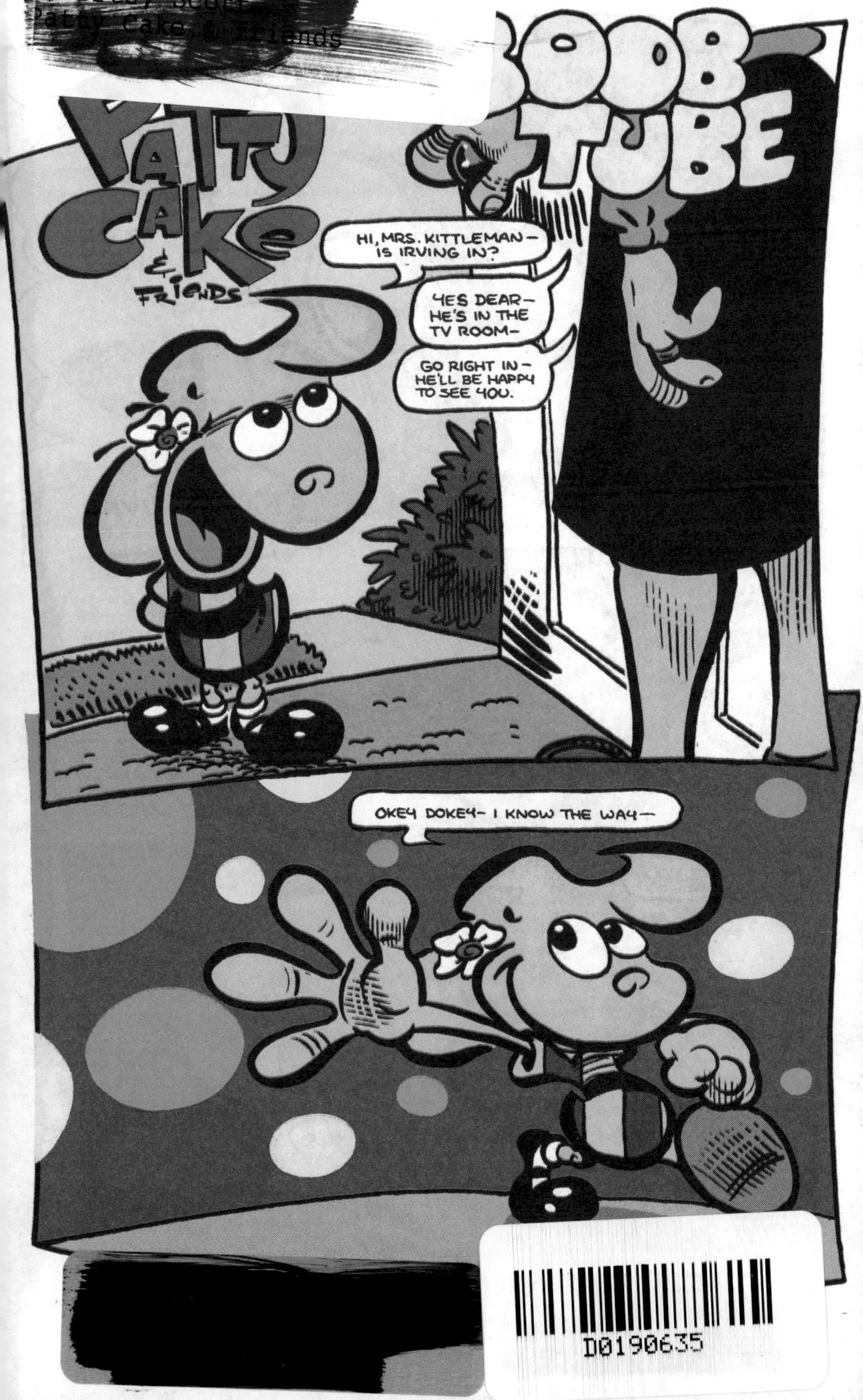
PATTY CAKE & FRIENDS
BOOB TUBE
HI, MRS. KITTLEMAN— IS IRVING IN?
YES DEAR— HE'S IN THE TV ROOM—
GO RIGHT IN— HE'LL BE HAPPY TO SEE YOU.
OKEY DOKEY— I KNOW THE WAY—

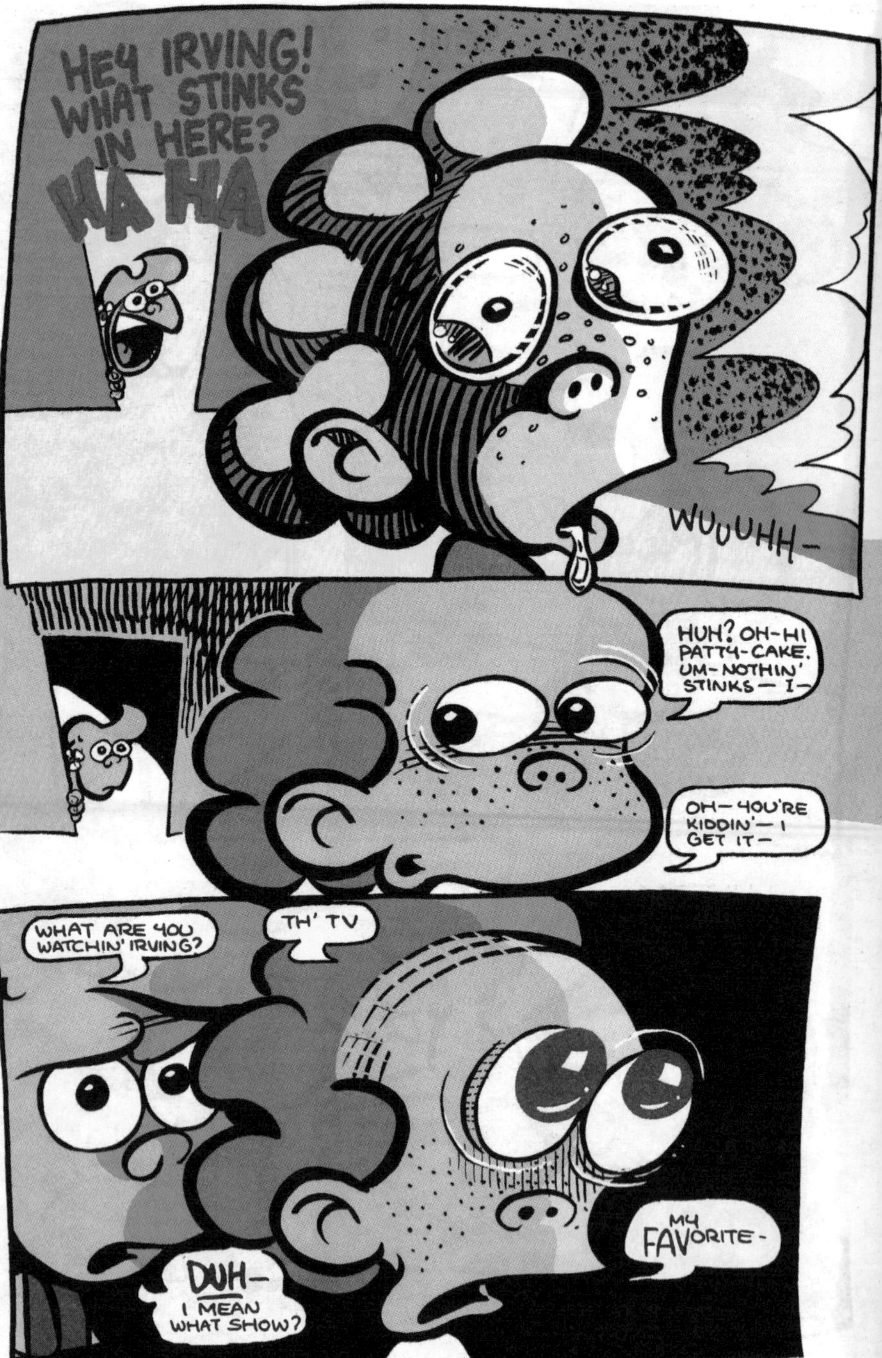
HEY IRVING! WHAT STINKS IN HERE?
HA HA
WUUUHH-
HUH? OH-HI PATTY-CAKE. UM-NOTHIN' STINKS — I—
OH— YOU'RE KIDDIN'— I GET IT—
WHAT ARE YOU WATCHIN' IRVING?
TH' TV
DUH- I MEAN WHAT SHOW?
MY FAVORITE-

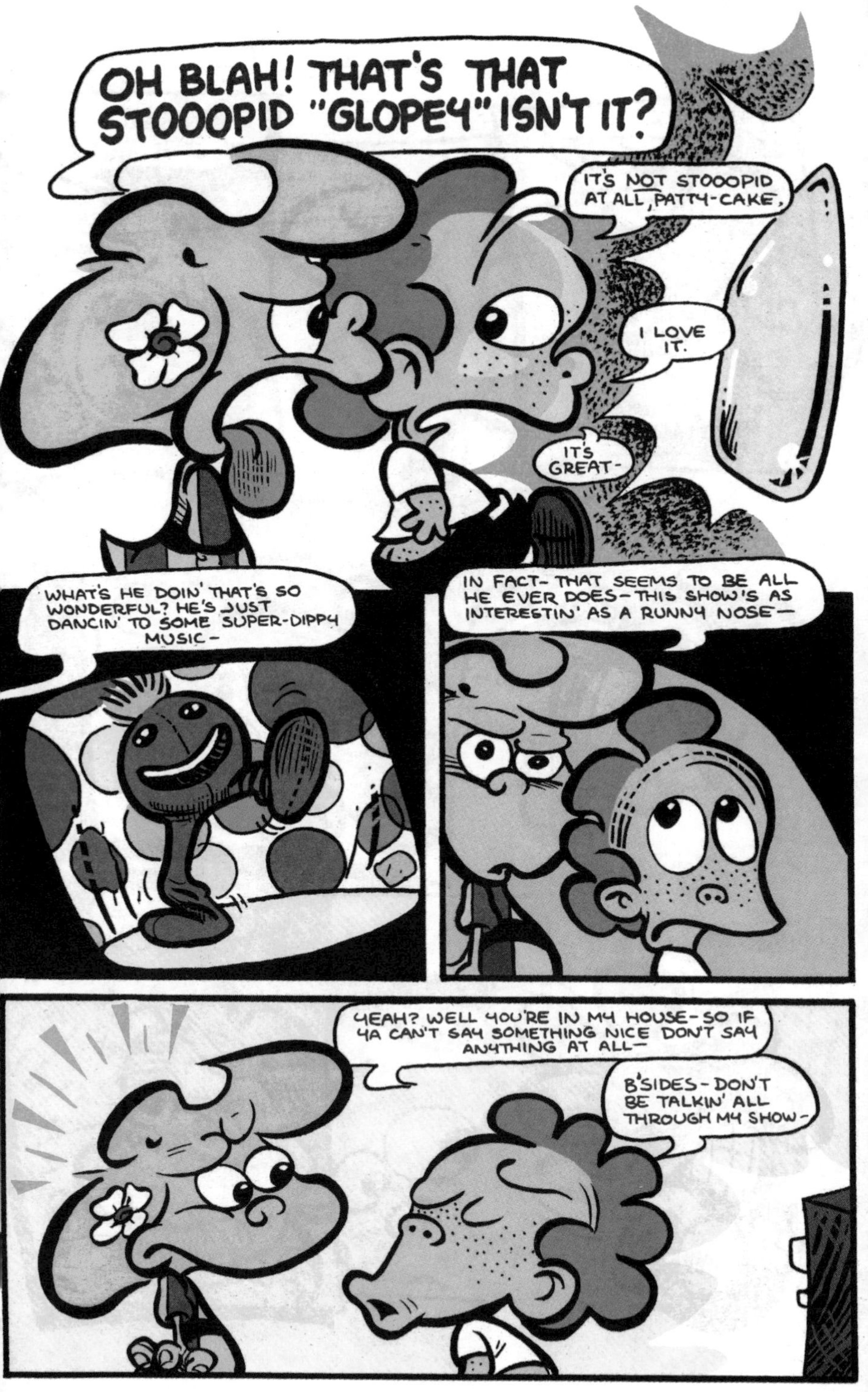
OH BLAH! THAT'S THAT STOOOPID "GLOPEY" ISN'T IT?
IT'S NOT STOOOPID AT ALL, PATTY-CAKE,
I LOVE IT.
IT'S GREAT-
WHAT'S HE DOIN' THAT'S SO WONDERFUL? HE'S JUST DANCIN' TO SOME SUPER-DIPPY MUSIC-
IN FACT- THAT SEEMS TO BE ALL HE EVER DOES- THIS SHOW'S AS INTERESTIN' AS A RUNNY NOSE-
YEAH? WELL YOU'RE IN MY HOUSE- SO IF YA CAN'T SAY SOMETHING NICE DON'T SAY ANYTHING AT ALL-
B'SIDES- DON'T BE TALKIN' ALL THROUGH MY SHOW-

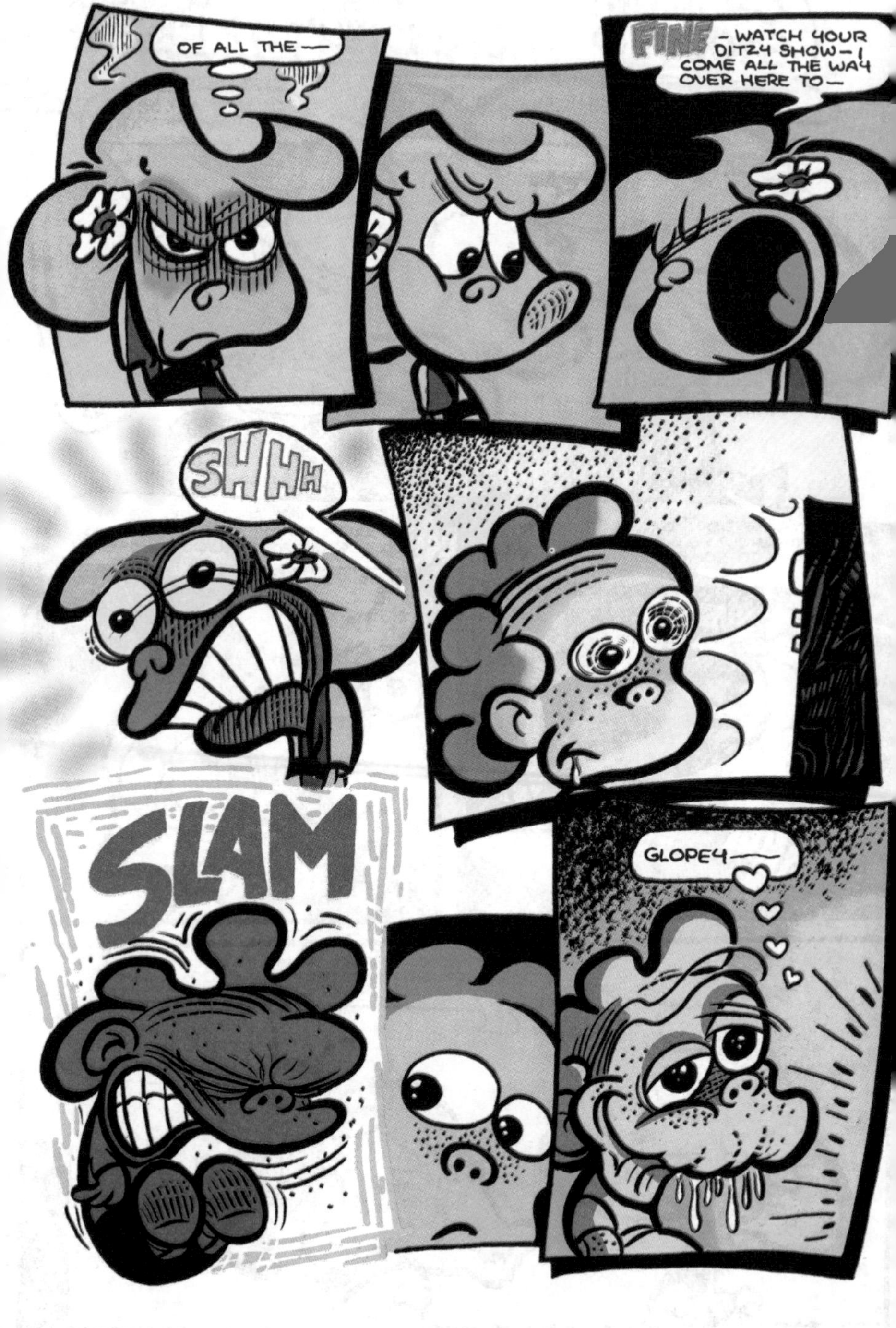

OF ALL THE—
FINE—WATCH YOUR DITZY SHOW—I COME ALL THE WAY OVER HERE TO—
SHHH
SLAM
GLOPEY——

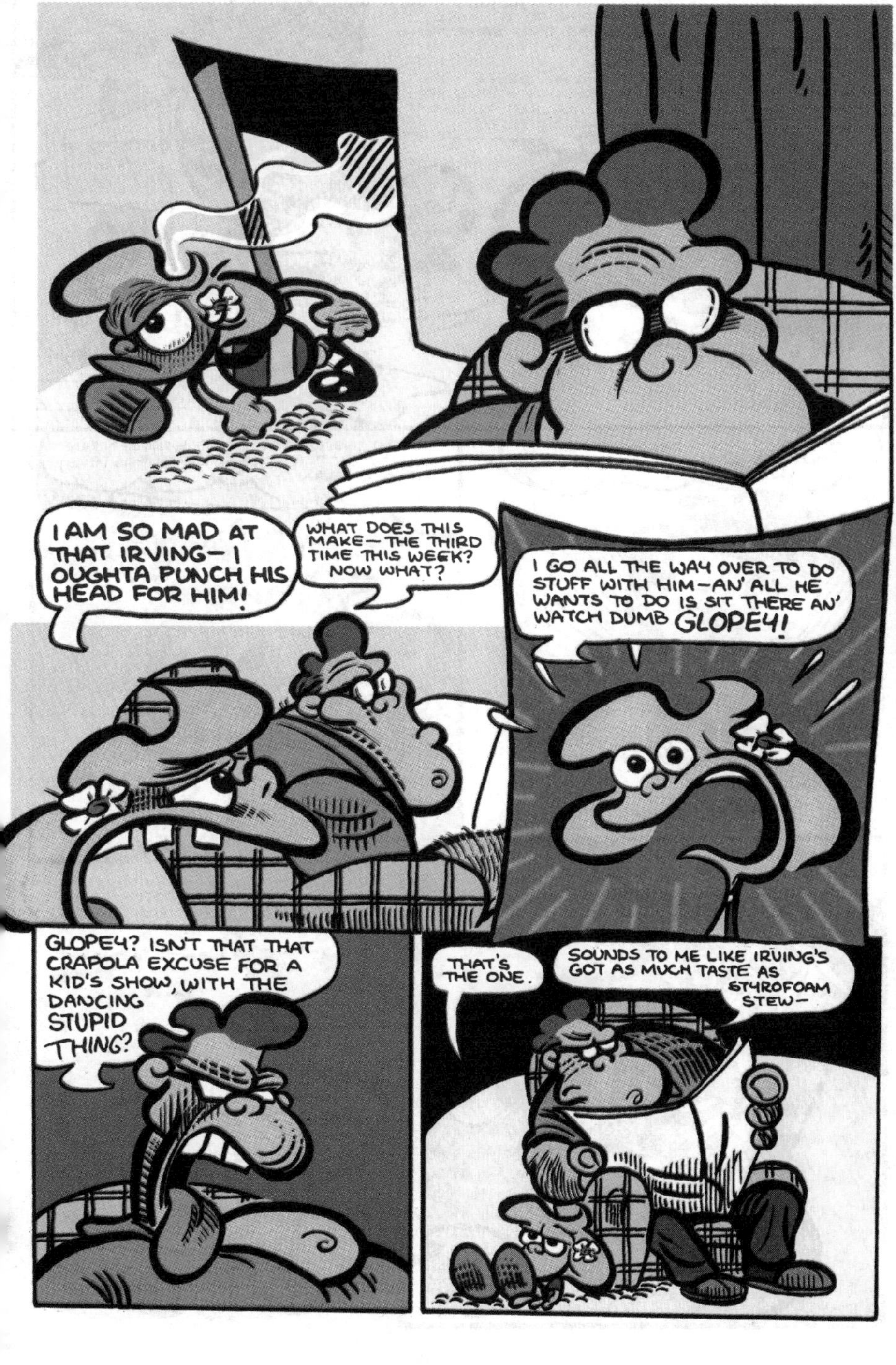
I AM SO MAD AT THAT IRVING— I OUGHTA PUNCH HIS HEAD FOR HIM!
WHAT DOES THIS MAKE— THE THIRD TIME THIS WEEK? NOW WHAT?
I GO ALL THE WAY OVER TO DO STUFF WITH HIM—AN' ALL HE WANTS TO DO IS SIT THERE AN' WATCH DUMB GLOPEY!
GLOPEY? ISN'T THAT THAT CRAPOLA EXCUSE FOR A KID'S SHOW, WITH THE DANCING STUPID THING?
THAT'S THE ONE.
SOUNDS TO ME LIKE IRVING'S GOT AS MUCH TASTE AS STYROFOAM STEW—

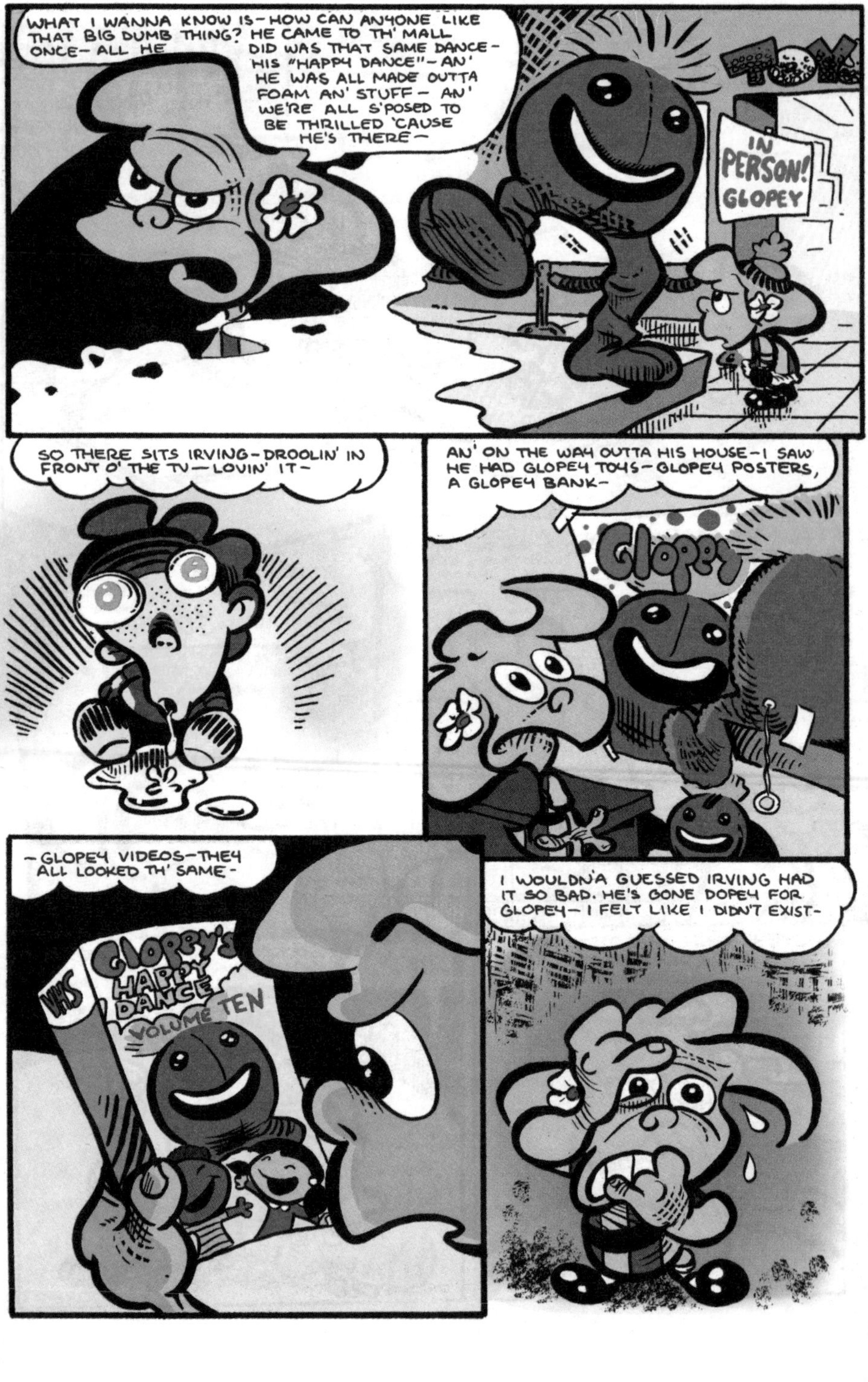
WHAT I WANNA KNOW IS— HOW CAN ANYONE LIKE THAT BIG DUMB THING? HE CAME TO TH' MALL ONCE— ALL HE DID WAS THAT SAME DANCE— HIS "HAPPY DANCE"— AN' HE WAS ALL MADE OUTTA FOAM AN' STUFF— AN' WE'RE ALL S'POSED TO BE THRILLED 'CAUSE HE'S THERE—
TOYS
IN PERSON! GLOPEY
SO THERE SITS IRVING— DROOLIN' IN FRONT O' THE TV— LOVIN' IT—
AN' ON THE WAY OUTTA HIS HOUSE— I SAW HE HAD GLOPEY TOYS— GLOPEY POSTERS, A GLOPEY BANK—
Glopey
—GLOPEY VIDEOS— THEY ALL LOOKED TH' SAME—
VHS
GLOPEY'S HAPPY DANCE
VOLUME TEN
I WOULDN'A GUESSED IRVING HAD IT SO BAD. HE'S GONE DOPEY FOR GLOPEY— I FELT LIKE I DIDN'T EXIST—

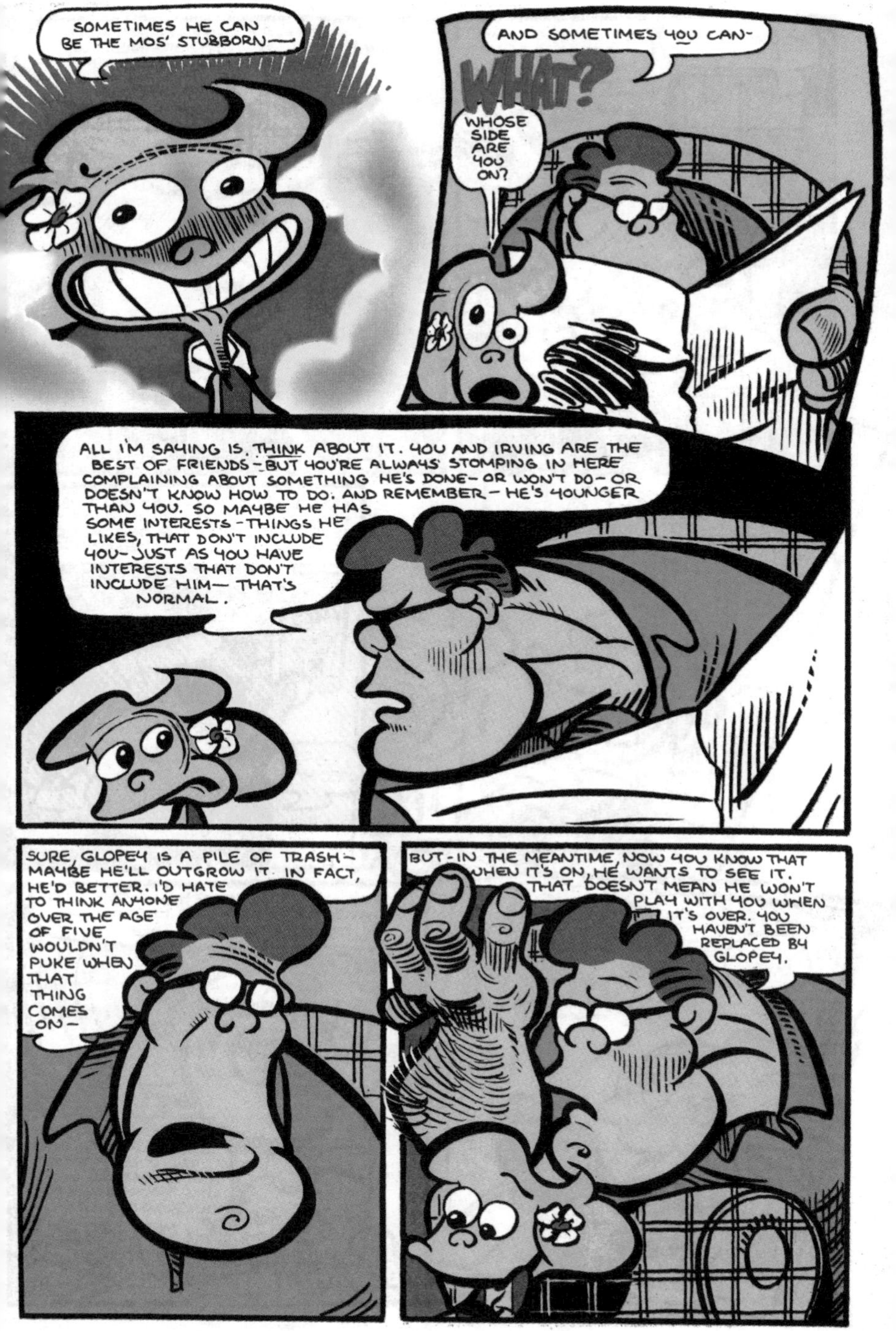

SOMETIMES HE CAN BE THE MOS' STUBBORN—
AND SOMETIMES YOU CAN-
WHAT?
WHOSE SIDE ARE YOU ON?
ALL I'M SAYING IS, THINK ABOUT IT. YOU AND IRVING ARE THE BEST OF FRIENDS - BUT YOU'RE ALWAYS STOMPING IN HERE COMPLAINING ABOUT SOMETHING HE'S DONE - OR WON'T DO - OR DOESN'T KNOW HOW TO DO. AND REMEMBER - HE'S YOUNGER THAN YOU. SO MAYBE HE HAS SOME INTERESTS - THINGS HE LIKES, THAT DON'T INCLUDE YOU - JUST AS YOU HAVE INTERESTS THAT DON'T INCLUDE HIM— THAT'S NORMAL.
SURE, GLOPEY IS A PILE OF TRASH— MAYBE HE'LL OUTGROW IT. IN FACT, HE'D BETTER. I'D HATE TO THINK ANYONE OVER THE AGE OF FIVE WOULDN'T PUKE WHEN THAT THING COMES ON—
BUT - IN THE MEANTIME, NOW YOU KNOW THAT WHEN IT'S ON, HE WANTS TO SEE IT. THAT DOESN'T MEAN HE WON'T PLAY WITH YOU WHEN IT'S OVER. YOU HAVEN'T BEEN REPLACED BY GLOPEY.

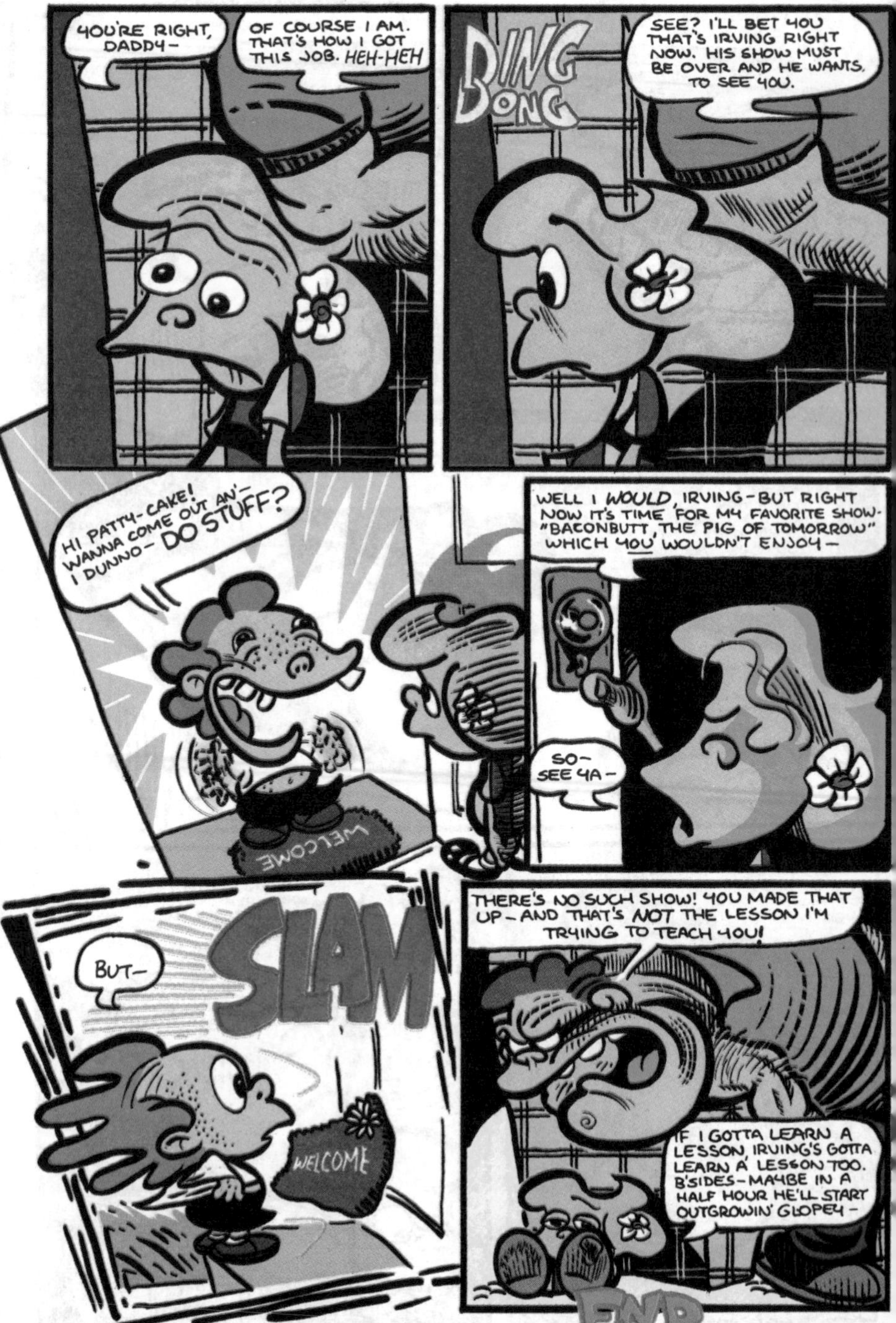
YOU'RE RIGHT, DADDY—
OF COURSE I AM. THAT'S HOW I GOT THIS JOB. HEH-HEH
DING DONG
SEE? I'LL BET YOU THAT'S IRVING RIGHT NOW. HIS SHOW MUST BE OVER AND HE WANTS TO SEE YOU.
HI PATTY-CAKE! WANNA COME OUT AN'— I DUNNO— DO STUFF?
WELCOME
WELL I WOULD, IRVING—BUT RIGHT NOW IT'S TIME FOR MY FAVORITE SHOW—"BACONBUTT, THE PIG OF TOMORROW" WHICH YOU WOULDN'T ENJOY—
SO— SEE YA—
BUT—
SLAM
WELCOME
THERE'S NO SUCH SHOW! YOU MADE THAT UP—AND THAT'S NOT THE LESSON I'M TRYING TO TEACH YOU!
IF I GOTTA LEARN A LESSON, IRVING'S GOTTA LEARN A LESSON TOO. B'SIDES—MAYBE IN A HALF HOUR HE'LL START OUTGROWIN' GLOPEY—
END

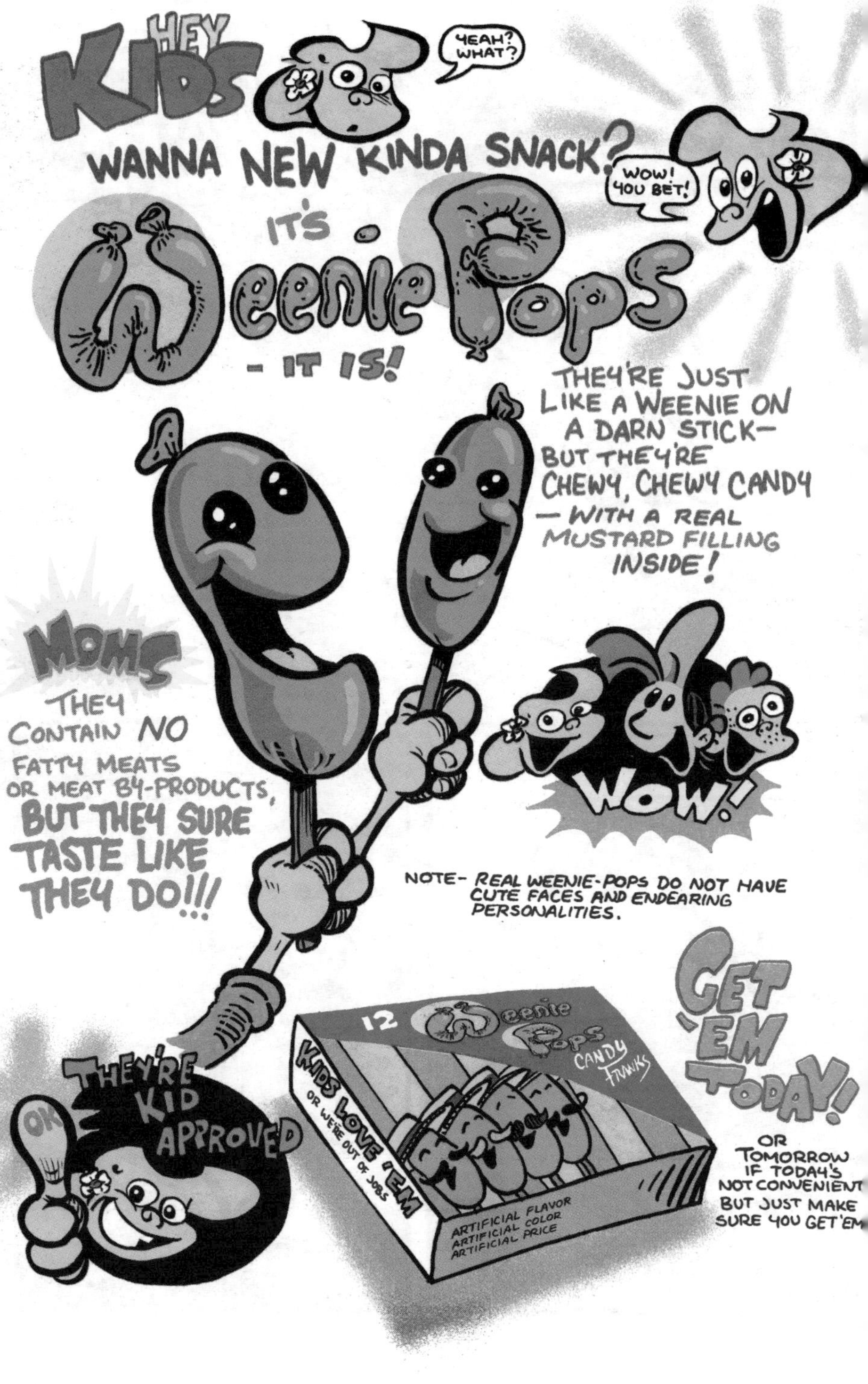
HEY KIDS
YEAH? WHAT?
WANNA NEW KINDA SNACK?
WOW! YOU BET!
IT'S - WEENIE POPS - IT IS!
THEY'RE JUST LIKE A WEENIE ON A DARN STICK— BUT THEY'RE CHEWY, CHEWY CANDY — WITH A REAL MUSTARD FILLING INSIDE!
MOMS
THEY CONTAIN NO FATTY MEATS OR MEAT BY-PRODUCTS, BUT THEY SURE TASTE LIKE THEY DO!!!
WOW!
NOTE- REAL WEENIE-POPS DO NOT HAVE CUTE FACES AND ENDEARING PERSONALITIES.
GET 'EM TODAY!
OR TOMORROW IF TODAY'S NOT CONVENIENT BUT JUST MAKE SURE YOU GET 'EM
12 WEENIE POPS CANDY FRANKS
KIDS LOVE 'EM
OR WE'RE OUT OF JOBS
ARTIFICIAL FLAVOR
ARTIFICIAL COLOR
ARTIFICIAL PRICE
OK
THEY'RE KID APPROVED

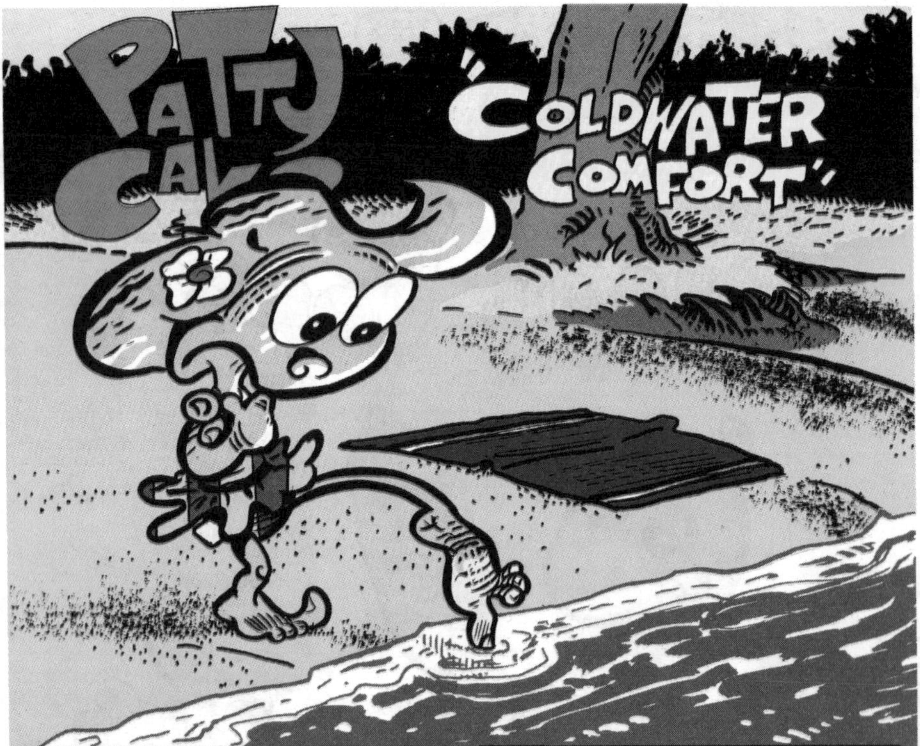
PATTY CAKE
"COLDWATER COMFORT"

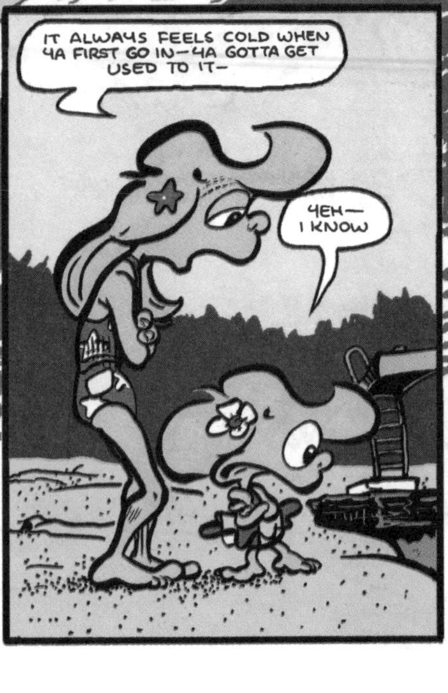
IT ALWAYS FEELS COLD WHEN YA FIRST GO IN—YA GOTTA GET USED TO IT—
YEH— I KNOW

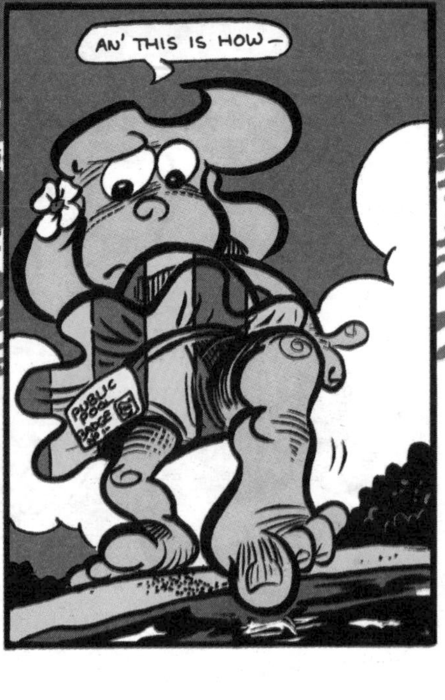
AN' THIS IS HOW—
PUBLIC POOL

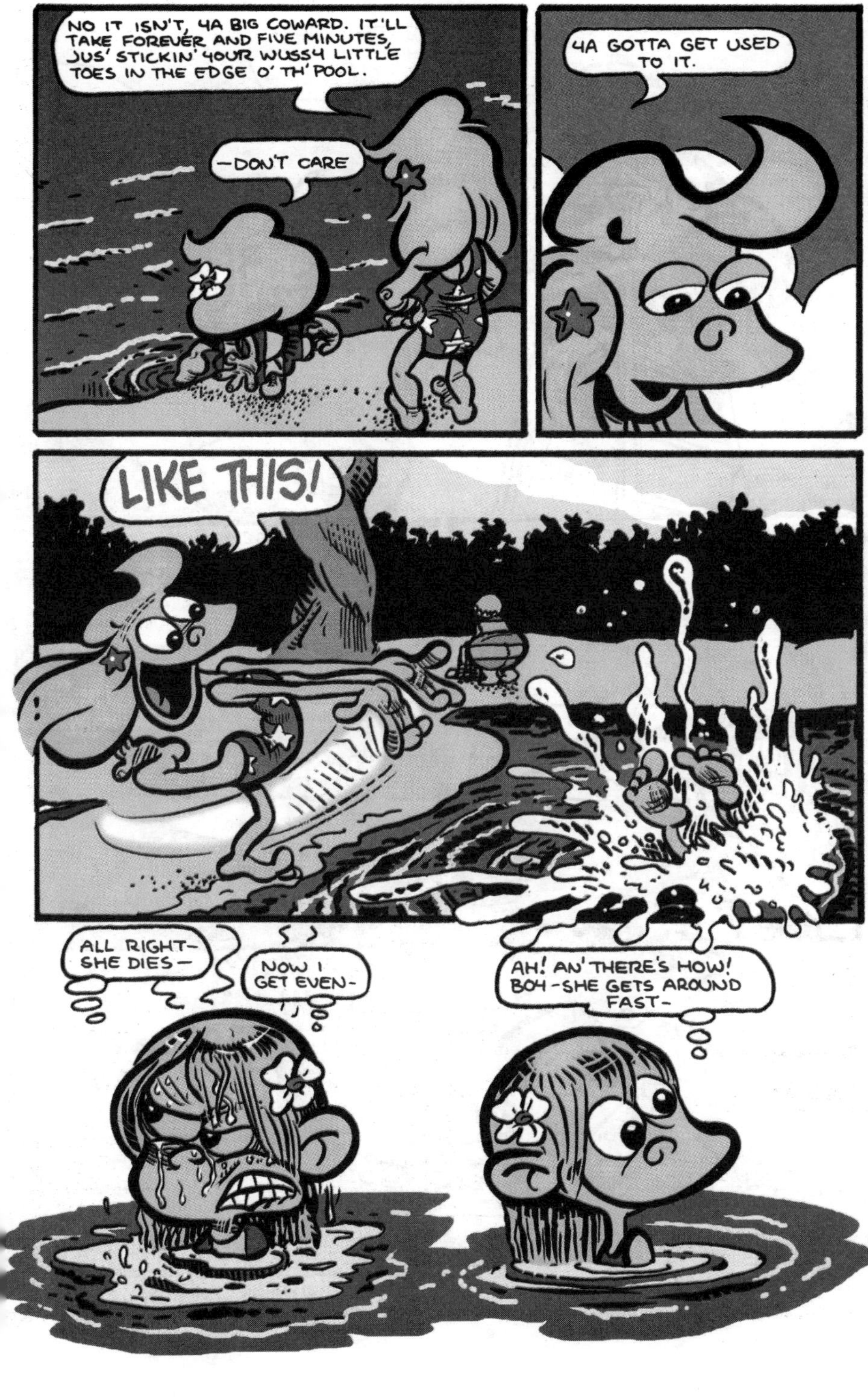
NO IT ISN'T, YA BIG COWARD. IT'LL TAKE FOREVER AND FIVE MINUTES, JUS' STICKIN' YOUR WUSSY LITTLE TOES IN THE EDGE O' TH' POOL.
—DON'T CARE
YA GOTTA GET USED TO IT.
LIKE THIS!
ALL RIGHT-SHE DIES—
NOW I GET EVEN-
AH! AN' THERE'S HOW! BOY -SHE GETS AROUND FAST-

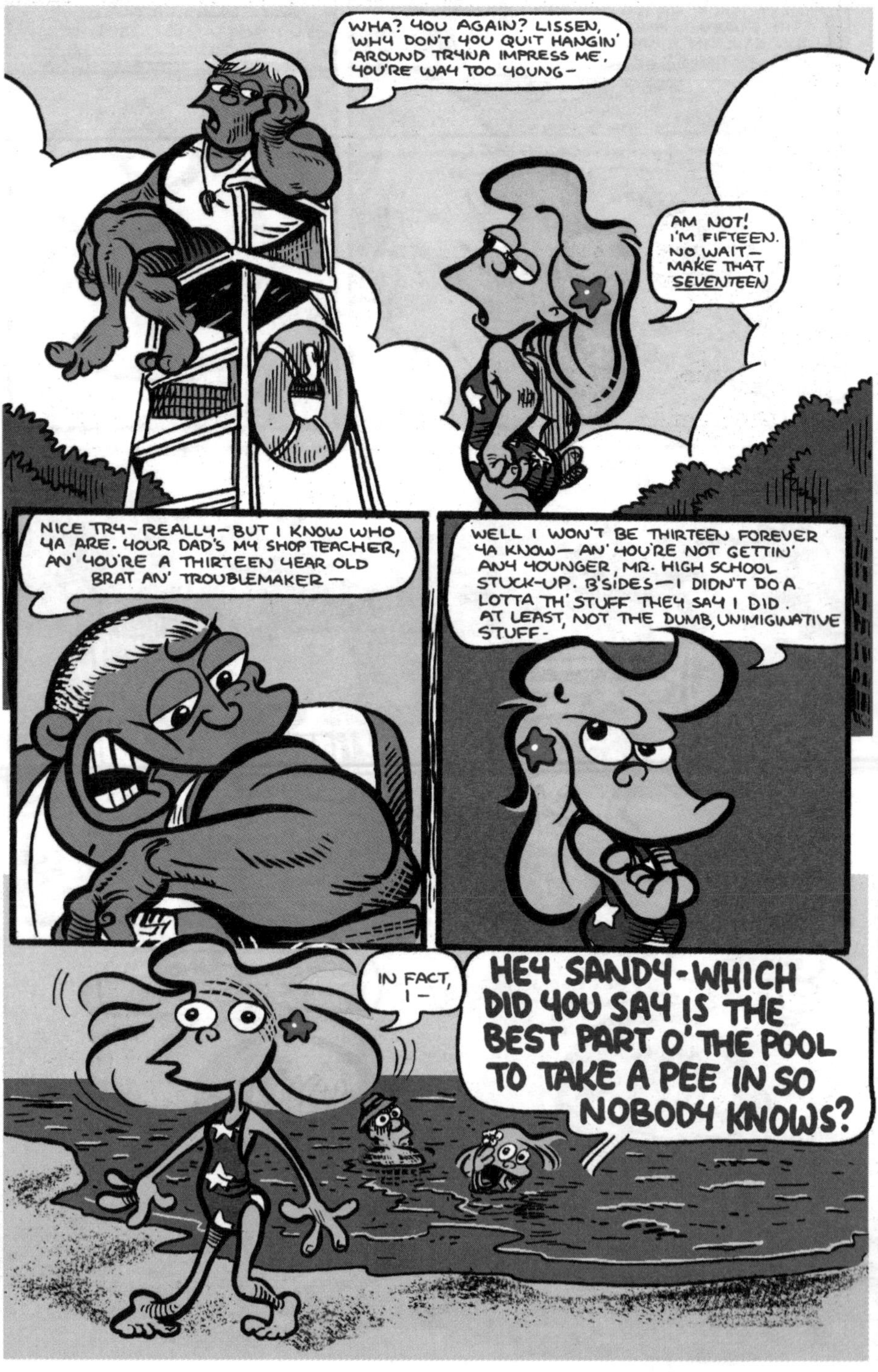
WHA? YOU AGAIN? LISSEN, WHY DON'T YOU QUIT HANGIN' AROUND TRYNA IMPRESS ME. YOU'RE WAY TOO YOUNG—
AM NOT! I'M FIFTEEN. NO WAIT— MAKE THAT SEVENTEEN
NICE TRY— REALLY— BUT I KNOW WHO YA ARE. YOUR DAD'S MY SHOP TEACHER, AN' YOU'RE A THIRTEEN YEAR OLD BRAT AN' TROUBLEMAKER—
WELL I WON'T BE THIRTEEN FOREVER YA KNOW— AN' YOU'RE NOT GETTIN' ANY YOUNGER, MR. HIGH SCHOOL STUCK-UP. B'SIDES—I DIDN'T DO A LOTTA TH' STUFF THEY SAY I DID. AT LEAST, NOT THE DUMB, UNIMIGINATIVE STUFF-
IN FACT, I—
HEY SANDY-WHICH DID YOU SAY IS THE BEST PART O' THE POOL TO TAKE A PEE IN SO NOBODY KNOWS?

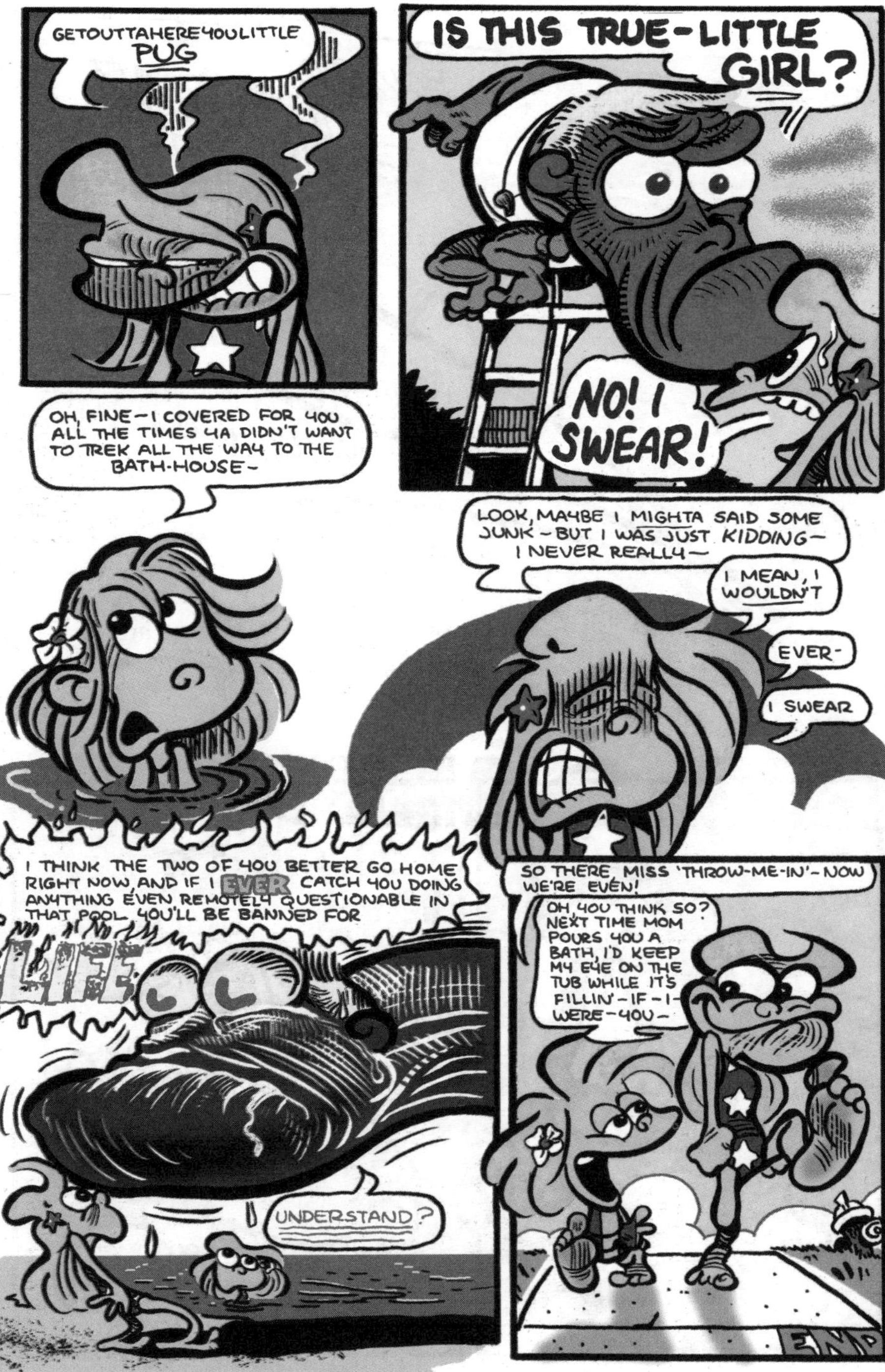
GETOUTTAHEREYOULITTLE PUG
IS THIS TRUE-LITTLE GIRL?
NO! I SWEAR!
OH, FINE-I COVERED FOR YOU ALL THE TIMES YA DIDN'T WANT TO TREK ALL THE WAY TO THE BATH-HOUSE-
LOOK, MAYBE I MIGHTA SAID SOME JUNK-BUT I WAS JUST KIDDING-I NEVER REALLY-
I MEAN, I WOULDN'T
EVER-
I SWEAR
I THINK THE TWO OF YOU BETTER GO HOME RIGHT NOW, AND IF I EVER CATCH YOU DOING ANYTHING EVEN REMOTELY QUESTIONABLE IN THAT POOL, YOU'LL BE BANNED FOR
LIFE
UNDERSTAND?
SO THERE, MISS 'THROW-ME-IN'-NOW WE'RE EVEN!
OH, YOU THINK SO? NEXT TIME MOM POURS YOU A BATH, I'D KEEP MY EYE ON THE TUB WHILE IT'S FILLIN'-IF-I WERE-YOU-
END

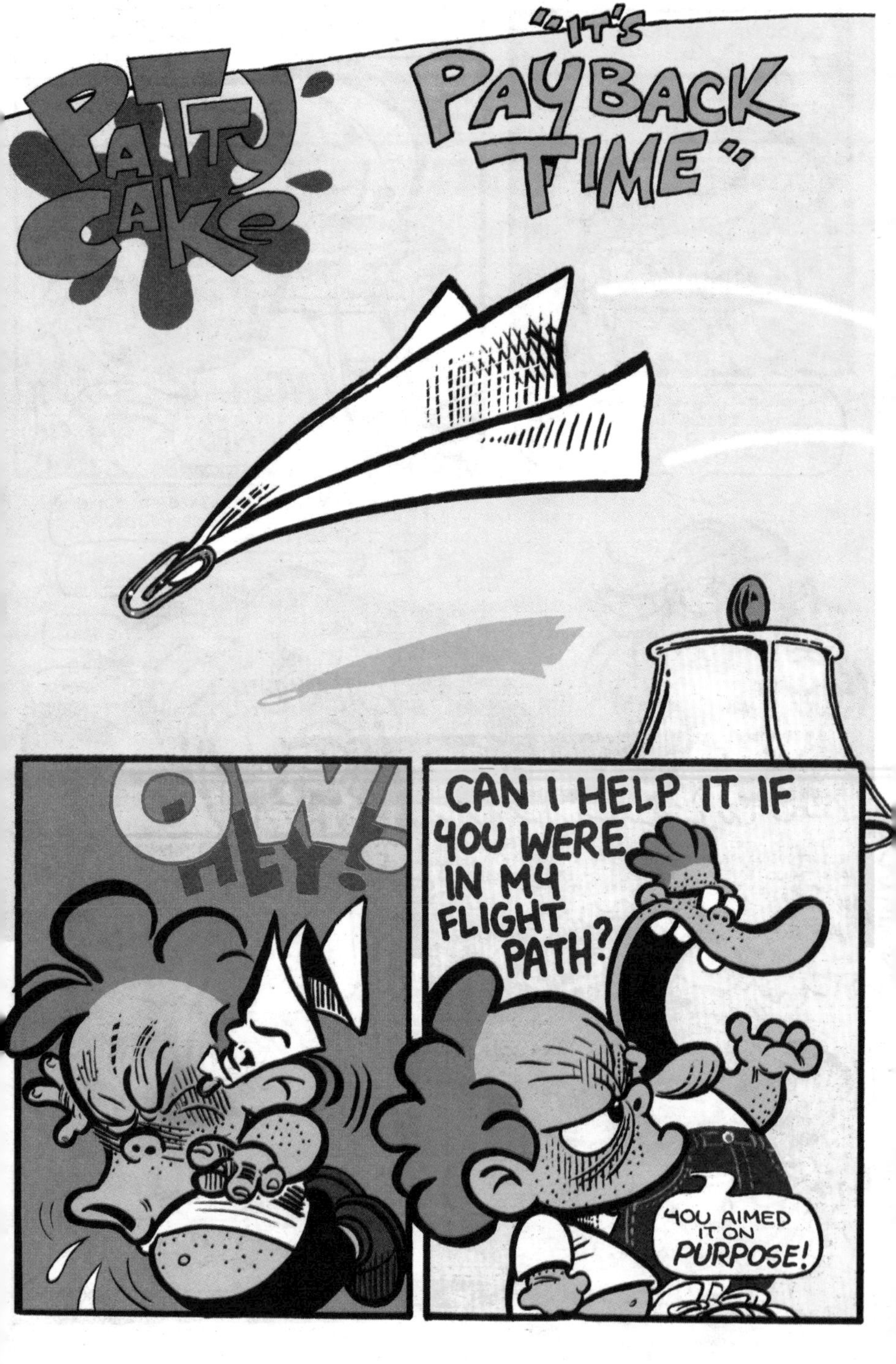
PATTY CAKE
"IT'S PAYBACK TIME"
OW!
HEY!
CAN I HELP IT IF YOU WERE IN MY FLIGHT PATH?
YOU AIMED IT ON PURPOSE!

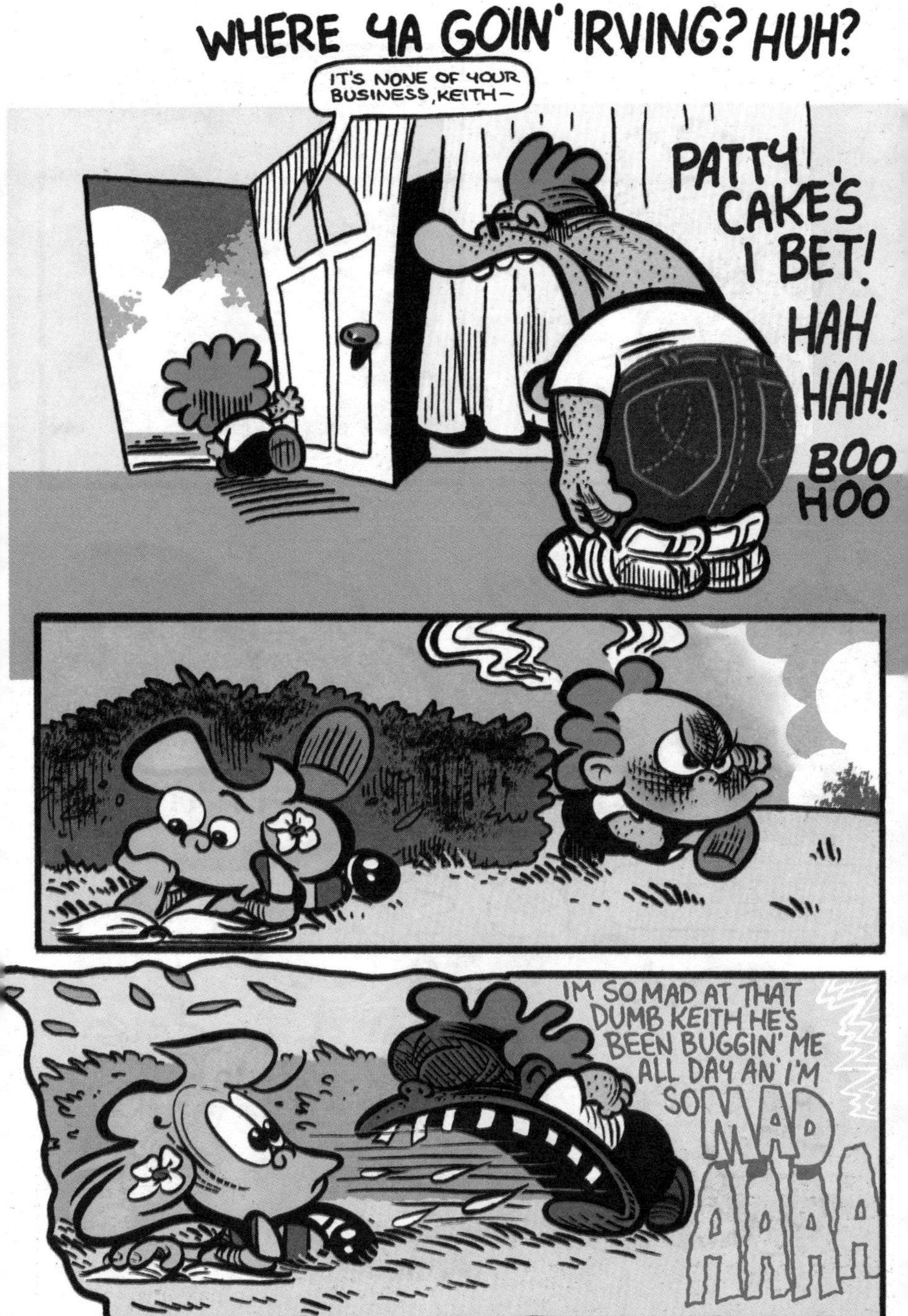
WHERE YA GOIN' IRVING? HUH?
IT'S NONE OF YOUR BUSINESS, KEITH—
PATTY CAKE'S I BET! HAH HAH! BOO HOO
IM SO MAD AT THAT DUMB KEITH HE'S BEEN BUGGIN' ME ALL DAY AN' I'M SO MAD
AAAA

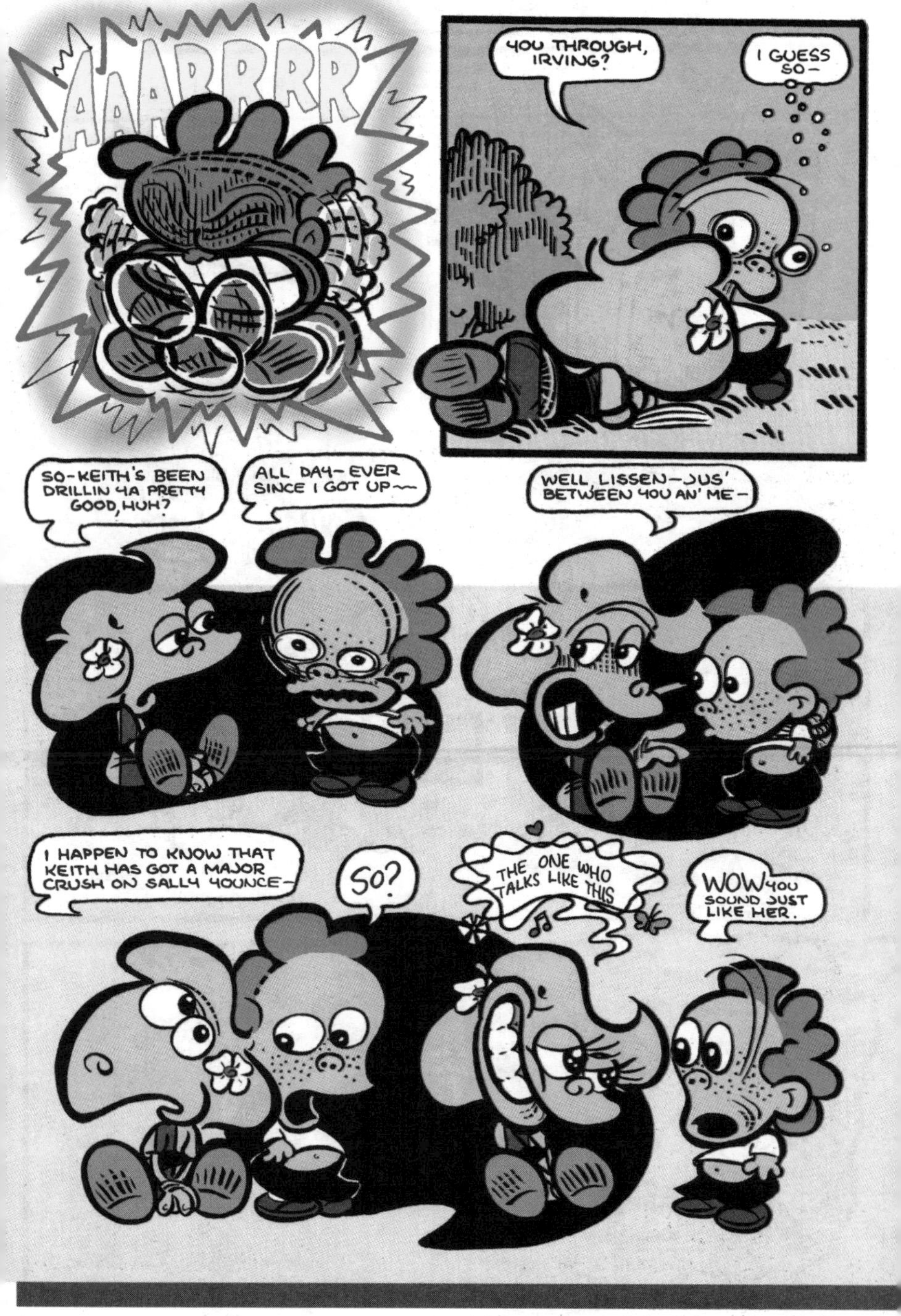
AAARRRR
YOU THROUGH, IRVING?
I GUESS SO—
SO—KEITH'S BEEN DRILLIN YA PRETTY GOOD, HUH?
ALL DAY—EVER SINCE I GOT UP~~
WELL LISSEN—JUS' BETWEEN YOU AN' ME—
I HAPPEN TO KNOW THAT KEITH HAS GOT A MAJOR CRUSH ON SALLY YOUNCE—
SO?
THE ONE WHO TALKS LIKE THIS
WOW YOU SOUND JUST LIKE HER.

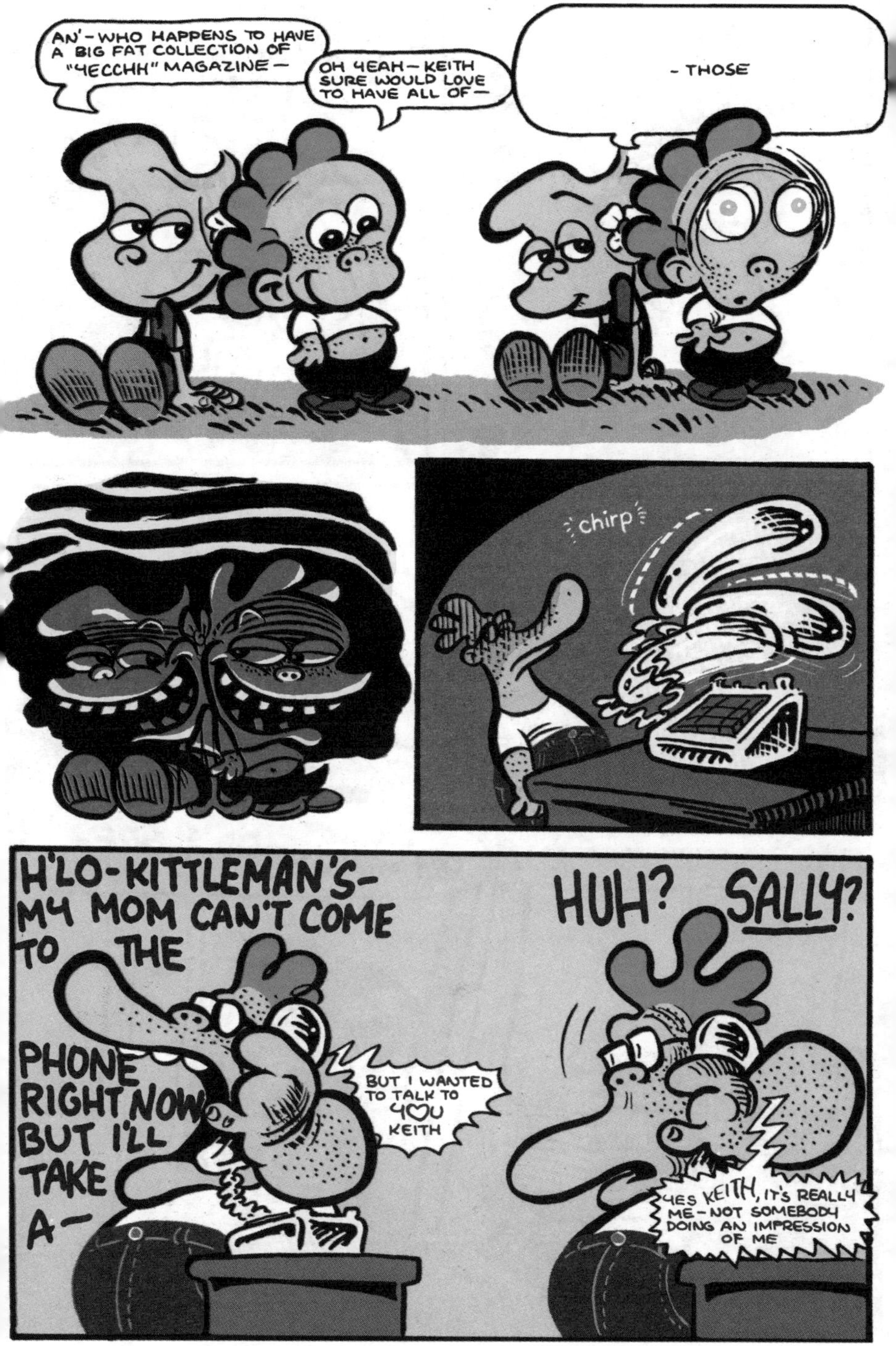
AN' - WHO HAPPENS TO HAVE A BIG FAT COLLECTION OF "YECCHH" MAGAZINE -
OH YEAH - KEITH SURE WOULD LOVE TO HAVE ALL OF -
- THOSE
chirp
H'LO-KITTLEMAN'S- MY MOM CAN'T COME TO THE PHONE RIGHT NOW BUT I'LL TAKE A -
BUT I WANTED TO TALK TO YOU KEITH
HUH? SALLY?
YES KEITH, IT'S REALLY ME - NOT SOMEBODY DOING AN IMPRESSION OF ME

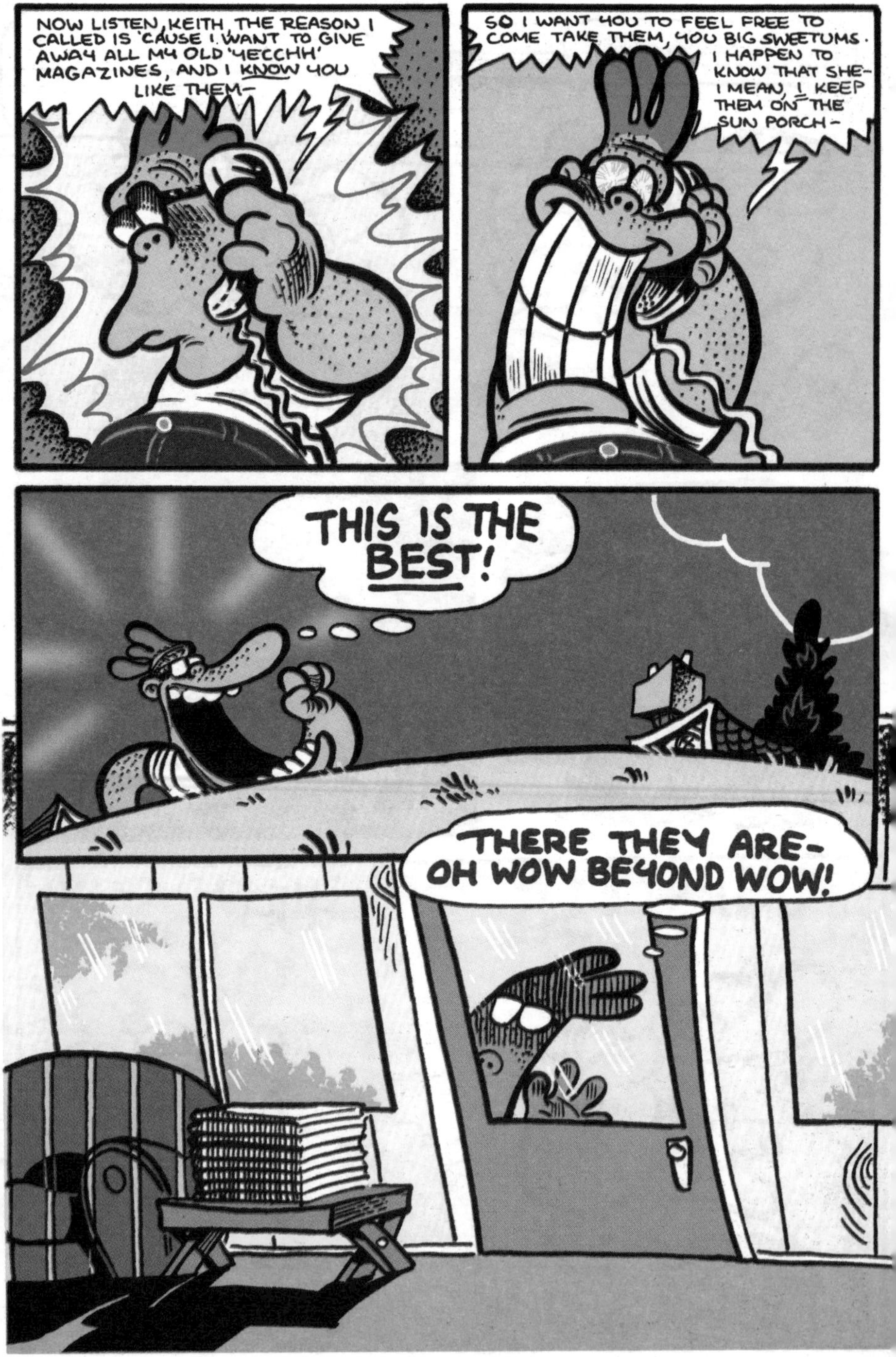
NOW LISTEN, KEITH, THE REASON I CALLED IS 'CAUSE I WANT TO GIVE AWAY ALL MY OLD 'YECCHH' MAGAZINES, AND I KNOW YOU LIKE THEM-
SO I WANT YOU TO FEEL FREE TO COME TAKE THEM, YOU BIG SWEETUMS. I HAPPEN TO KNOW THAT SHE- I MEAN, I KEEP THEM ON THE SUN PORCH-
THIS IS THE BEST!
THERE THEY ARE- OH WOW BEYOND WOW!

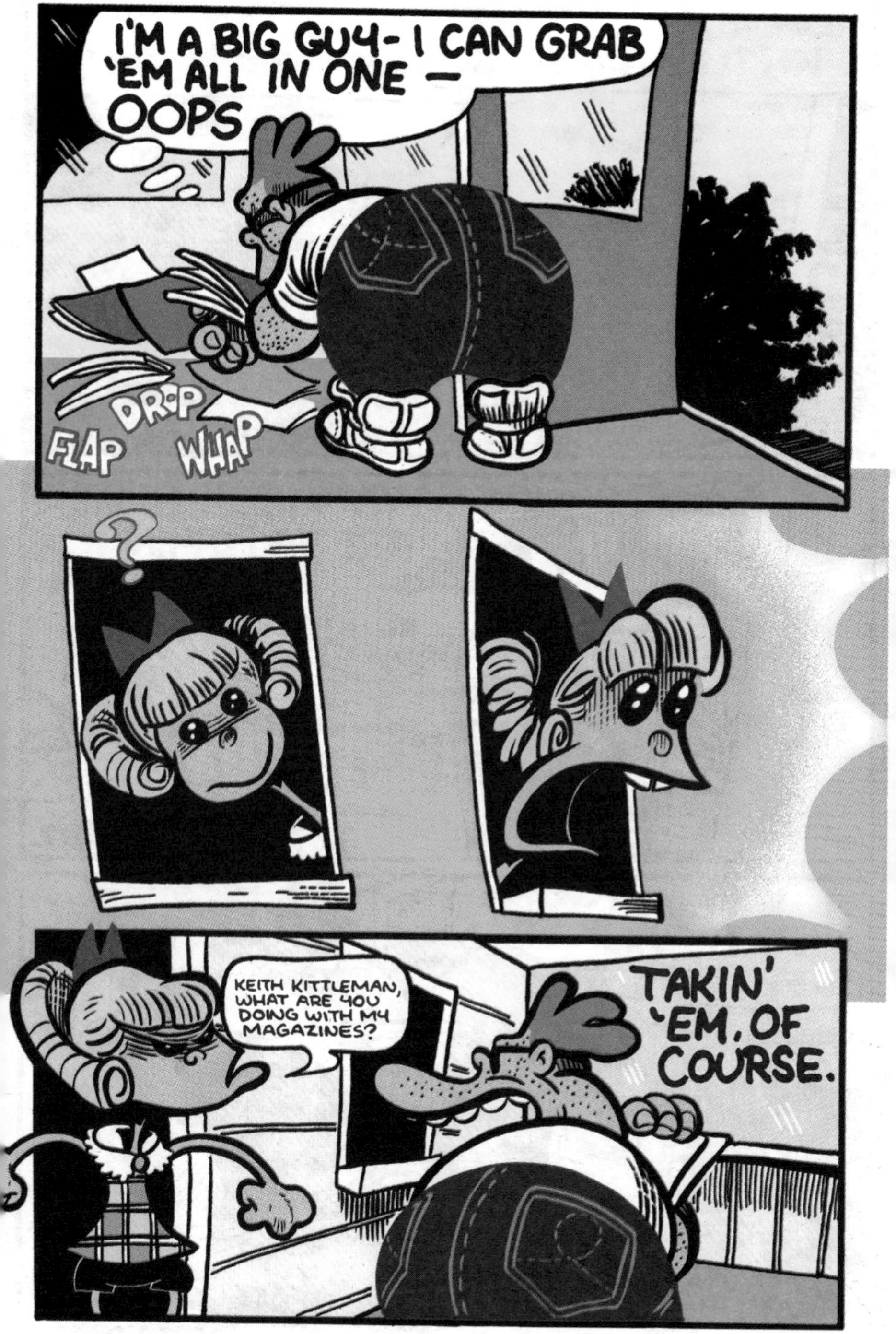
I'M A BIG GUY- I CAN GRAB 'EM ALL IN ONE — OOPS
DROP
FLAP
WHAP
KEITH KITTLEMAN, WHAT ARE YOU DOING WITH MY MAGAZINES?
TAKIN' 'EM, OF COURSE.

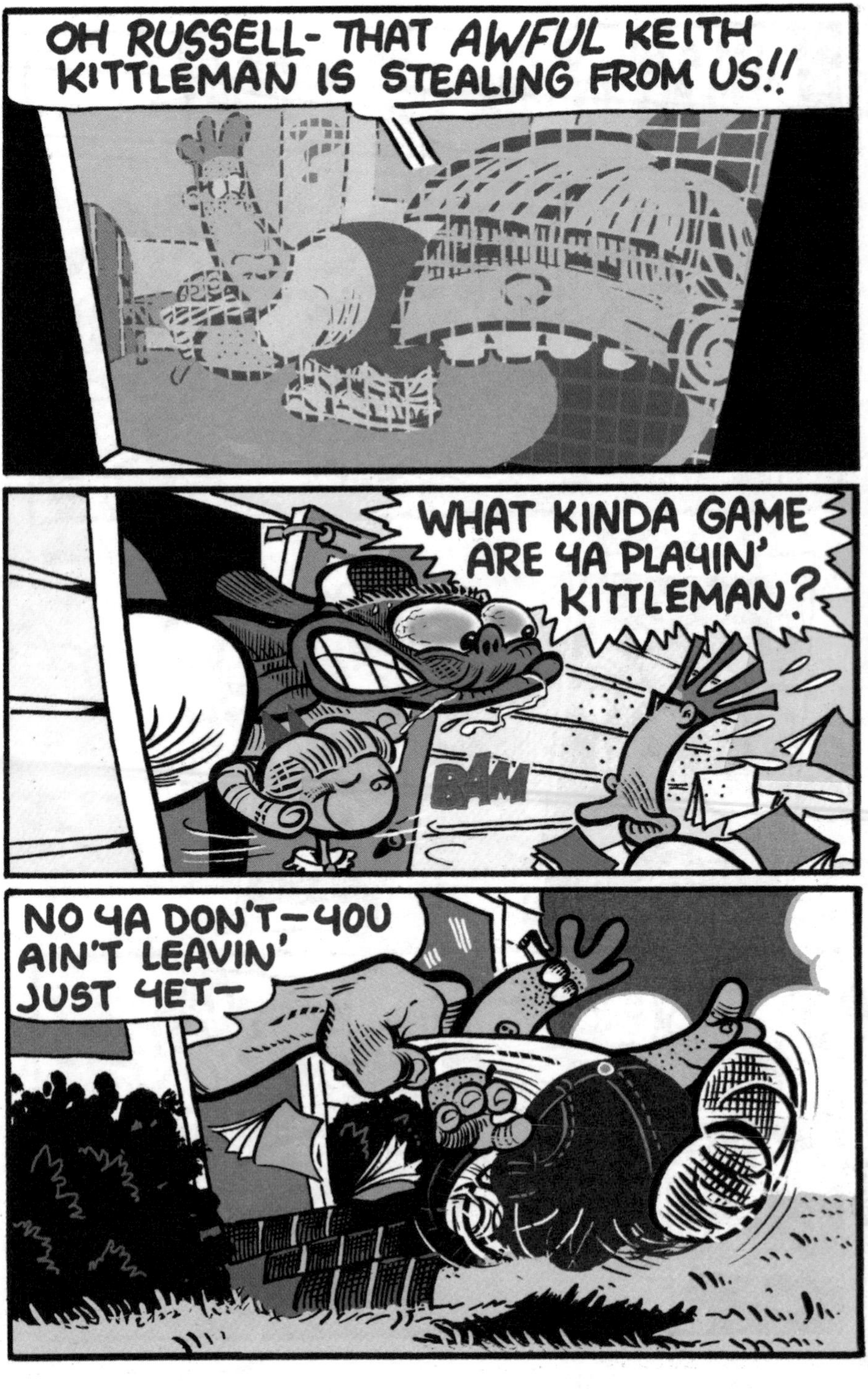
OH RUSSELL- THAT AWFUL KEITH KITTLEMAN IS STEALING FROM US!!
WHAT KINDA GAME ARE YA PLAYIN' KITTLEMAN?
BAM
NO YA DON'T- YOU AIN'T LEAVIN' JUST YET-

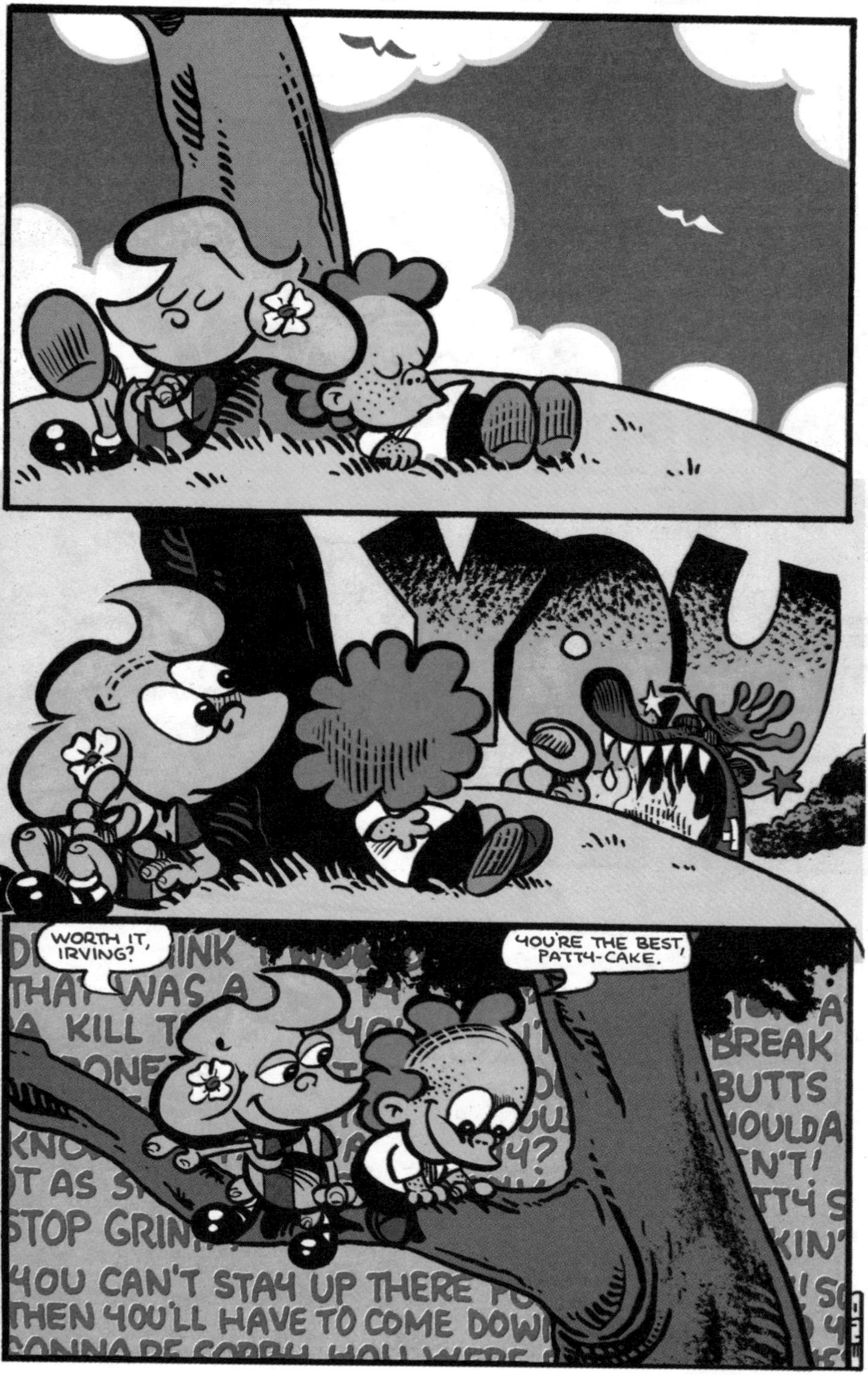
YOU
WORTH IT, IRVING?
YOU'RE THE BEST, PATTY-CAKE.
THAT WAS A
KILL
BREAK
BUTTS
STOP GRIN
YOU CAN'T STAY UP THERE
THEN YOU'LL HAVE TO COME DOW

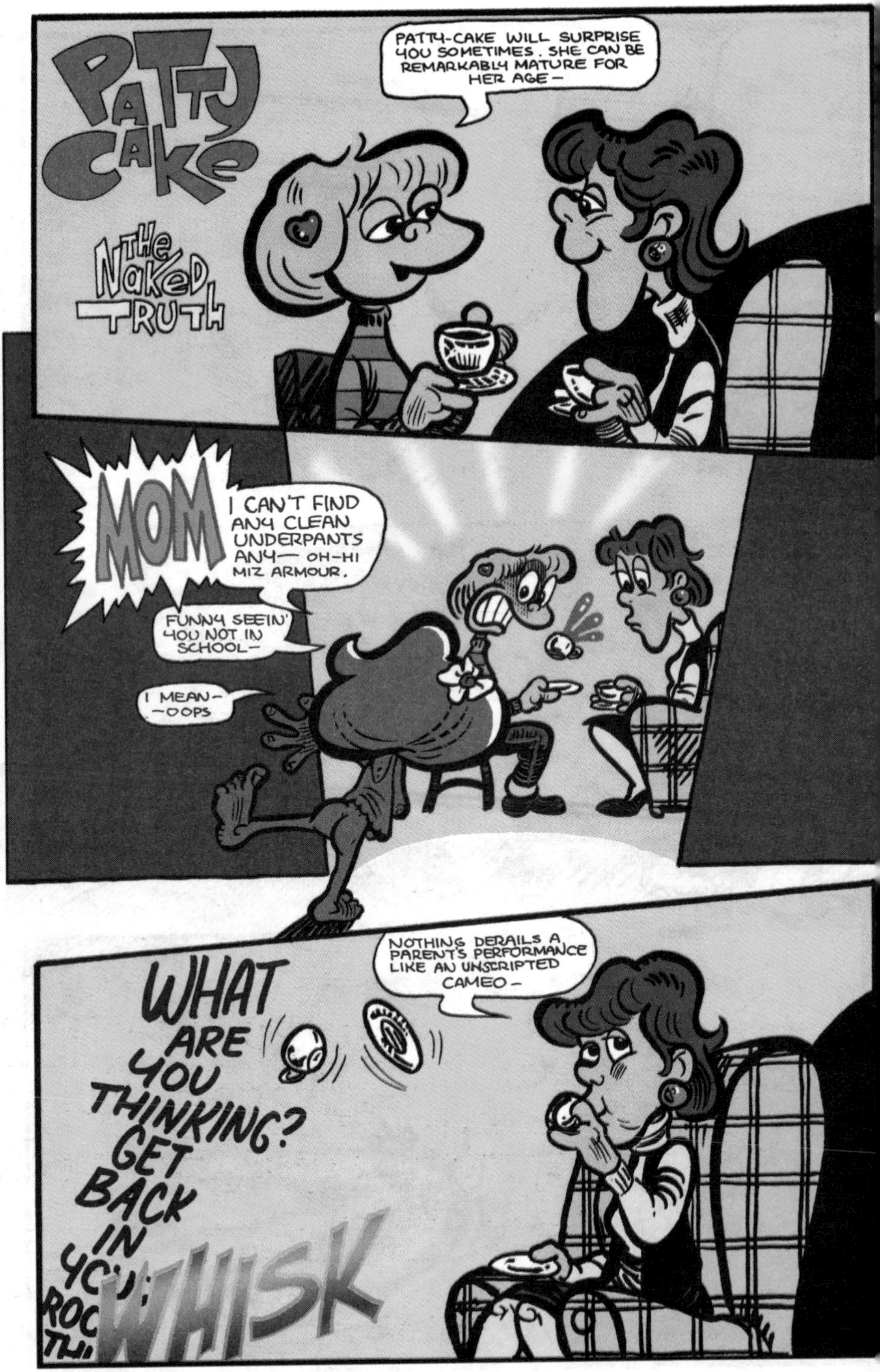
PATTY CAKE
THE NAKED TRUTH
PATTY-CAKE WILL SURPRISE YOU SOMETIMES. SHE CAN BE REMARKABLY MATURE FOR HER AGE–
MOM
I CAN'T FIND ANY CLEAN UNDERPANTS ANY— OH-HI MIZ ARMOUR.
FUNNY SEEIN' YOU NOT IN SCHOOL–
I MEAN– –OOPS
NOTHING DERAILS A PARENT'S PERFORMANCE LIKE AN UNSCRIPTED CAMEO–
WHAT ARE YOU THINKING? GET BACK IN
WHISK

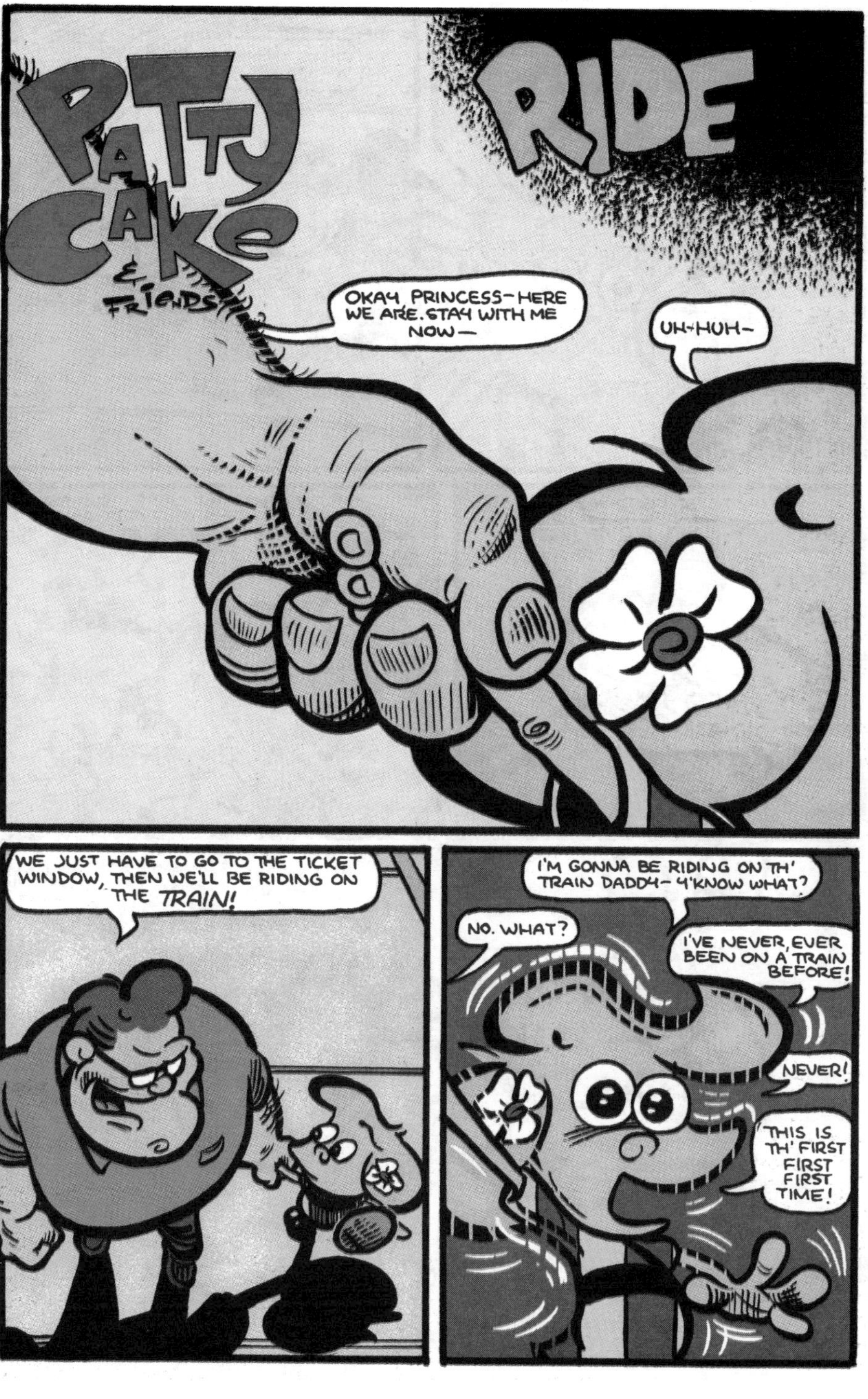
PATTY CAKE & FRIENDS
RIDE
OKAY PRINCESS—HERE WE ARE. STAY WITH ME NOW—
UH-HUH—
WE JUST HAVE TO GO TO THE TICKET WINDOW, THEN WE'LL BE RIDING ON THE TRAIN!
I'M GONNA BE RIDING ON TH' TRAIN DADDY—Y'KNOW WHAT?
NO. WHAT?
I'VE NEVER, EVER BEEN ON A TRAIN BEFORE!
NEVER!
THIS IS TH' FIRST FIRST FIRST TIME!

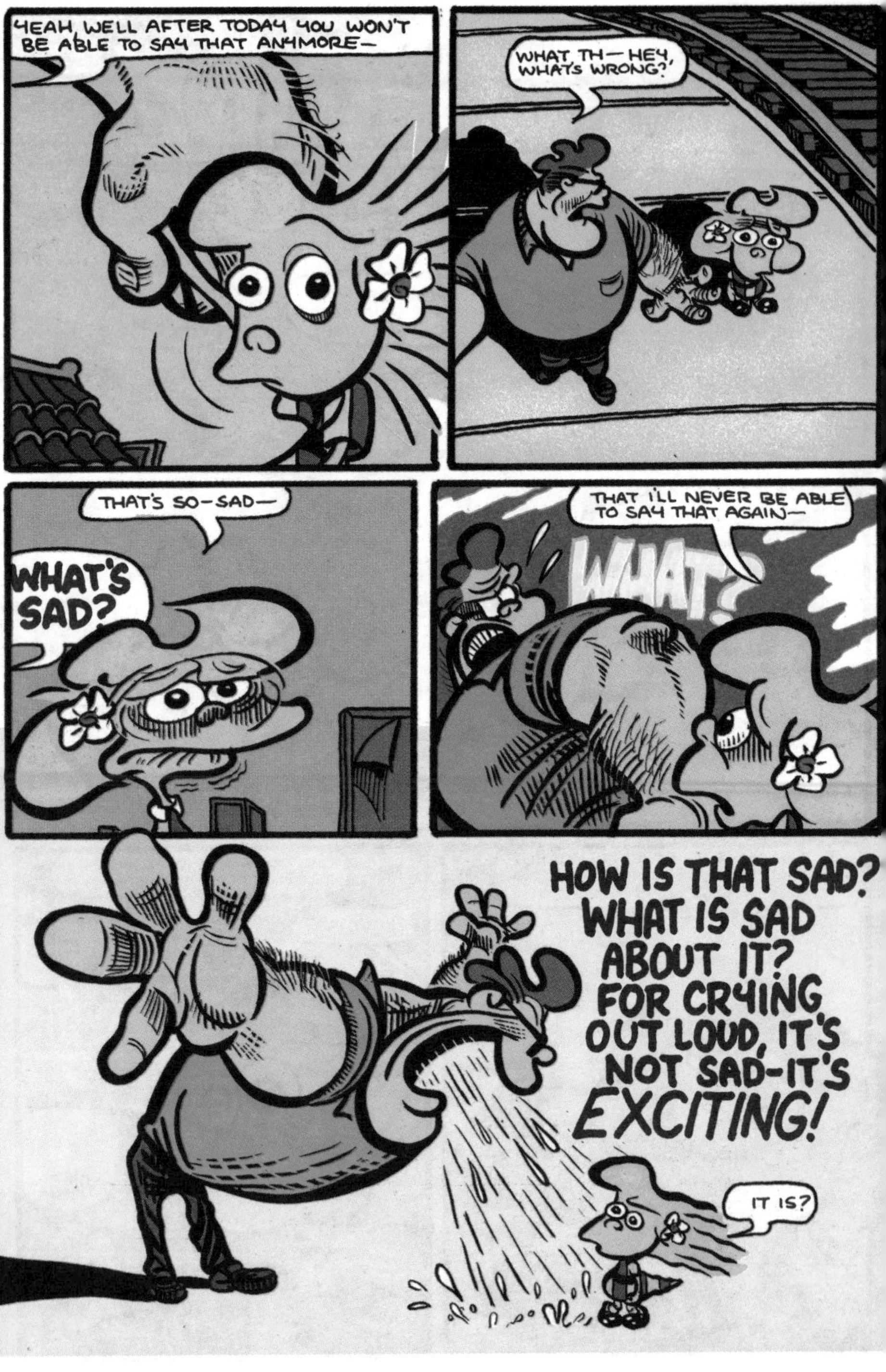
YEAH, WELL AFTER TODAY YOU WON'T BE ABLE TO SAY THAT ANYMORE—
WHAT TH—HEY, WHAT'S WRONG?
THAT'S SO—SAD—
WHAT'S SAD?
THAT I'LL NEVER BE ABLE TO SAY THAT AGAIN—
WHAT?
HOW IS THAT SAD? WHAT IS SAD ABOUT IT? FOR CRYING OUT LOUD, IT'S NOT SAD-IT'S EXCITING!
IT IS?

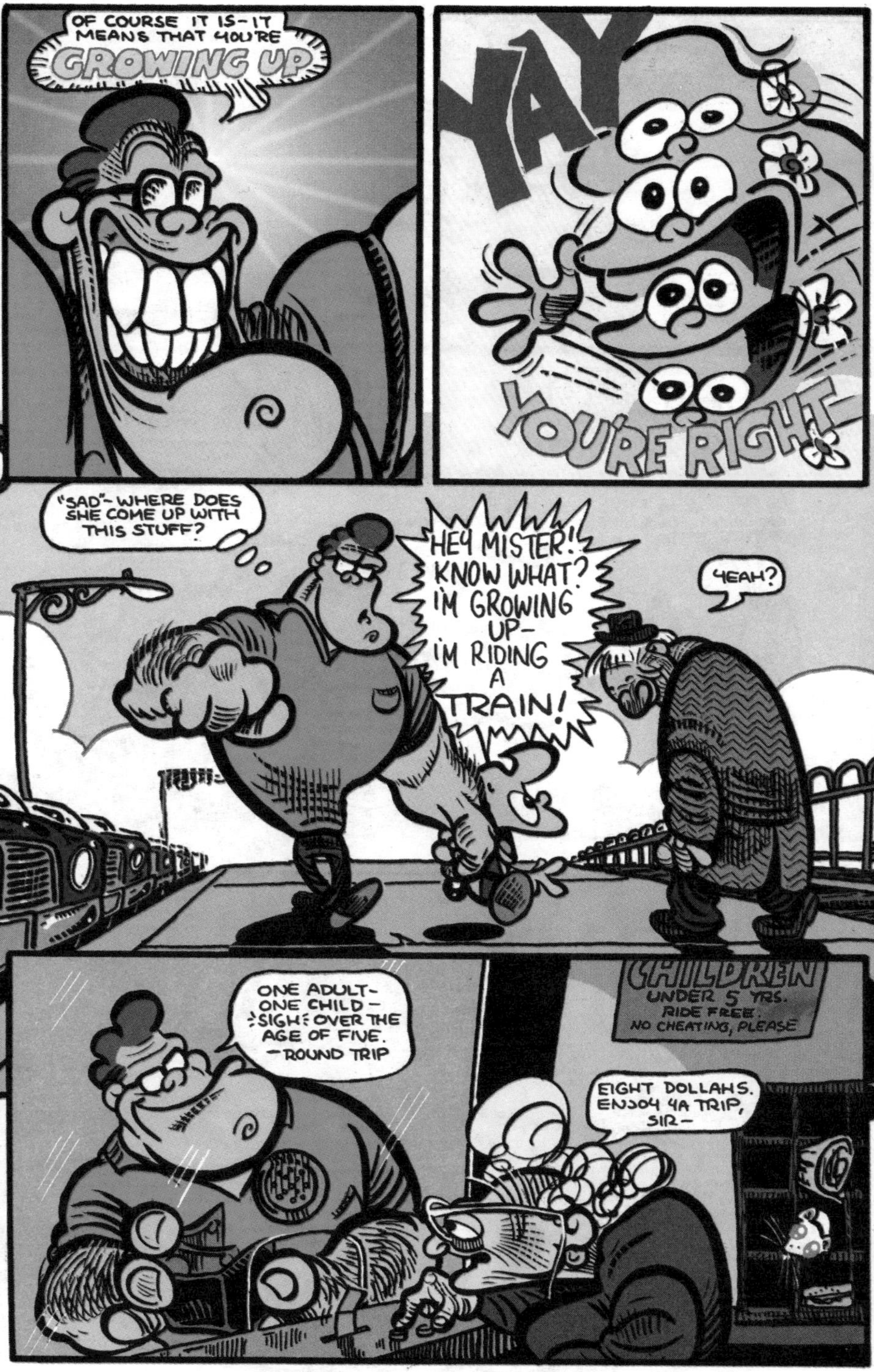
OF COURSE IT IS—IT MEANS THAT YOU'RE GROWING UP
YAY
YOU'RE RIGHT!
"SAD"—WHERE DOES SHE COME UP WITH THIS STUFF?
HEY MISTER! KNOW WHAT? I'M GROWING UP— I'M RIDING A TRAIN!
YEAH?
ONE ADULT—ONE CHILD— :SIGH: OVER THE AGE OF FIVE. —ROUND TRIP
CHILDREN UNDER 5 YRS. RIDE FREE. NO CHEATING, PLEASE
EIGHT DOLLAHS. ENJOY YA TRIP, SIR—

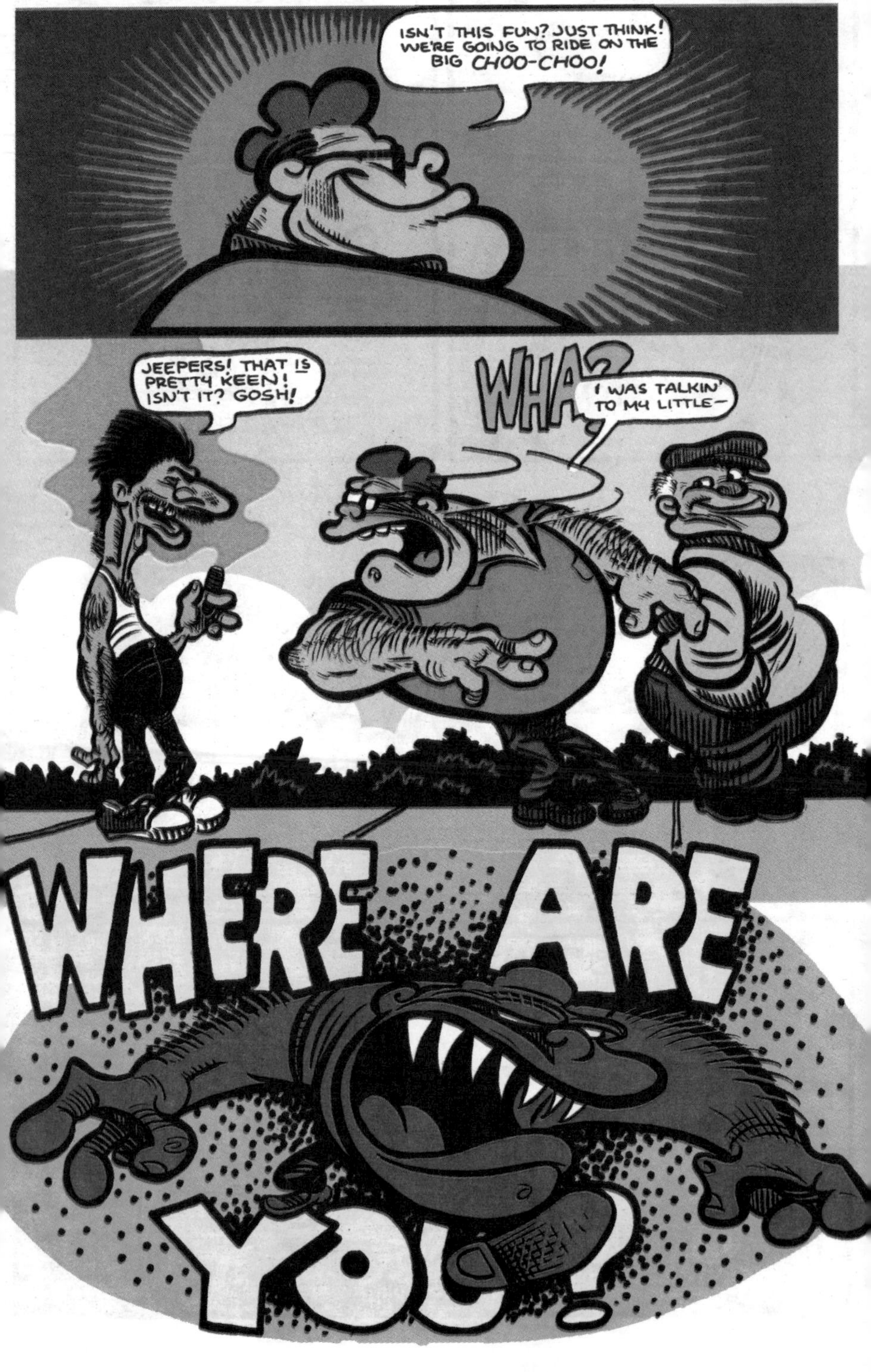
ISN'T THIS FUN? JUST THINK! WE'RE GOING TO RIDE ON THE BIG CHOO-CHOO!
JEEPERS! THAT IS PRETTY KEEN! ISN'T IT? GOSH!
WHA?
I WAS TALKIN' TO MY LITTLE—
WHERE ARE YOU?

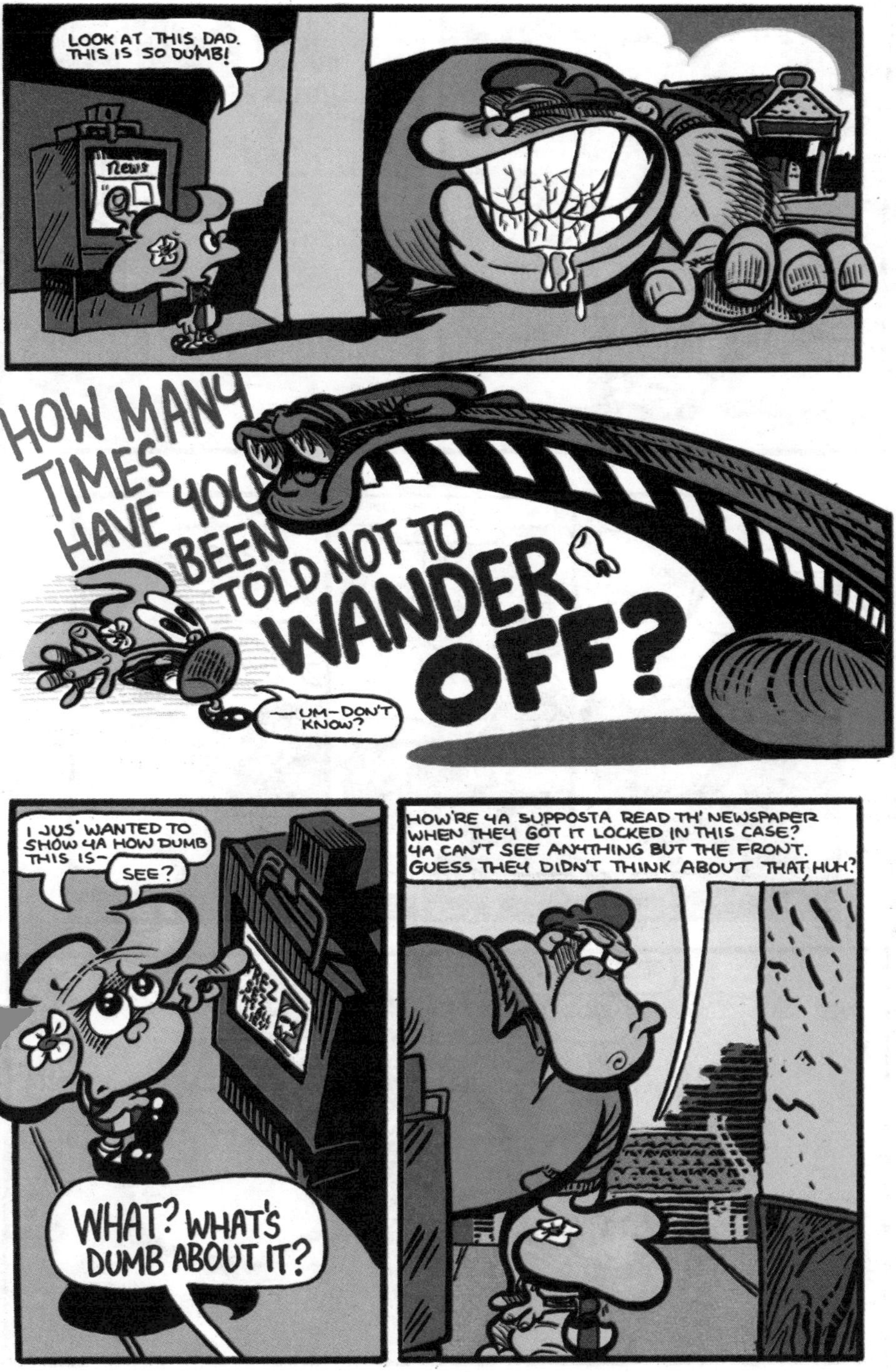
LOOK AT THIS DAD. THIS IS SO DUMB!
HOW MANY TIMES HAVE YOU BEEN TOLD NOT TO WANDER OFF?
—UM—DON'T KNOW?
I JUS' WANTED TO SHOW YA HOW DUMB THIS IS—
SEE?
WHAT? WHAT'S DUMB ABOUT IT?
HOW'RE YA SUPPOSTA READ TH' NEWSPAPER WHEN THEY GOT IT LOCKED IN THIS CASE? YA CAN'T SEE ANYTHING BUT THE FRONT. GUESS THEY DIDN'T THINK ABOUT THAT, HUH?

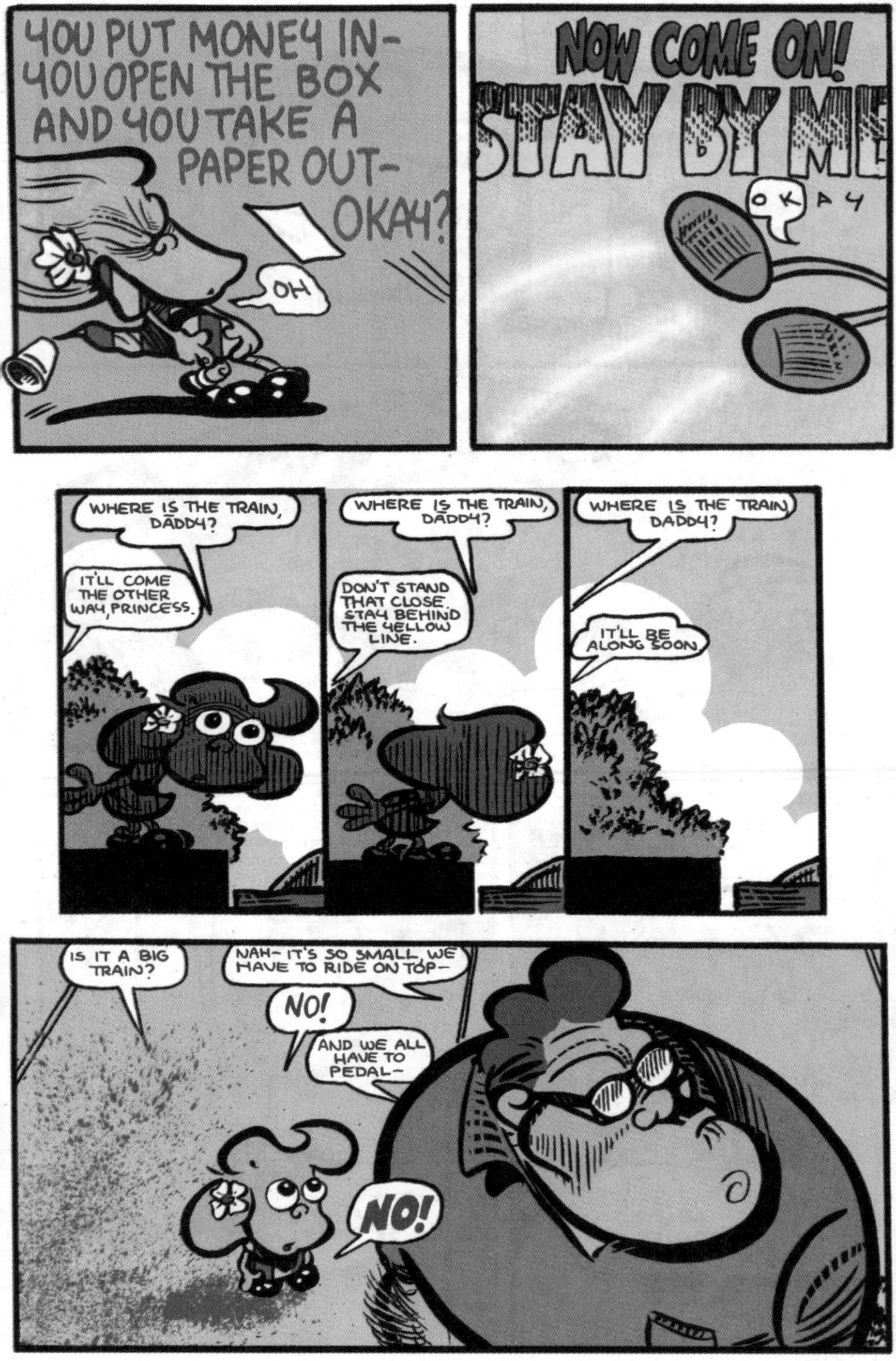
YOU PUT MONEY IN-
YOU OPEN THE BOX
AND YOU TAKE A
PAPER OUT-
OKAY?
OH
NOW COME ON!
STAY BY ME
OKAY
WHERE IS THE TRAIN, DADDY?
IT'LL COME THE OTHER WAY, PRINCESS.
WHERE IS THE TRAIN, DADDY?
DON'T STAND THAT CLOSE. STAY BEHIND THE YELLOW LINE.
WHERE IS THE TRAIN, DADDY?
IT'LL BE ALONG SOON.
IS IT A BIG TRAIN?
NAH- IT'S SO SMALL, WE HAVE TO RIDE ON TOP-
NO!
AND WE ALL HAVE TO PEDAL-
NO!

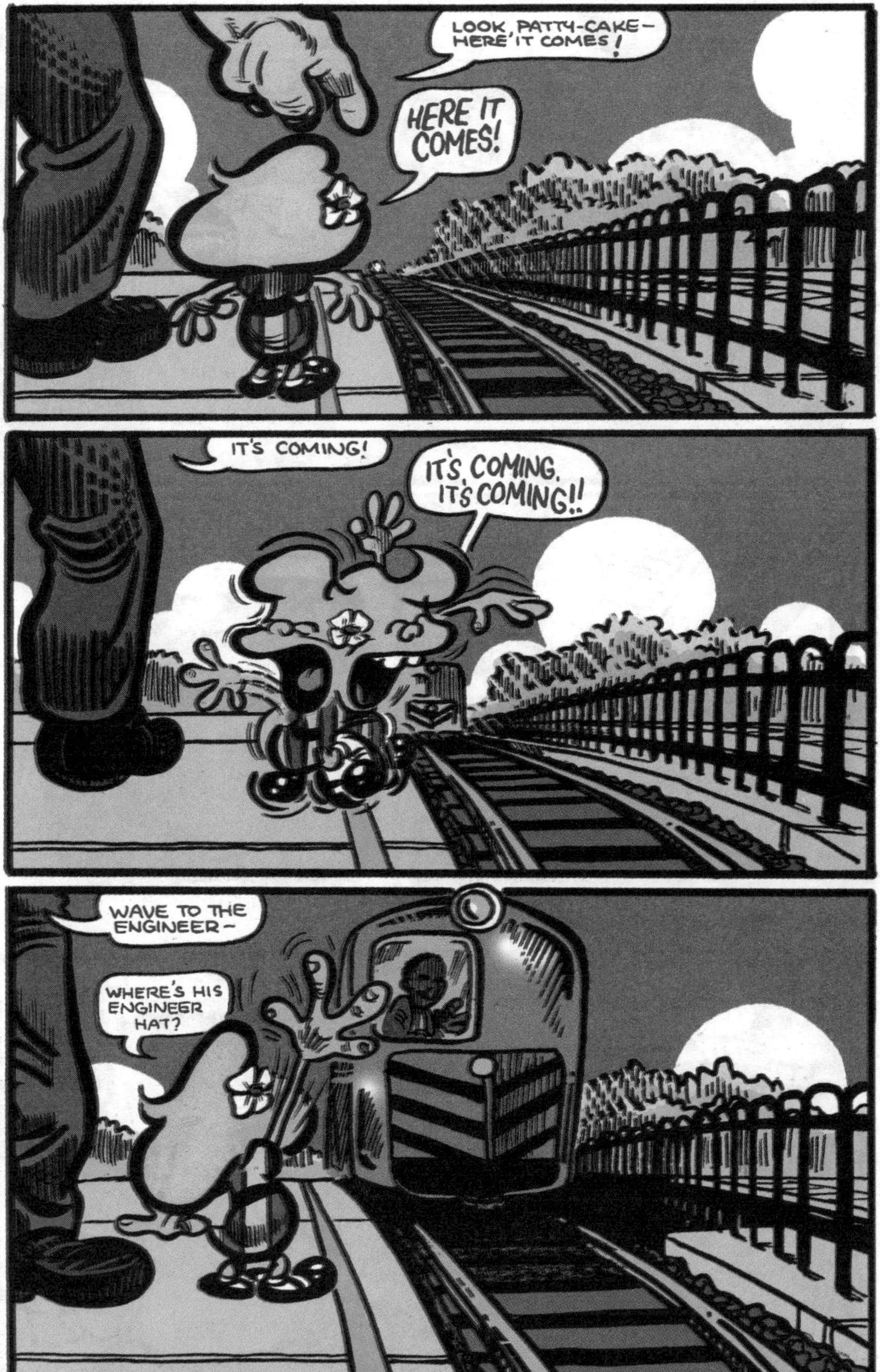
LOOK, PATTY-CAKE— HERE IT COMES!
HERE IT COMES!
IT'S COMING!
IT'S COMING. IT'S COMING!!
WAVE TO THE ENGINEER—
WHERE'S HIS ENGINEER HAT?

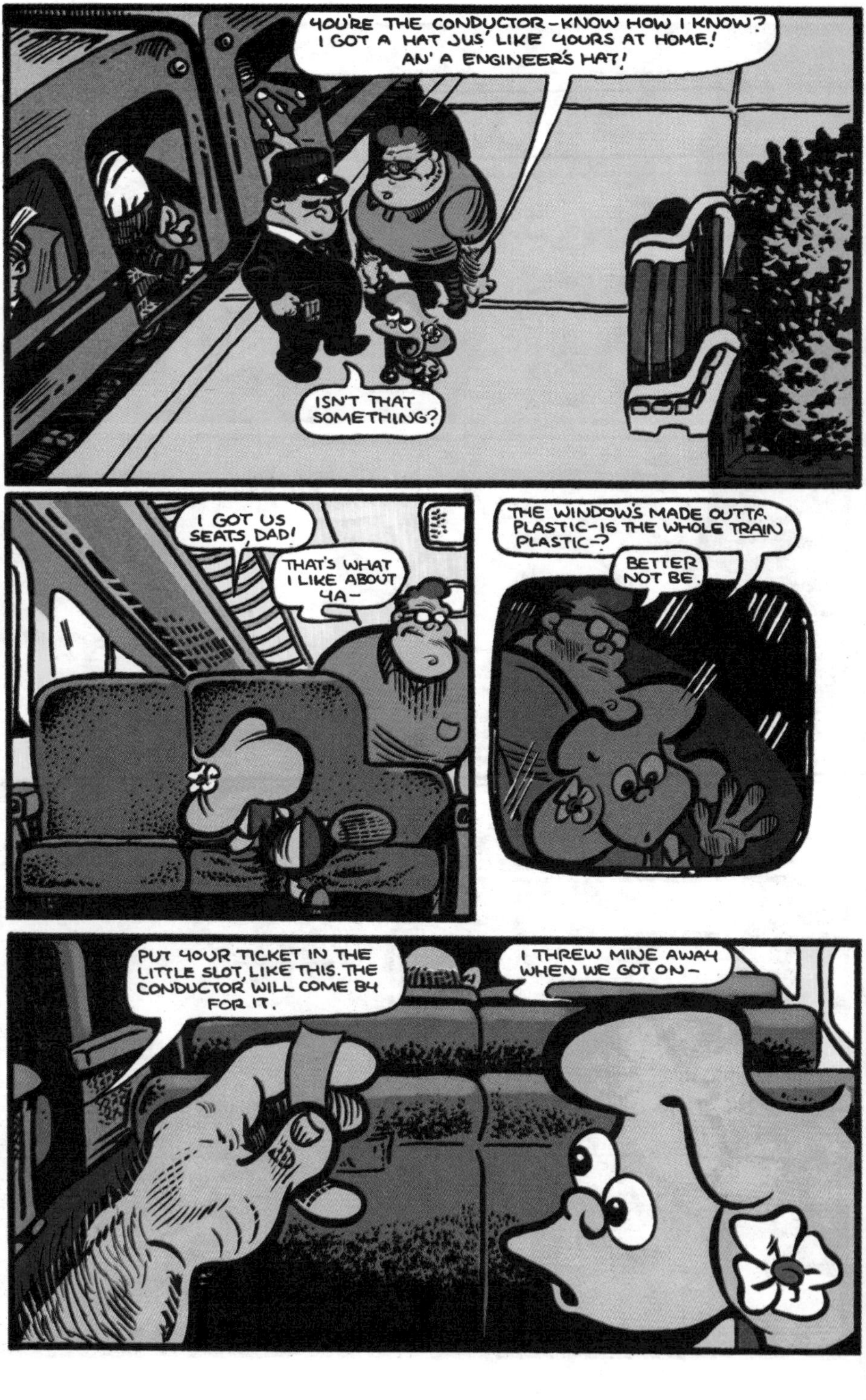
YOU'RE THE CONDUCTOR–KNOW HOW I KNOW? I GOT A HAT JUS' LIKE YOURS AT HOME! AN' A ENGINEER'S HAT!
ISN'T THAT SOMETHING?
I GOT US SEATS, DAD!
THAT'S WHAT I LIKE ABOUT YA–
THE WINDOW'S MADE OUTTA PLASTIC–IS THE WHOLE TRAIN PLASTIC–?
BETTER NOT BE.
PUT YOUR TICKET IN THE LITTLE SLOT, LIKE THIS. THE CONDUCTOR WILL COME BY FOR IT.
I THREW MINE AWAY WHEN WE GOT ON–

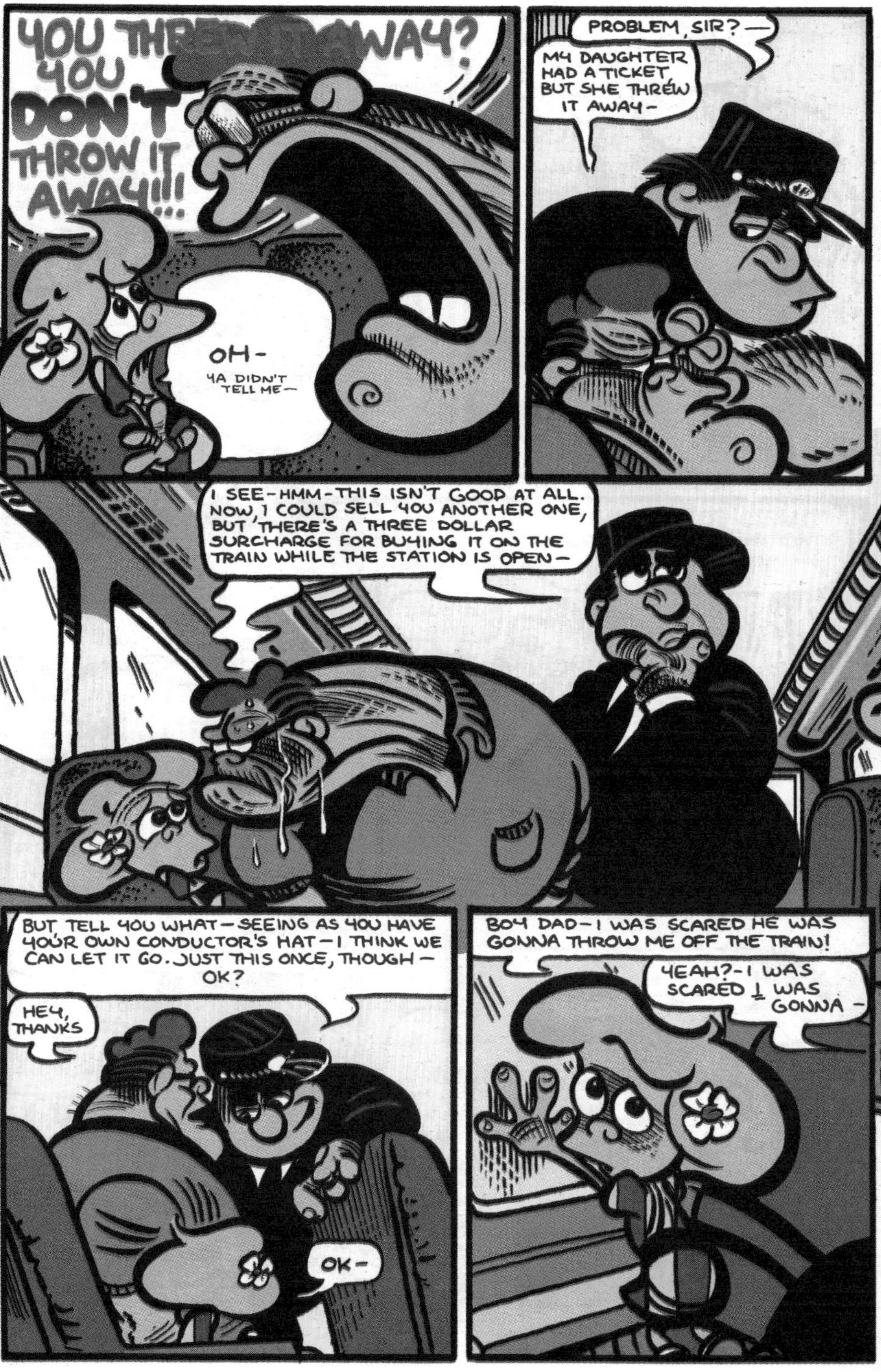

YOU THRE AWAY? YOU DON'T THROW IT AWAY!!!
OH- YA DIDN'T TELL ME-
PROBLEM, SIR?-
MY DAUGHTER HAD A TICKET BUT SHE THREW IT AWAY-
I SEE-HMM-THIS ISN'T GOOD AT ALL. NOW, I COULD SELL YOU ANOTHER ONE, BUT THERE'S A THREE DOLLAR SURCHARGE FOR BUYING IT ON THE TRAIN WHILE THE STATION IS OPEN-
BUT TELL YOU WHAT-SEEING AS YOU HAVE YOUR OWN CONDUCTOR'S HAT-I THINK WE CAN LET IT GO. JUST THIS ONCE, THOUGH- OK?
HEY, THANKS
OK-
BOY DAD-I WAS SCARED HE WAS GONNA THROW ME OFF THE TRAIN!
YEAH?-I WAS SCARED I WAS GONNA-

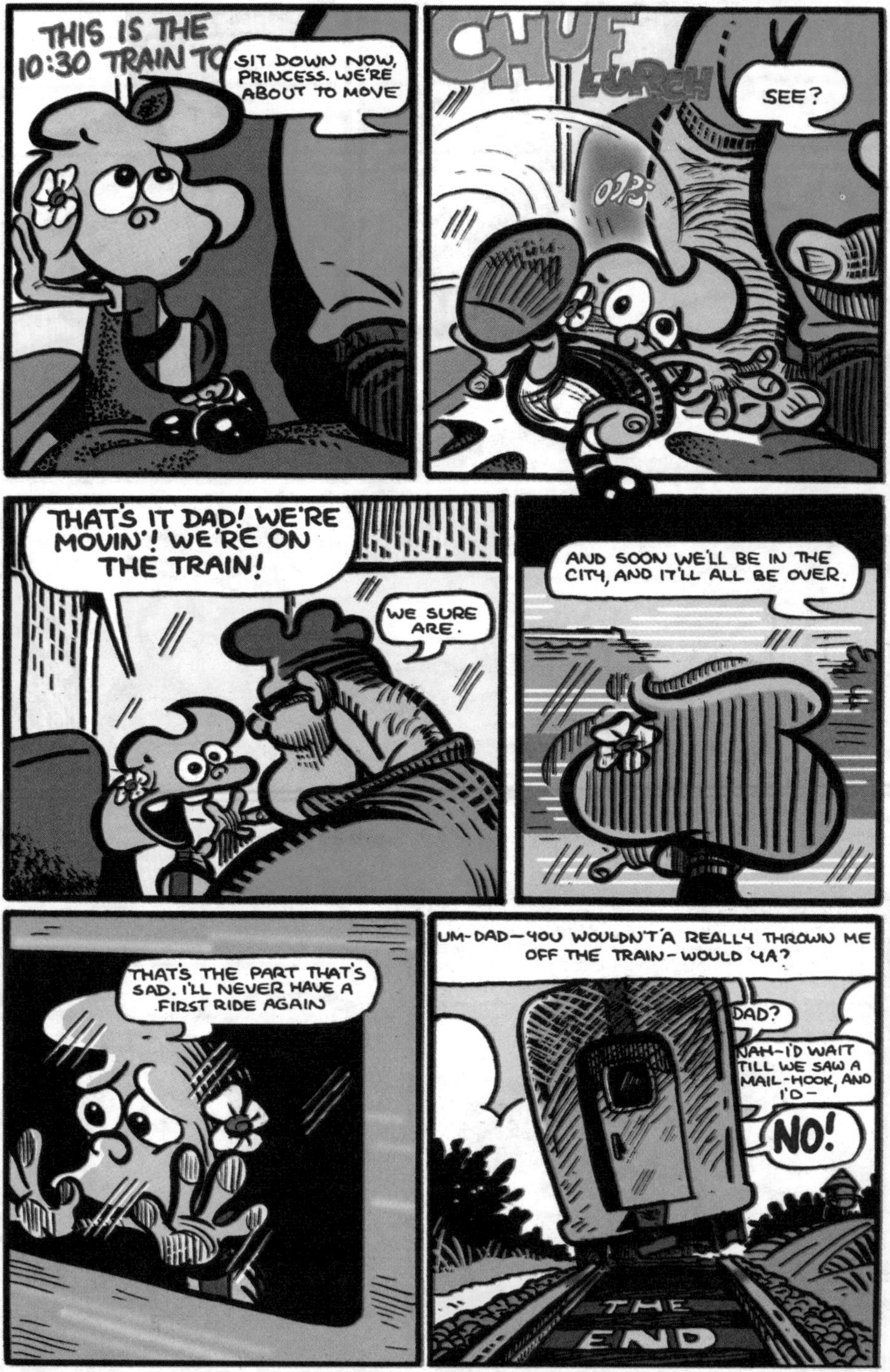
THIS IS THE 10:30 TRAIN TO
SIT DOWN NOW, PRINCESS. WE'RE ABOUT TO MOVE
CHUF
LURCH
SEE?
THAT'S IT DAD! WE'RE MOVIN'! WE'RE ON THE TRAIN!
WE SURE ARE.
AND SOON WE'LL BE IN THE CITY, AND IT'LL ALL BE OVER.
THAT'S THE PART THAT'S SAD. I'LL NEVER HAVE A FIRST RIDE AGAIN
UM-DAD—YOU WOULDN'T'A REALLY THROWN ME OFF THE TRAIN—WOULD YA?
DAD?
NAH—I'D WAIT TILL WE SAW A MAIL-HOOK, AND I'D—
NO!
THE END

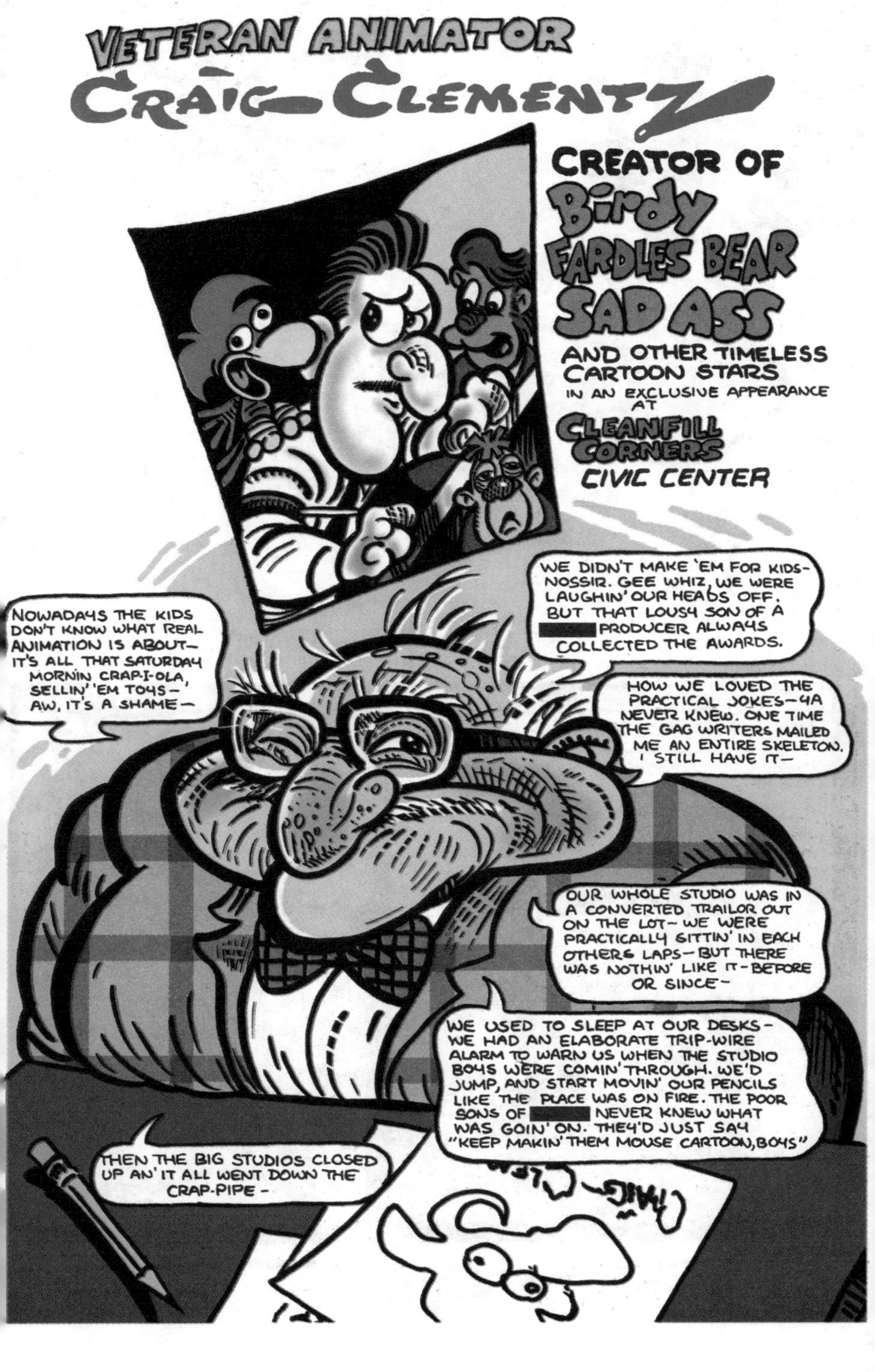
VETERAN ANIMATOR
CRAIG CLEMENTZ
CREATOR OF
Birdy
FARDLES BEAR
SAD ASS
AND OTHER TIMELESS CARTOON STARS
IN AN EXCLUSIVE APPEARANCE AT
CLEANFILL CORNERS
CIVIC CENTER
NOWADAYS THE KIDS DON'T KNOW WHAT REAL ANIMATION IS ABOUT— IT'S ALL THAT SATURDAY MORNIN CRAP-I-OLA, SELLIN' 'EM TOYS— AW, IT'S A SHAME—
WE DIDN'T MAKE 'EM FOR KIDS-NOSSIR. GEE WHIZ, WE WERE LAUGHIN' OUR HEADS OFF. BUT THAT LOUSY SON OF A [redacted] PRODUCER ALWAYS COLLECTED THE AWARDS.
HOW WE LOVED THE PRACTICAL JOKES—YA NEVER KNEW. ONE TIME THE GAG WRITERS MAILED ME AN ENTIRE SKELETON. I STILL HAVE IT—
OUR WHOLE STUDIO WAS IN A CONVERTED TRAILOR OUT ON THE LOT- WE WERE PRACTICALLY SITTIN' IN EACH OTHERS LAPS- BUT THERE WAS NOTHIN' LIKE IT- BEFORE OR SINCE-
WE USED TO SLEEP AT OUR DESKS- WE HAD AN ELABORATE TRIP-WIRE ALARM TO WARN US WHEN THE STUDIO BOYS WERE COMIN' THROUGH. WE'D JUMP, AND START MOVIN' OUR PENCILS LIKE THE PLACE WAS ON FIRE. THE POOR SONS OF [redacted] NEVER KNEW WHAT WAS GOIN' ON. THEY'D JUST SAY "KEEP MAKIN' THEM MOUSE CARTOON, BOYS"
THEN THE BIG STUDIOS CLOSED UP AN' IT ALL WENT DOWN THE CRAP-PIPE -

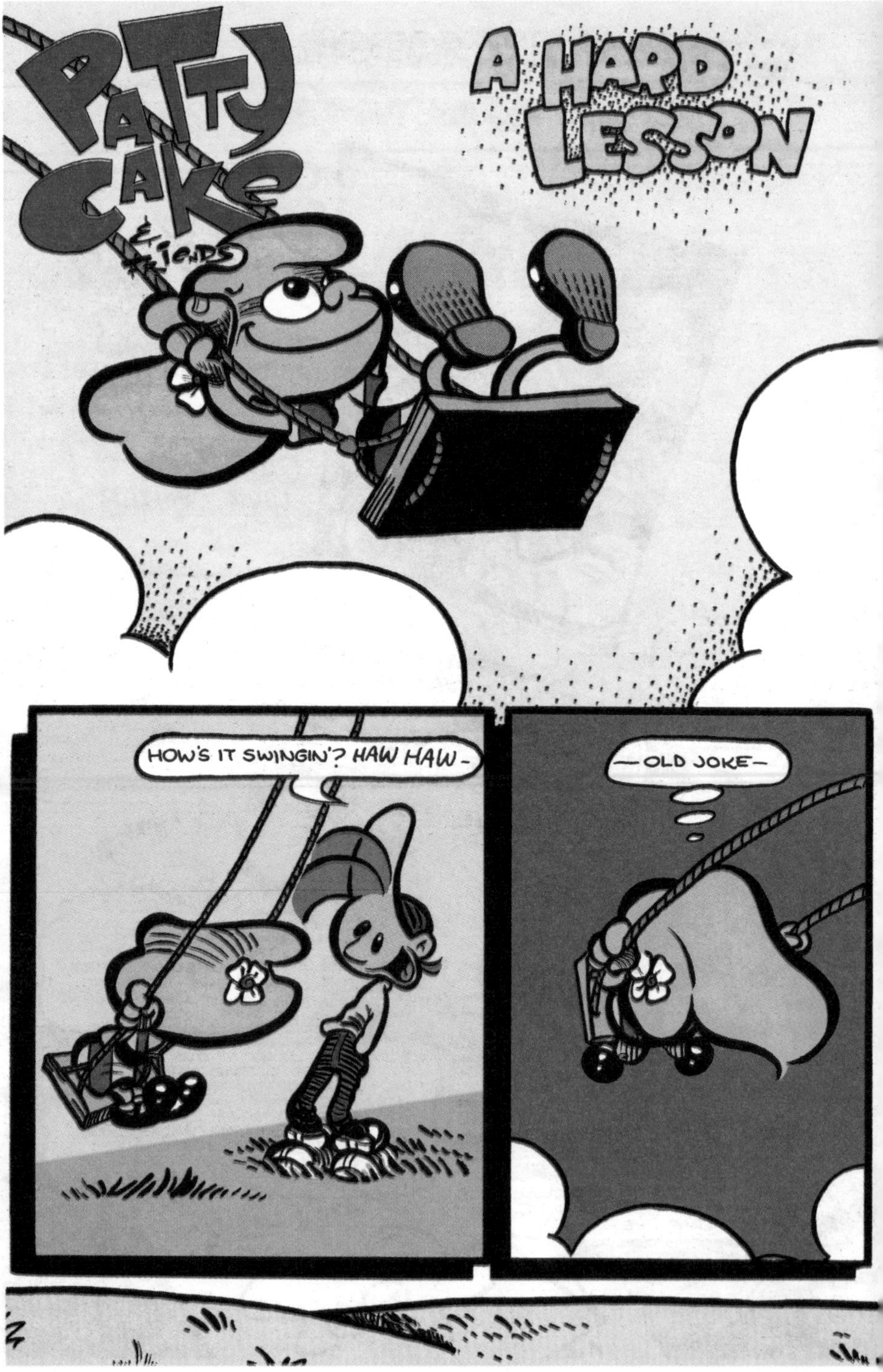
PATTY CAKE & FRIENDS
A HARD LESSON
HOW'S IT SWINGIN'? HAW HAW—
—OLD JOKE—

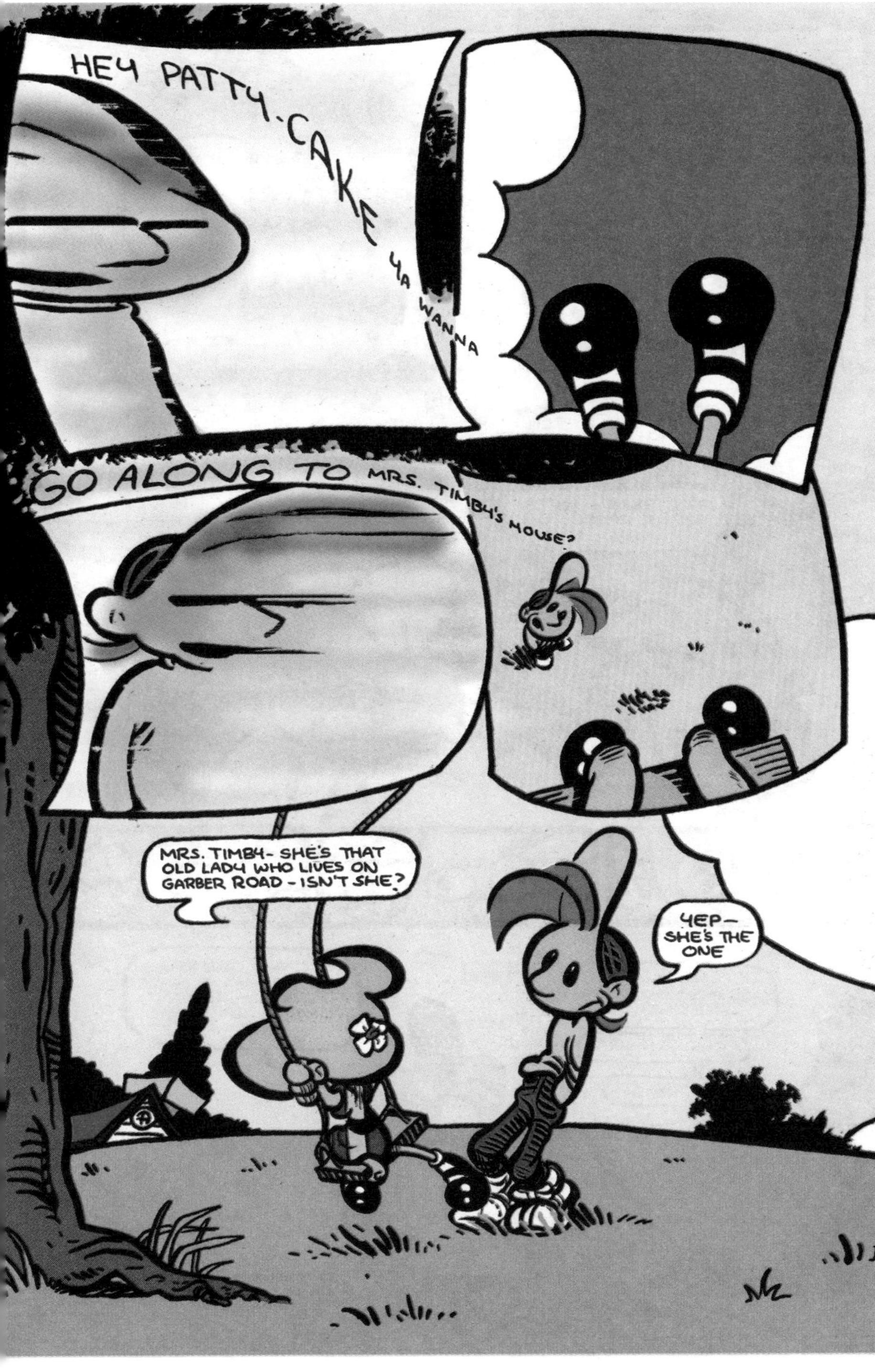
HEY PATTY-CAKE YA WANNA
GO ALONG TO MRS. TIMBY'S HOUSE?
MRS. TIMBY- SHE'S THAT OLD LADY WHO LIVES ON GARBER ROAD - ISN'T SHE?
YEP- SHE'S THE ONE

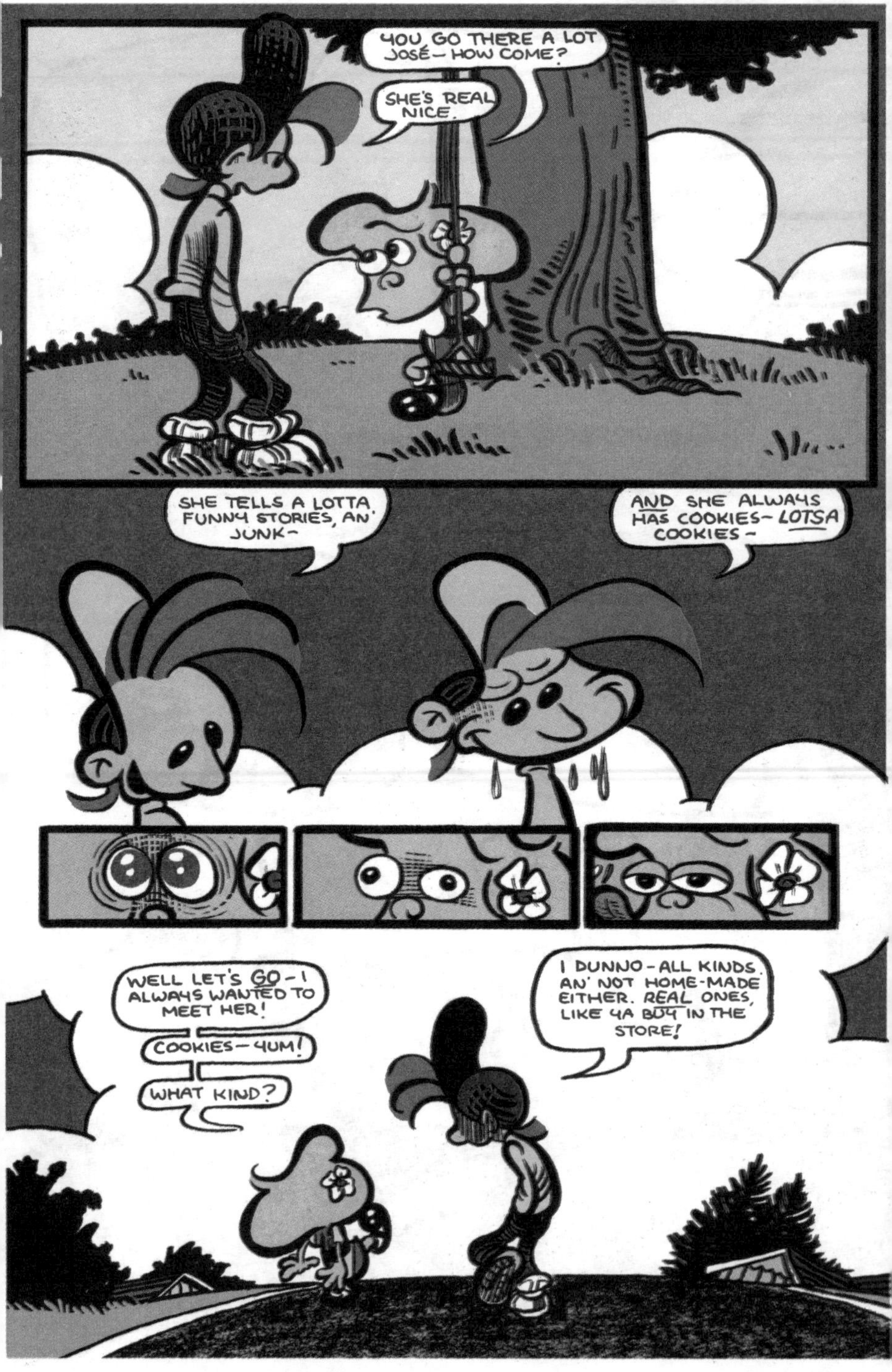

YOU GO THERE A LOT JOSÉ— HOW COME?
SHE'S REAL NICE.
SHE TELLS A LOTTA FUNNY STORIES, AN' JUNK—
AND SHE ALWAYS HAS COOKIES— LOTSA COOKIES—
WELL LET'S GO— I ALWAYS WANTED TO MEET HER!
COOKIES— YUM!
WHAT KIND?
I DUNNO— ALL KINDS AN' NOT HOME-MADE EITHER. REAL ONES, LIKE YA BUY IN THE STORE!

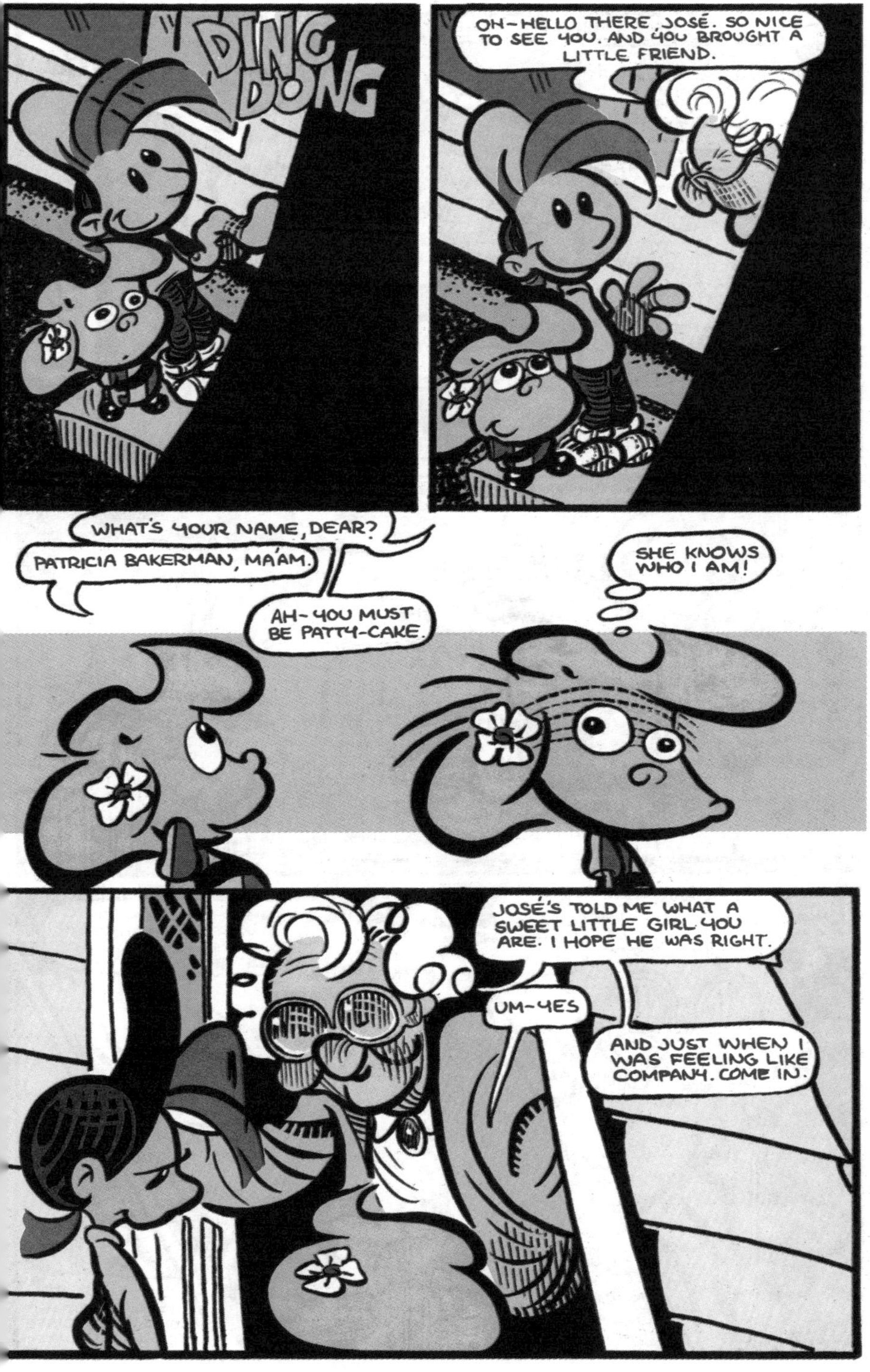
DING DONG
OH-HELLO THERE, JOSÉ. SO NICE TO SEE YOU. AND YOU BROUGHT A LITTLE FRIEND.
WHAT'S YOUR NAME, DEAR?
PATRICIA BAKERMAN, MA'AM.
AH- YOU MUST BE PATTY-CAKE.
SHE KNOWS WHO I AM!
JOSÉ'S TOLD ME WHAT A SWEET LITTLE GIRL YOU ARE. I HOPE HE WAS RIGHT.
UM-YES
AND JUST WHEN I WAS FEELING LIKE COMPANY. COME IN.

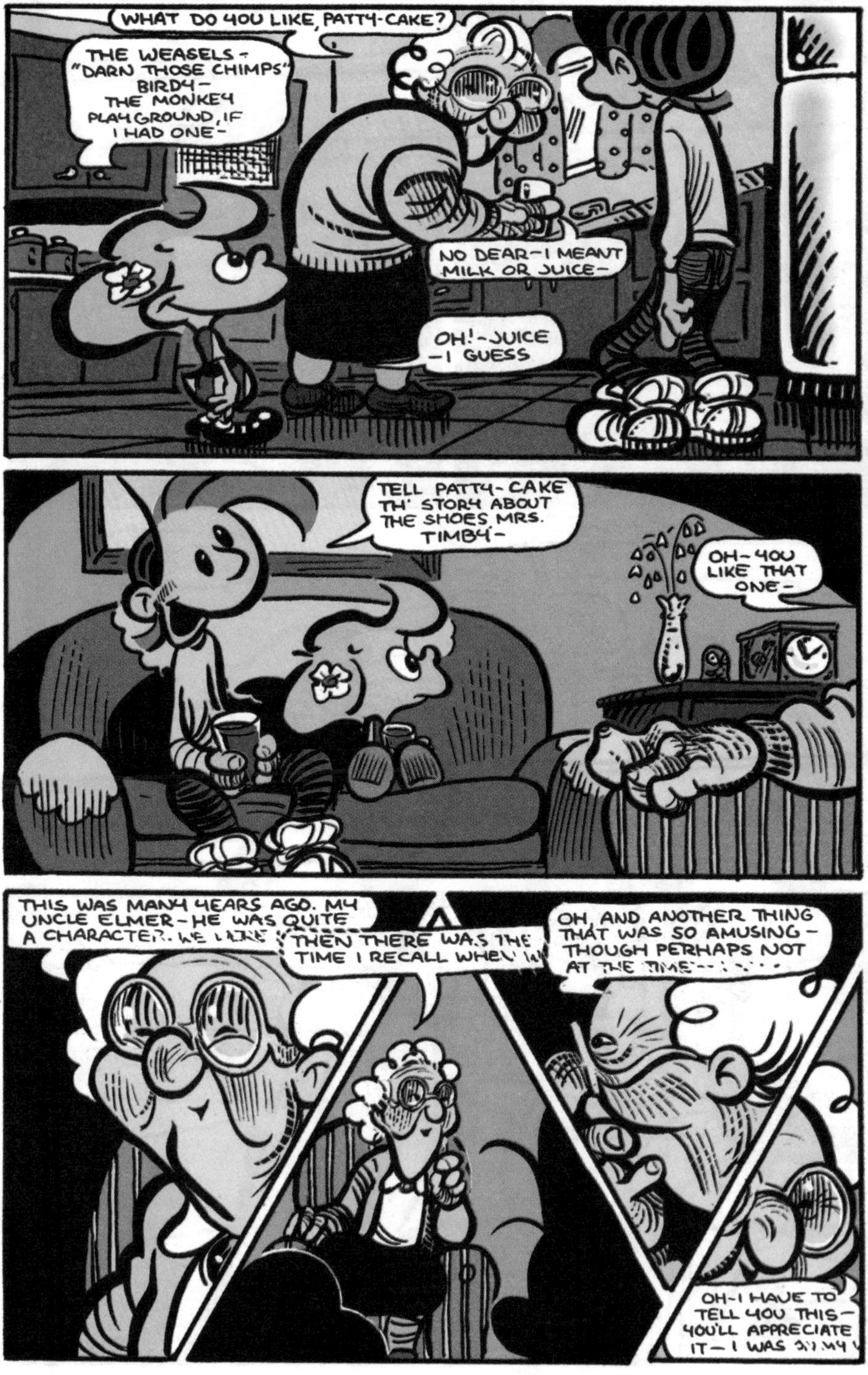
WHAT DO YOU LIKE, PATTY-CAKE?
THE WEASELS- "DARN THOSE CHIMPS" BIRDY- THE MONKEY PLAYGROUND, IF I HAD ONE-
NO DEAR-I MEANT MILK OR JUICE-
OH!-JUICE -I GUESS
TELL PATTY-CAKE TH' STORY ABOUT THE SHOES MRS. TIMBY-
OH-YOU LIKE THAT ONE-
THIS WAS MANY YEARS AGO. MY UNCLE ELMER-HE WAS QUITE A CHARACTER.
THEN THERE WAS THE TIME I RECALL WHEN
OH, AND ANOTHER THING THAT WAS SO AMUSING- THOUGH PERHAPS NOT AT THE TIME--
OH-I HAVE TO TELL YOU THIS- YOU'LL APPRECIATE IT- I WAS

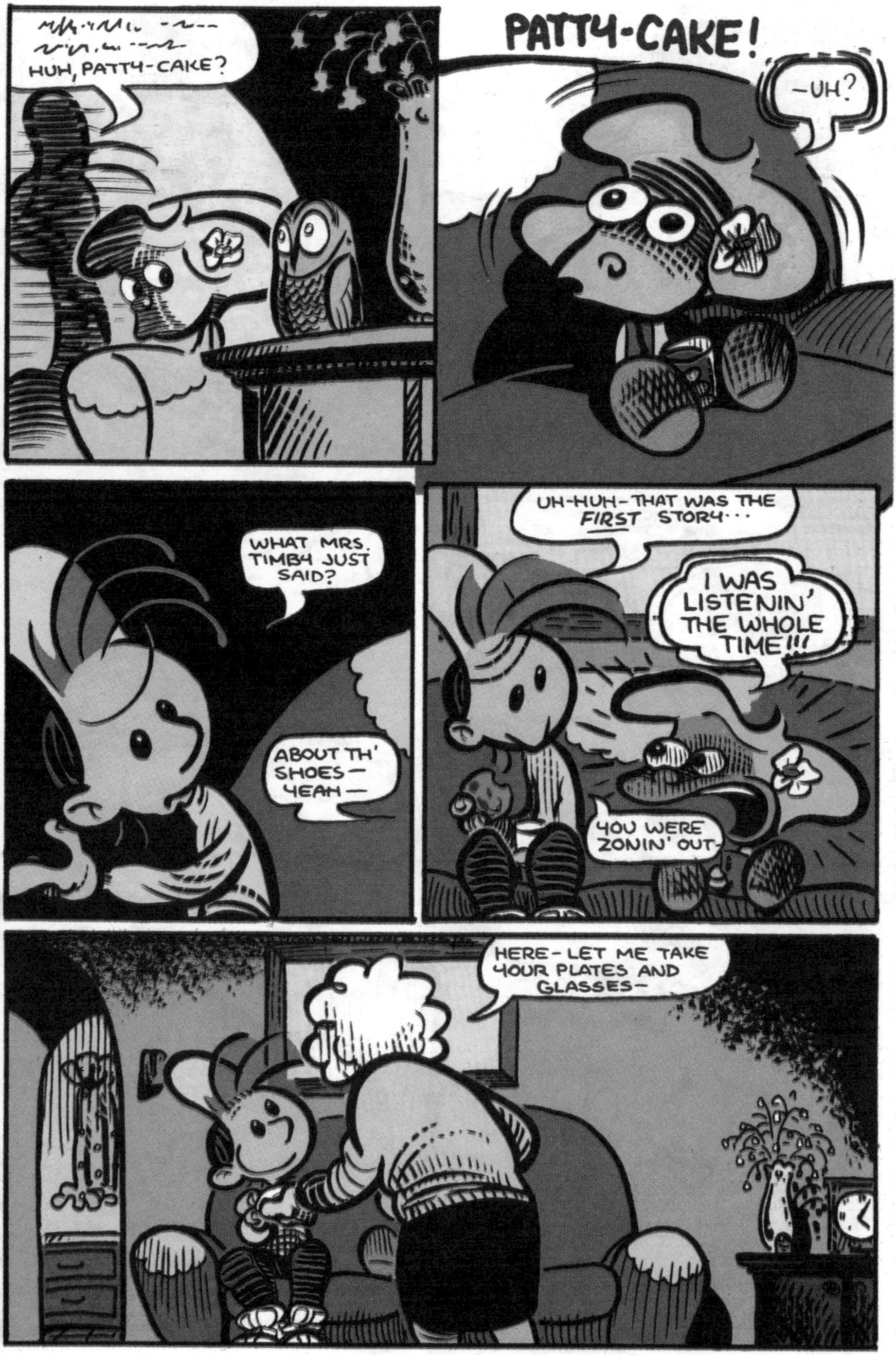
HUH, PATTY-CAKE?
PATTY-CAKE!
-UH?
WHAT MRS. TIMBY JUST SAID?
ABOUT TH' SHOES— YEAH—
UH-HUH- THAT WAS THE FIRST STORY...
I WAS LISTENIN' THE WHOLE TIME!!!
YOU WERE ZONIN' OUT-
HERE- LET ME TAKE YOUR PLATES AND GLASSES-

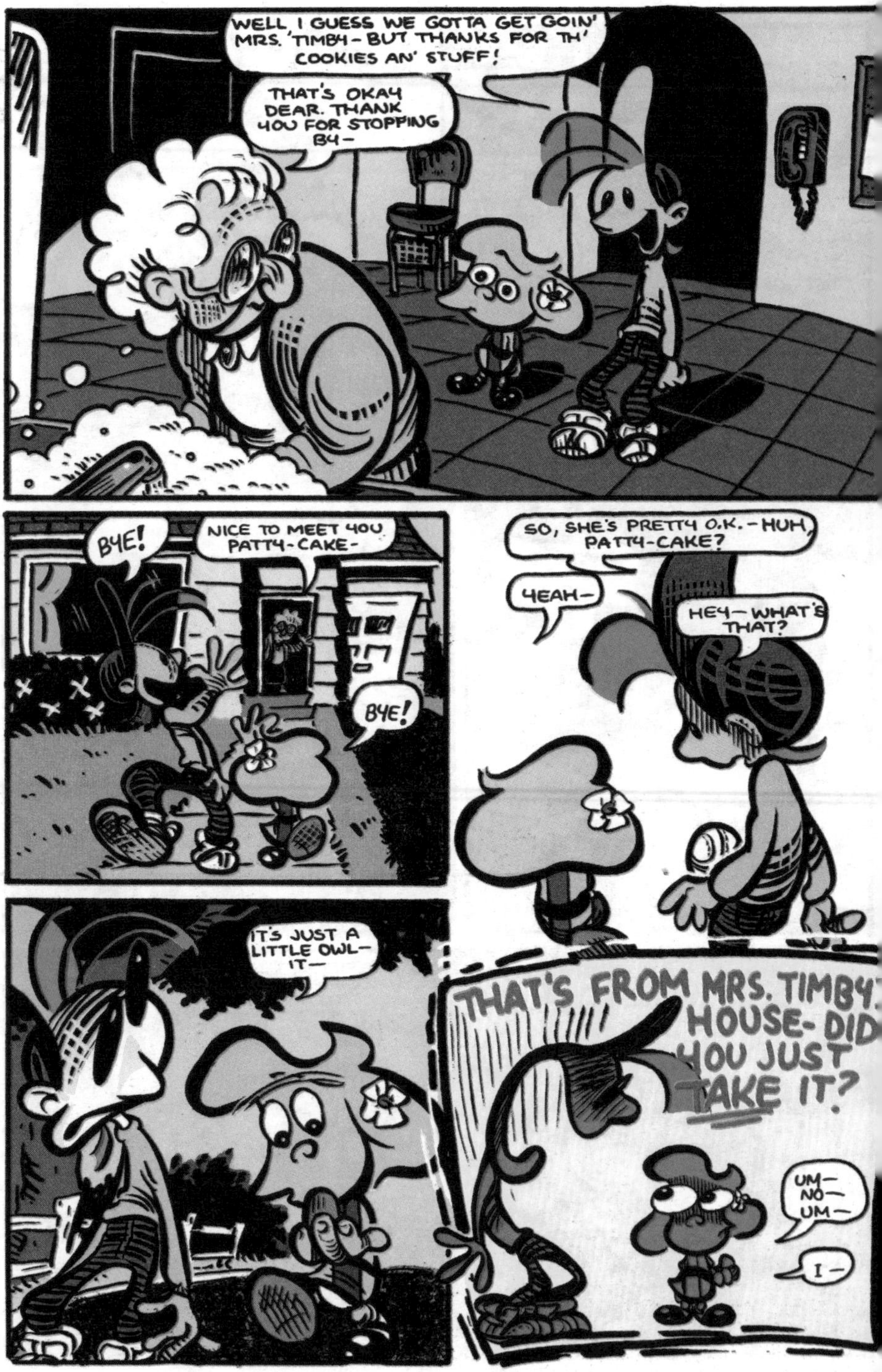

WELL, I GUESS WE GOTTA GET GOIN' MRS. 'TIMBY - BUT THANKS FOR TH' COOKIES AN' STUFF!
THAT'S OKAY DEAR. THANK YOU FOR STOPPING BY—
BYE!
NICE TO MEET YOU PATTY-CAKE-
BYE!
SO, SHE'S PRETTY O.K. - HUH, PATTY-CAKE?
YEAH—
HEY— WHAT'S THAT?
IT'S JUST A LITTLE OWL— IT—
THAT'S FROM MRS. TIMBY'S HOUSE- DID YOU JUST TAKE IT?
UM— NO— UM—
I—

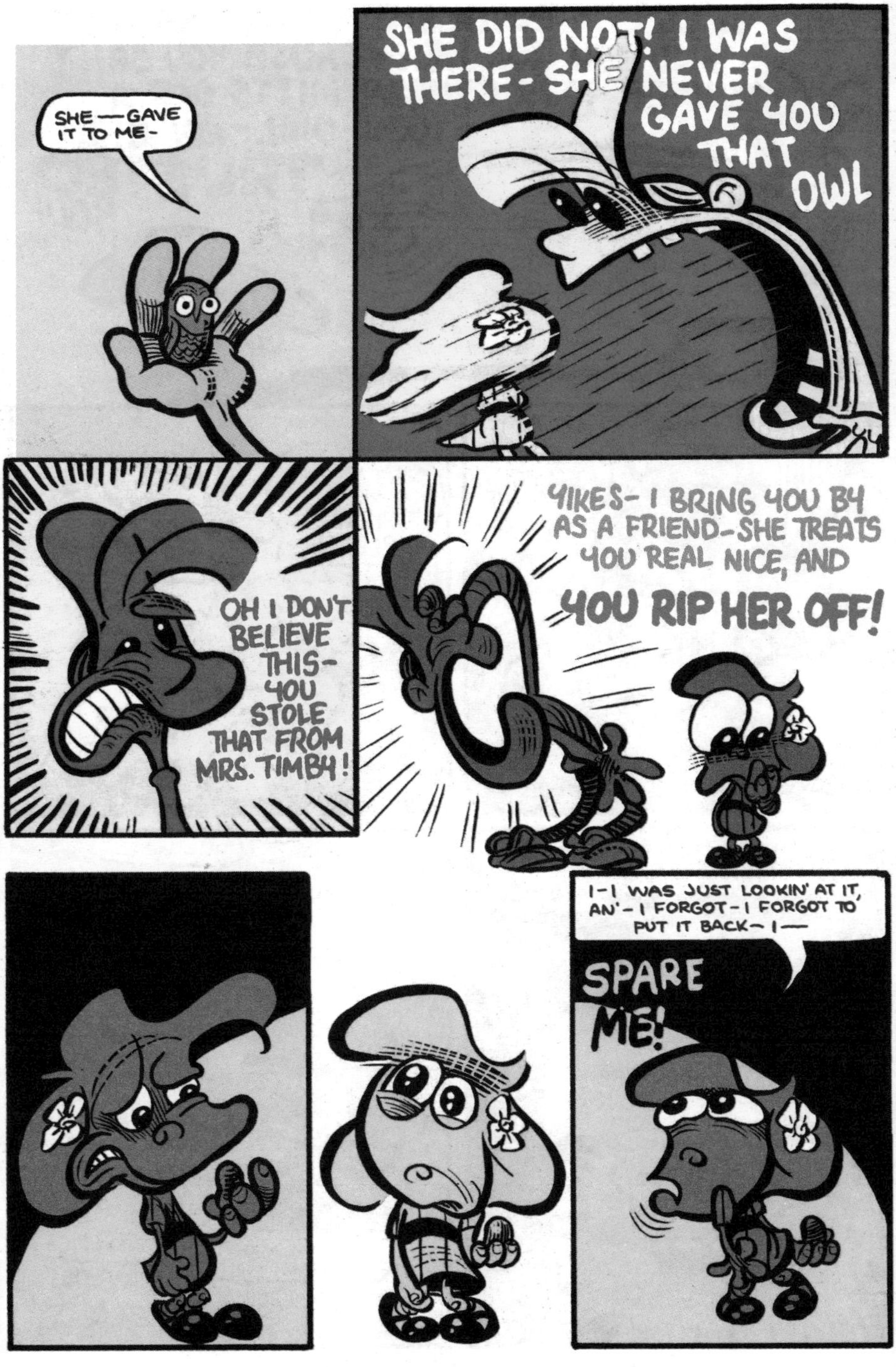
SHE —— GAVE IT TO ME-
SHE DID NOT! I WAS THERE- SHE NEVER GAVE YOU THAT OWL
OH I DON'T BELIEVE THIS- YOU STOLE THAT FROM MRS. TIMBY!
YIKES- I BRING YOU BY AS A FRIEND- SHE TREATS YOU REAL NICE, AND
YOU RIP HER OFF!
I-I WAS JUST LOOKIN' AT IT, AN' - I FORGOT - I FORGOT TO PUT IT BACK~ I—
SPARE ME!

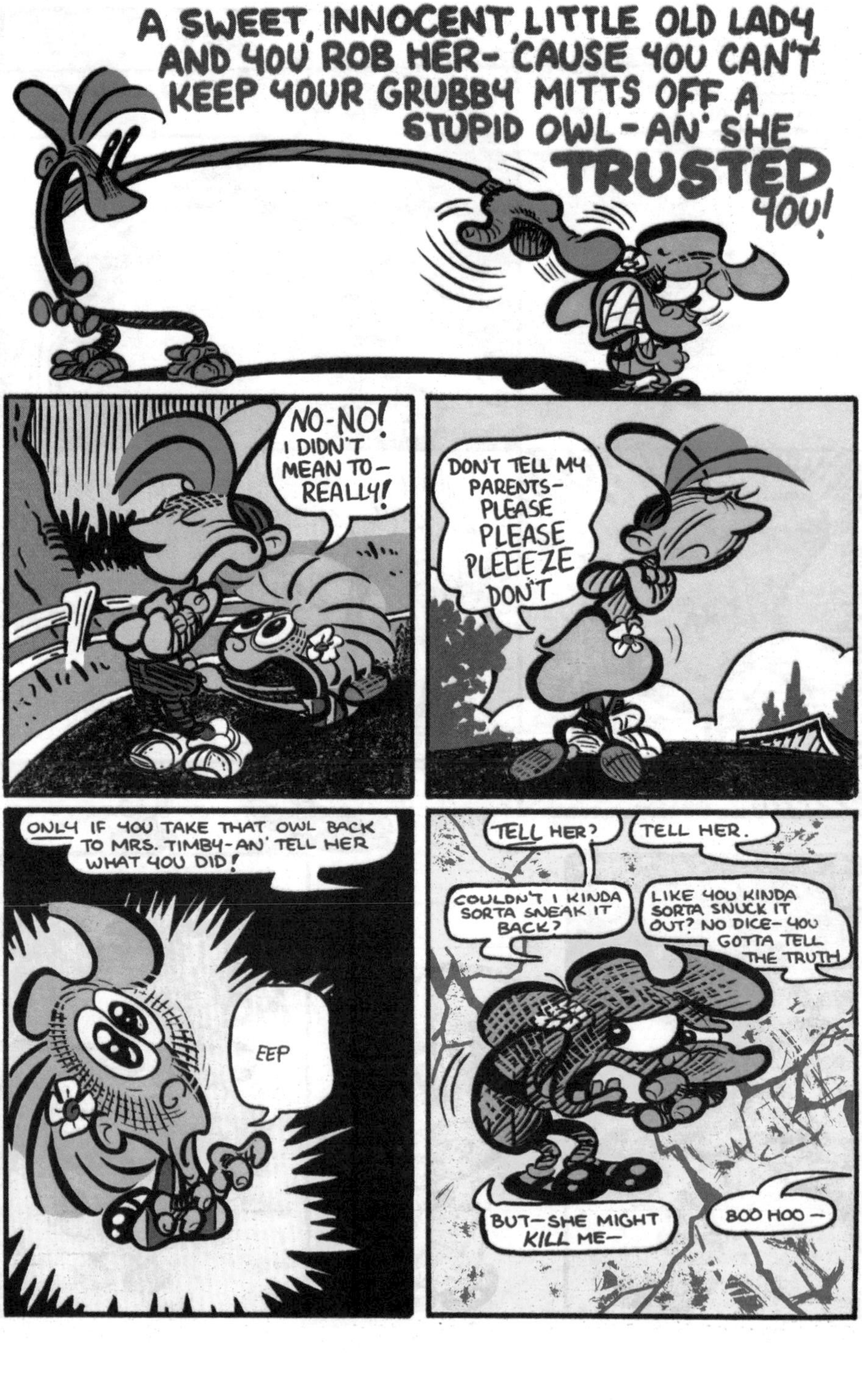
A SWEET, INNOCENT, LITTLE OLD LADY AND YOU ROB HER- 'CAUSE YOU CAN'T KEEP YOUR GRUBBY MITTS OFF A STUPID OWL-AN' SHE TRUSTED YOU!
NO-NO! I DIDN'T MEAN TO- REALLY!
DON'T TELL MY PARENTS- PLEASE PLEASE PLEEEZE DON'T
ONLY IF YOU TAKE THAT OWL BACK TO MRS. TIMBY-AN' TELL HER WHAT YOU DID!
EEP
TELL HER?
TELL HER.
COULDN'T I KINDA SORTA SNEAK IT BACK?
LIKE YOU KINDA SORTA SNUCK IT OUT? NO DICE- YOU GOTTA TELL THE TRUTH
BUT-SHE MIGHT KILL ME-
BOO HOO-

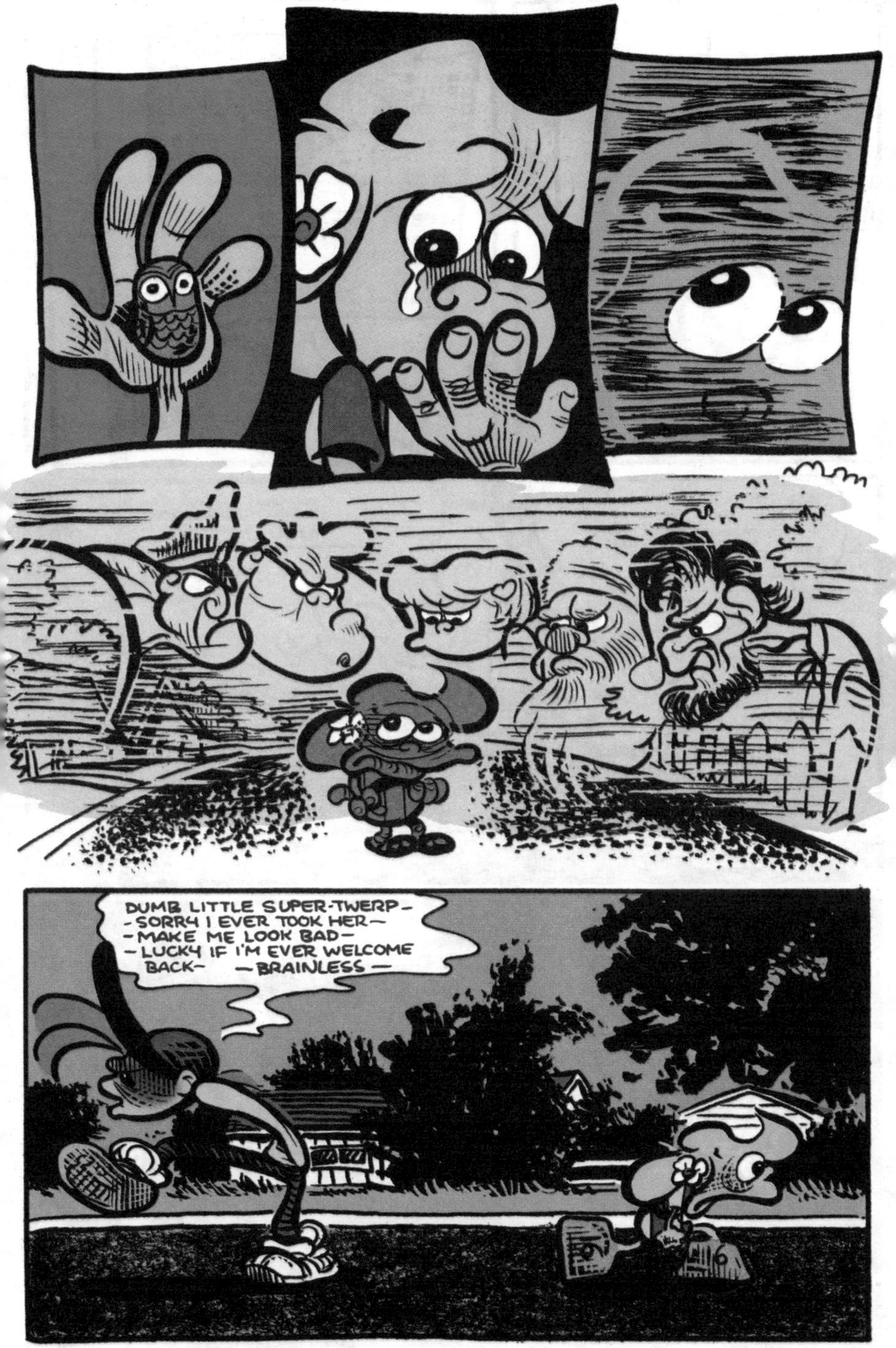
DUMB LITTLE SUPER-TWERP- -SORRY I EVER TOOK HER- -MAKE ME LOOK BAD- -LUCKY IF I'M EVER WELCOME BACK- -BRAINLESS-

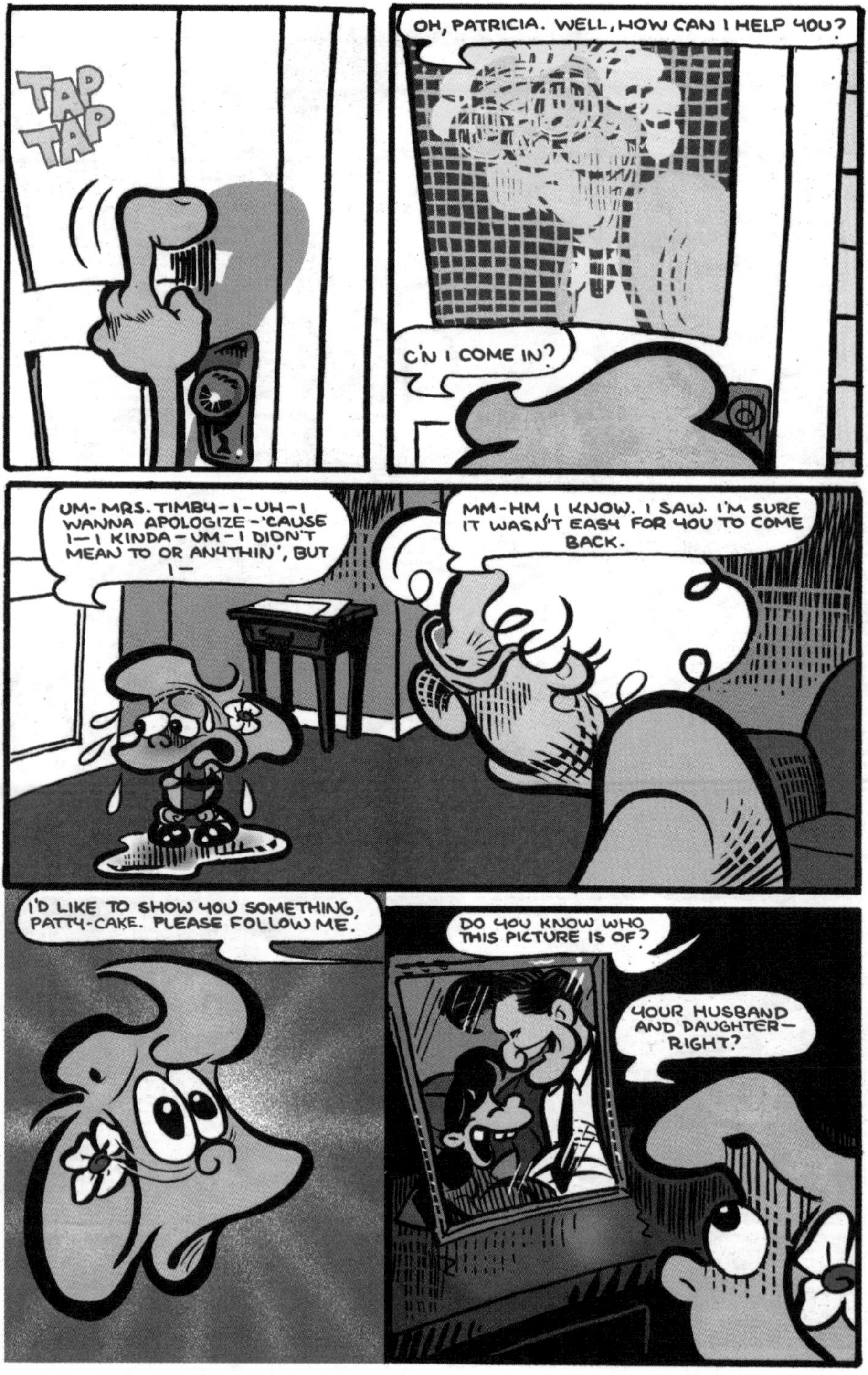
TAP TAP
OH, PATRICIA. WELL, HOW CAN I HELP YOU?
C'N I COME IN?
UM- MRS. TIMBY- I- UH- I WANNA APOLOGIZE- 'CAUSE I- I KINDA- UM- I DIDN'T MEAN TO OR ANYTHIN', BUT I-
MM-HM, I KNOW. I SAW. I'M SURE IT WASN'T EASY FOR YOU TO COME BACK.
I'D LIKE TO SHOW YOU SOMETHING, PATTY-CAKE. PLEASE FOLLOW ME.
DO YOU KNOW WHO THIS PICTURE IS OF?
YOUR HUSBAND AND DAUGHTER- RIGHT?

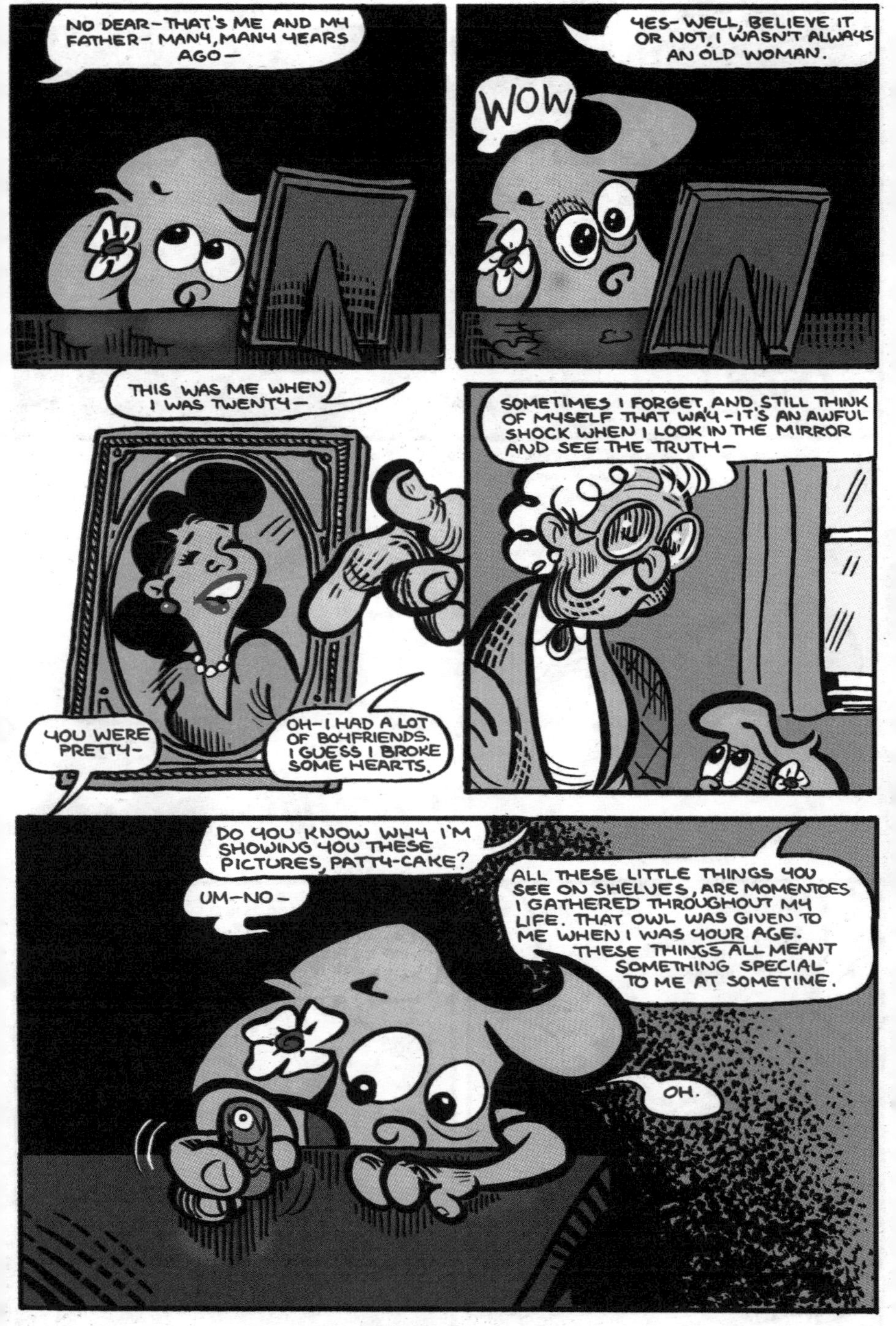

NO DEAR–THAT'S ME AND MY FATHER– MANY, MANY YEARS AGO–
YES– WELL, BELIEVE IT OR NOT, I WASN'T ALWAYS AN OLD WOMAN.
WOW
THIS WAS ME WHEN I WAS TWENTY–
YOU WERE PRETTY–
OH–I HAD A LOT OF BOYFRIENDS. I GUESS I BROKE SOME HEARTS.
SOMETIMES I FORGET, AND STILL THINK OF MYSELF THAT WAY–IT'S AN AWFUL SHOCK WHEN I LOOK IN THE MIRROR AND SEE THE TRUTH–
DO YOU KNOW WHY I'M SHOWING YOU THESE PICTURES, PATTY-CAKE?
UM–NO–
ALL THESE LITTLE THINGS YOU SEE ON SHELVES, ARE MOMENTOES I GATHERED THROUGHOUT MY LIFE. THAT OWL WAS GIVEN TO ME WHEN I WAS YOUR AGE. THESE THINGS ALL MEANT SOMETHING SPECIAL TO ME AT SOMETIME.
OH.

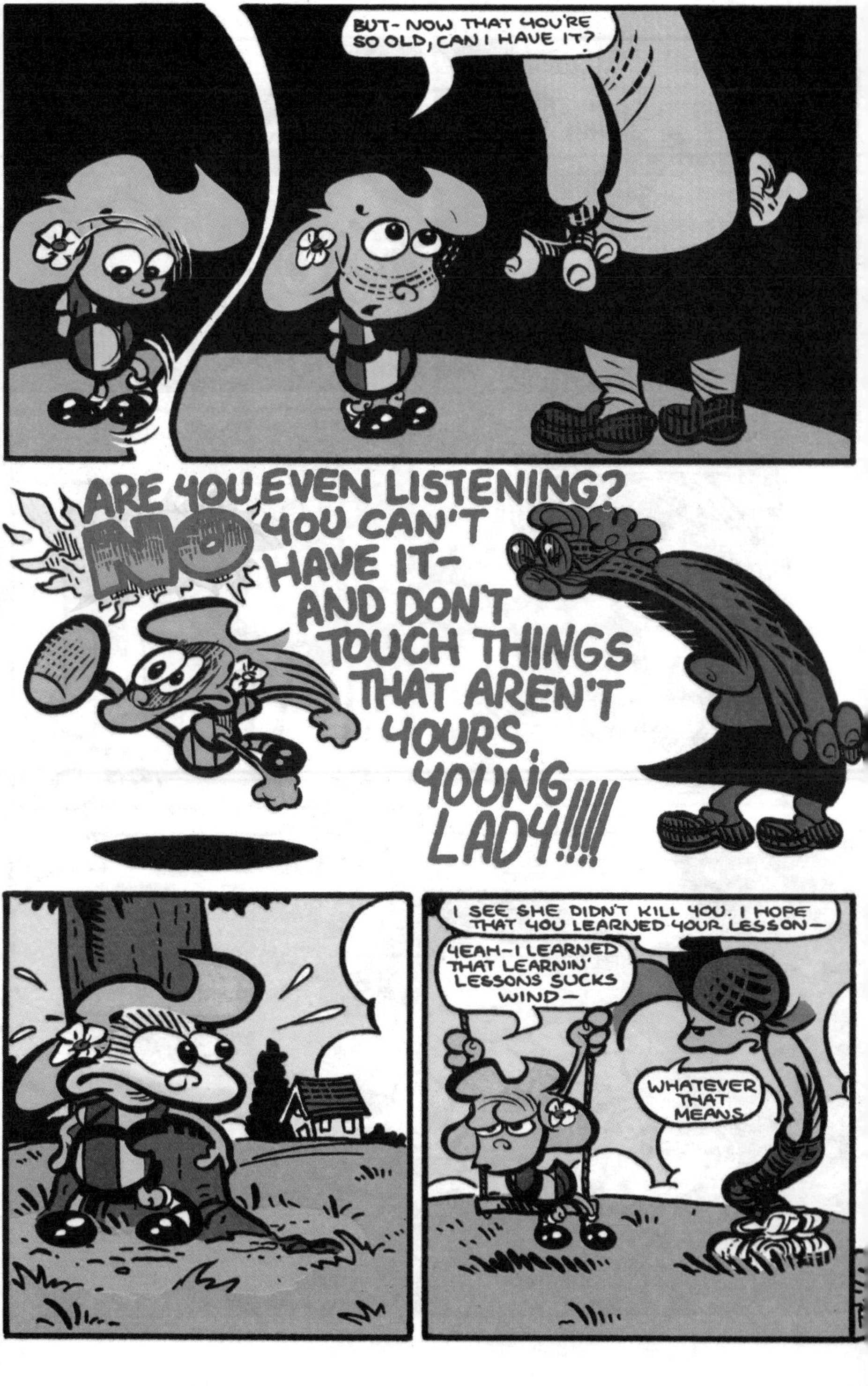
BUT- NOW THAT YOU'RE SO OLD, CAN I HAVE IT?
ARE YOU EVEN LISTENING?
NO
YOU CAN'T HAVE IT- AND DON'T TOUCH THINGS THAT AREN'T YOURS, YOUNG LADY!!!!
I SEE SHE DIDN'T KILL YOU. I HOPE THAT YOU LEARNED YOUR LESSON—
YEAH—I LEARNED THAT LEARNIN' LESSONS SUCKS WIND—
WHATEVER THAT MEANS

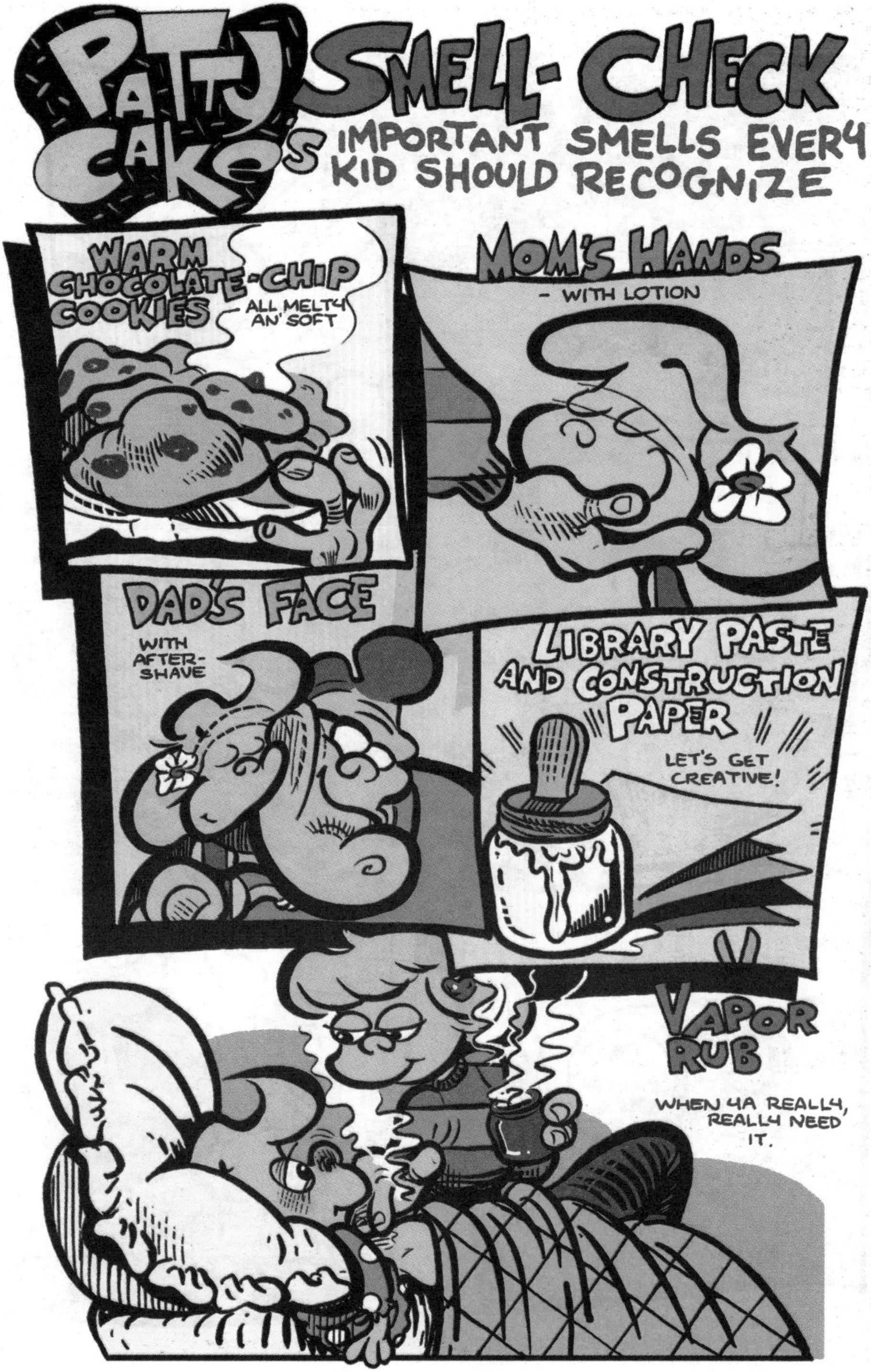
Patty Cake's
Smell-Check
important smells every kid should recognize
Warm Chocolate-Chip Cookies
All melty an' soft
Mom's Hands
- with lotion
Dad's Face
with after-shave
Library Paste and Construction Paper
Let's get creative!
Vapor Rub
When ya really, really need it.

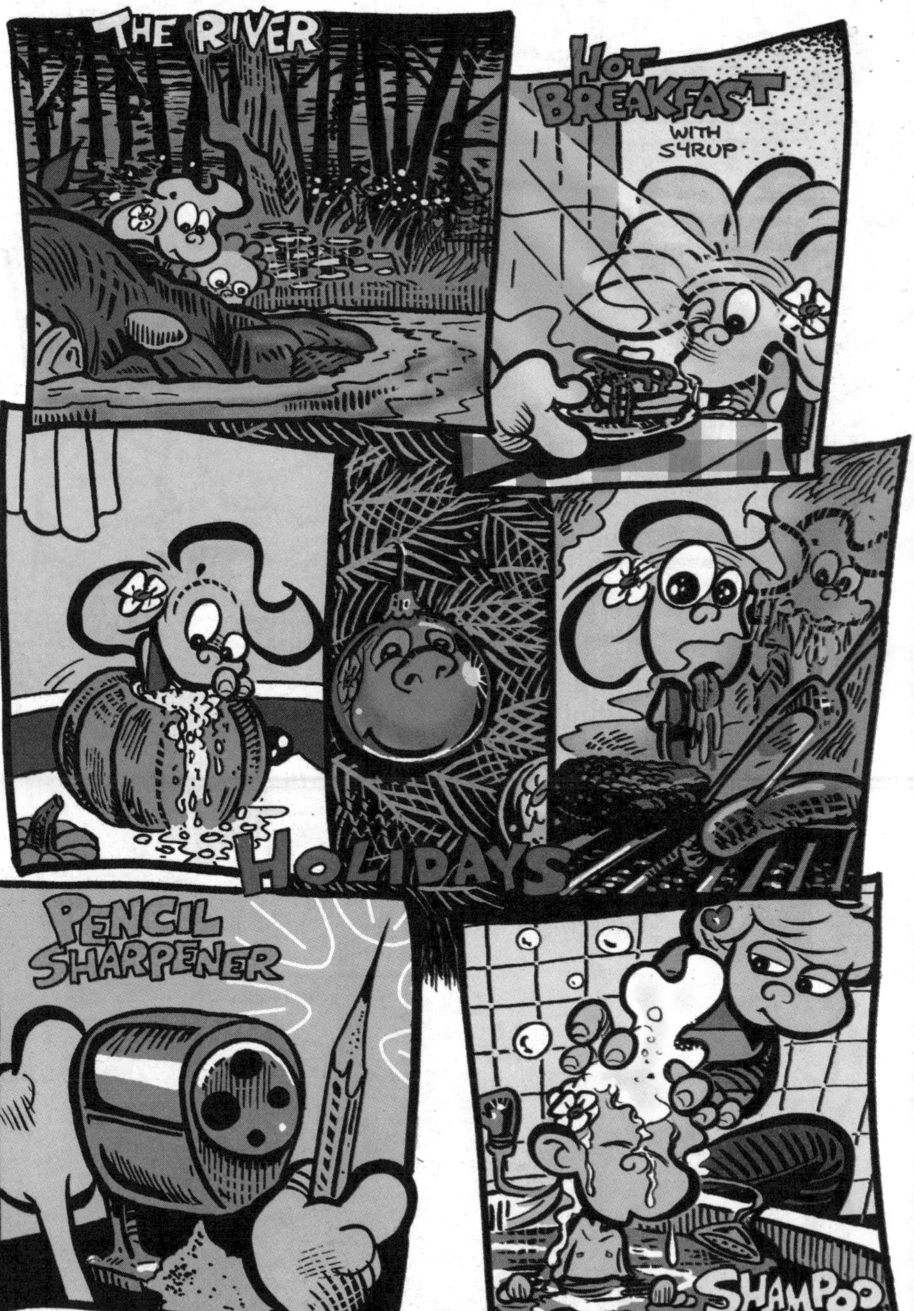
THE RIVER
HOT BREAKFAST
WITH SYRUP
HOLIDAYS
PENCIL SHARPENER
SHAMPOO

SOME BAD SMELLS

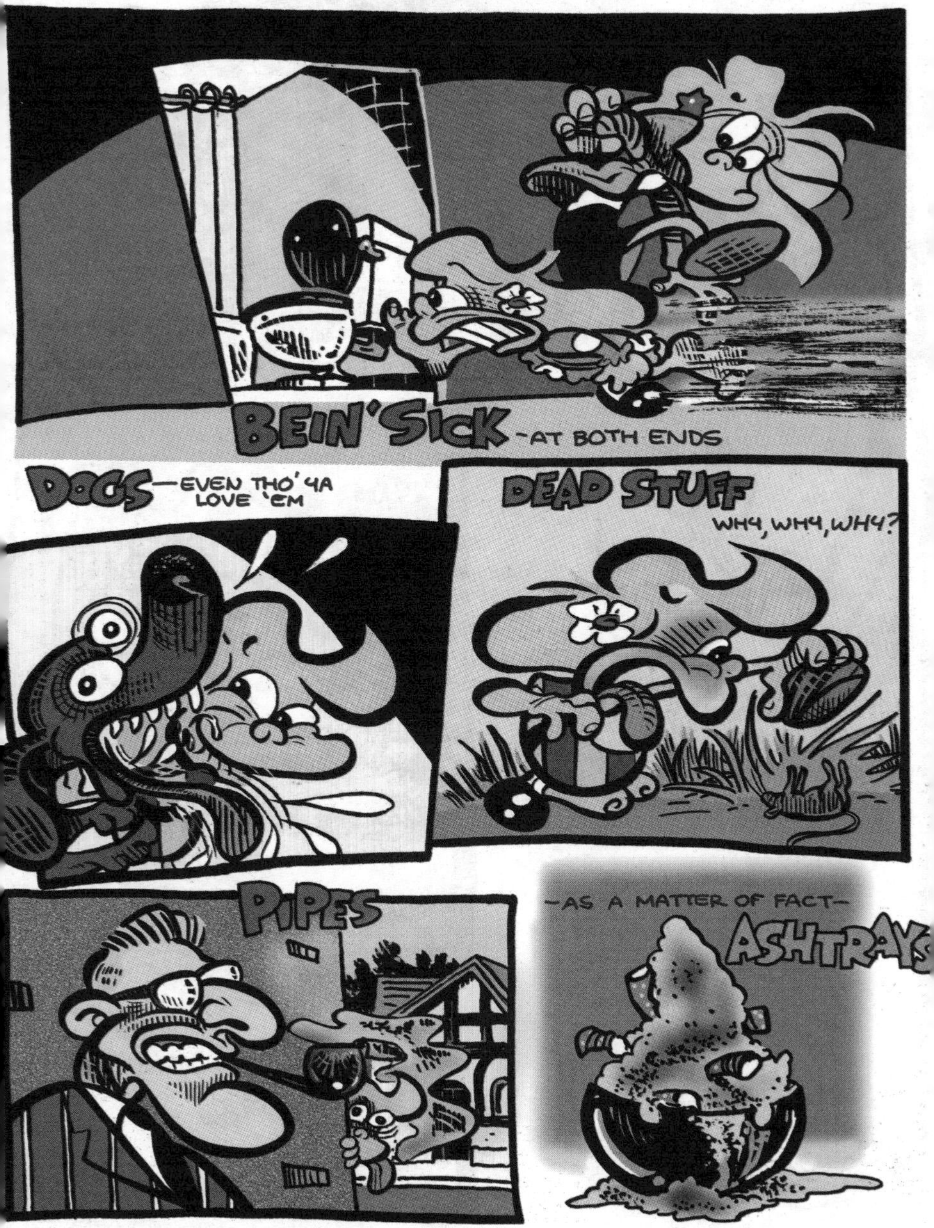

BEIN' SICK
-AT BOTH ENDS
DOGS
—EVEN THO' YA LOVE 'EM
DEAD STUFF
WHY, WHY, WHY?
PIPES
—AS A MATTER OF FACT—
ASHTRAYS

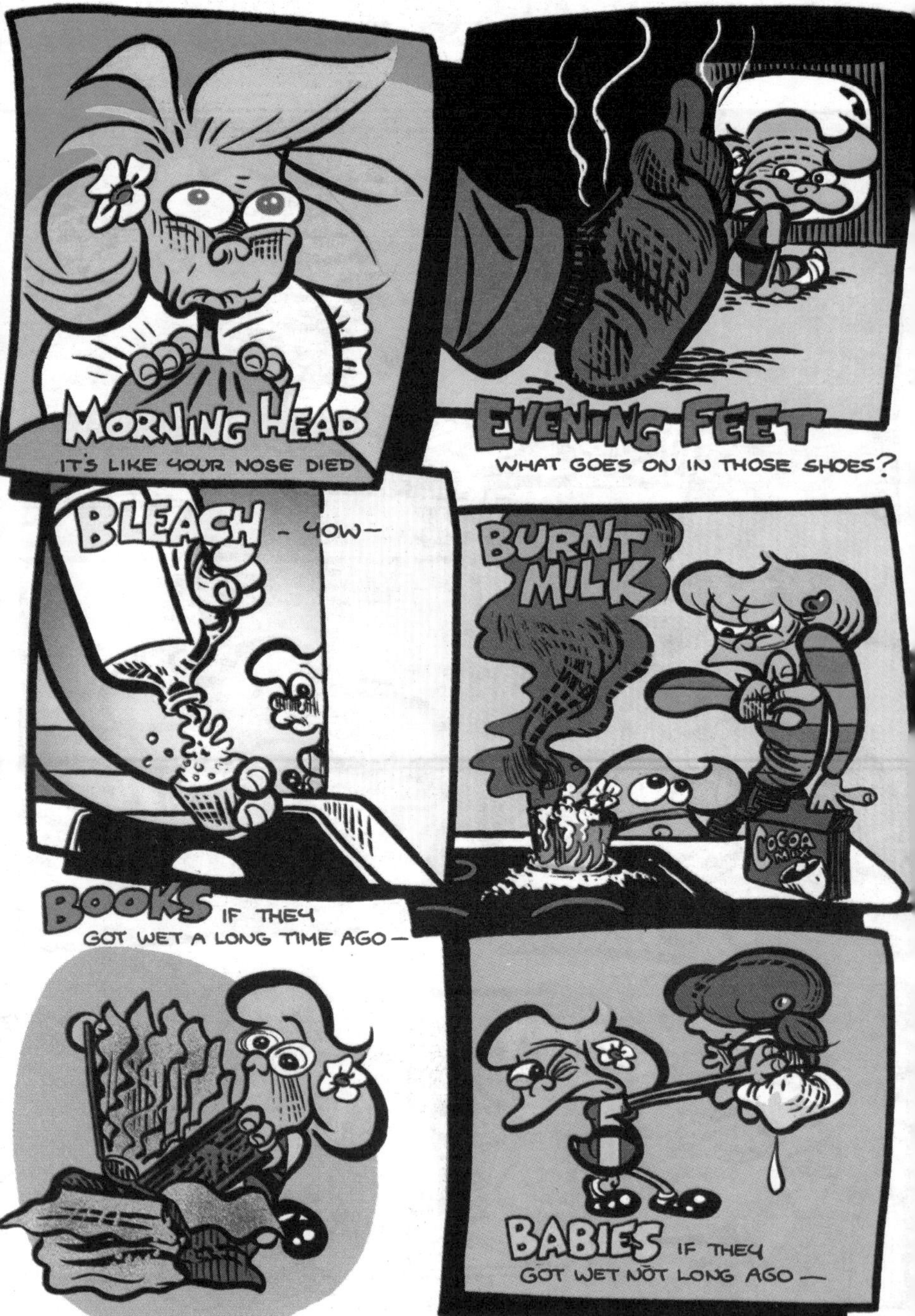
MORNING HEAD
IT'S LIKE YOUR NOSE DIED
EVENING FEET
WHAT GOES ON IN THOSE SHOES?
BLEACH - YOW-
BURNT MILK
COCOA MIX
BOOKS IF THEY
GOT WET A LONG TIME AGO—
BABIES IF THEY
GOT WET NOT LONG AGO—

WELL, THAT'S ENOUGH ABOUT (KOFF) BAD SMELLS FOR NOW. —IN FACT, THAT'S ENOUGH ABOUT SMELLIN' IN GENERAL. WE KNOW YOU'RE ALL ASKING "HEY, WHAT MAKES US SMELL ANYWAY?"— NOT TAKIN' A BATH!!— NO, SERIOUSLY— FOR THE SCIENCE-MINDED, HERE'S A CUTAWAY VIEW OF THE 'OL' FACTORY ITSELF.

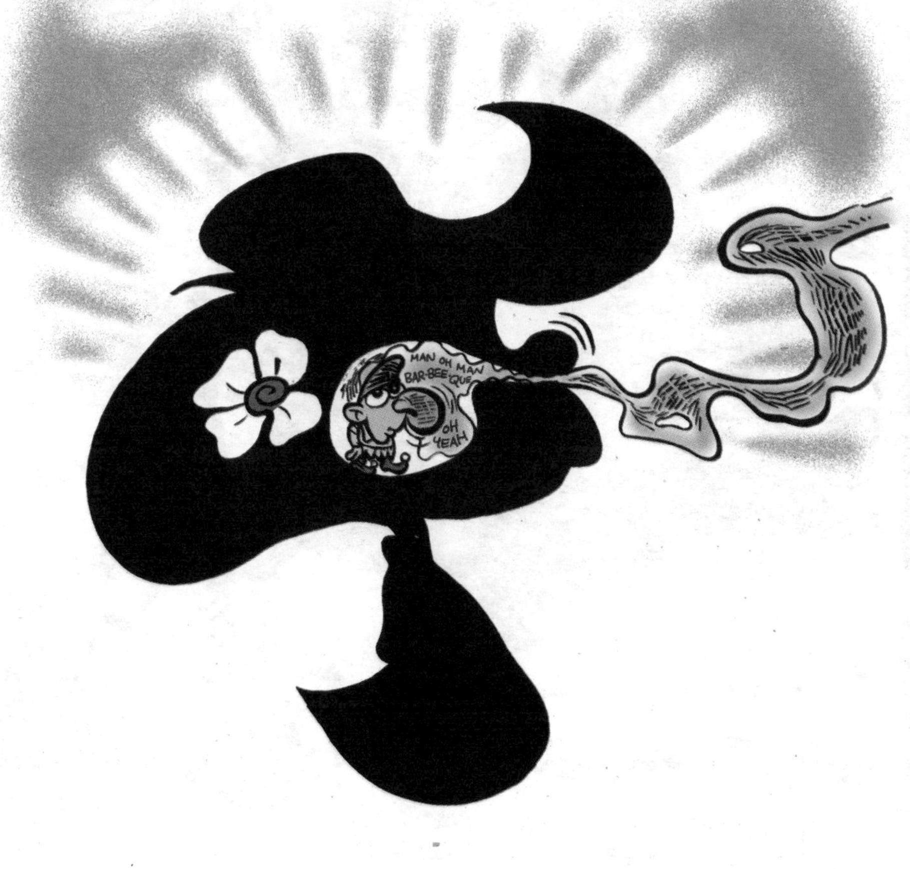
MAN OH MAN
BAR-BEE-QUE
OH YEAH

WE HOPE THIS HAS BEEN INFORMATIVE AS WELL AS SMELLY. THANK YOU FOR YOUR TIME.

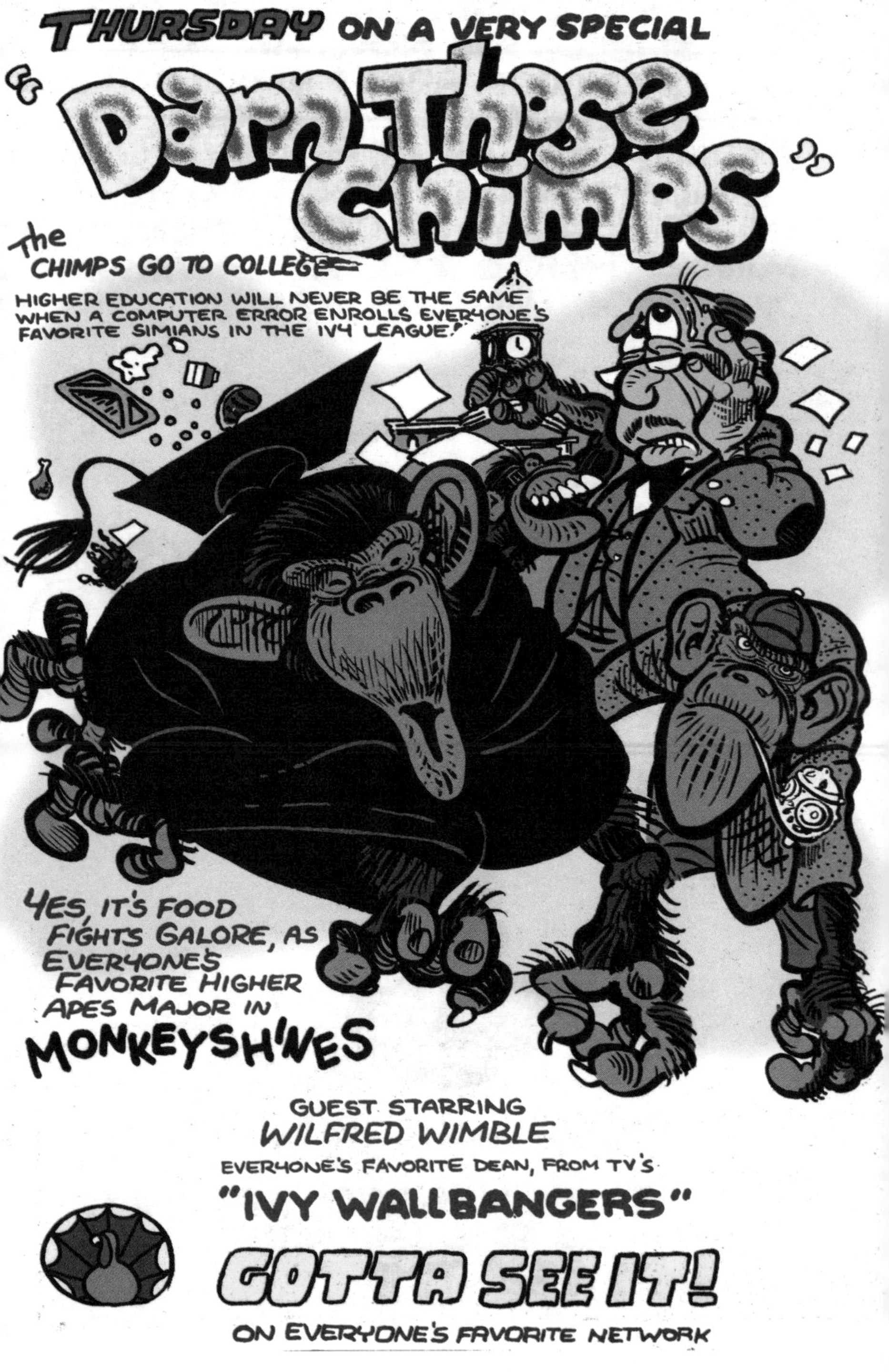
THURSDAY ON A VERY SPECIAL
"DARN THOSE CHIMPS"
THE CHIMPS GO TO COLLEGE
HIGHER EDUCATION WILL NEVER BE THE SAME WHEN A COMPUTER ERROR ENROLLS EVERYONE'S FAVORITE SIMIANS IN THE IVY LEAGUE!
YES, IT'S FOOD FIGHTS GALORE, AS EVERYONE'S FAVORITE HIGHER APES MAJOR IN
MONKEYSHINES
GUEST STARRING
WILFRED WIMBLE
EVERYONE'S FAVORITE DEAN, FROM TV'S
"IVY WALLBANGERS"
GOTTA SEE IT!
ON EVERYONE'S FAVORITE NETWORK

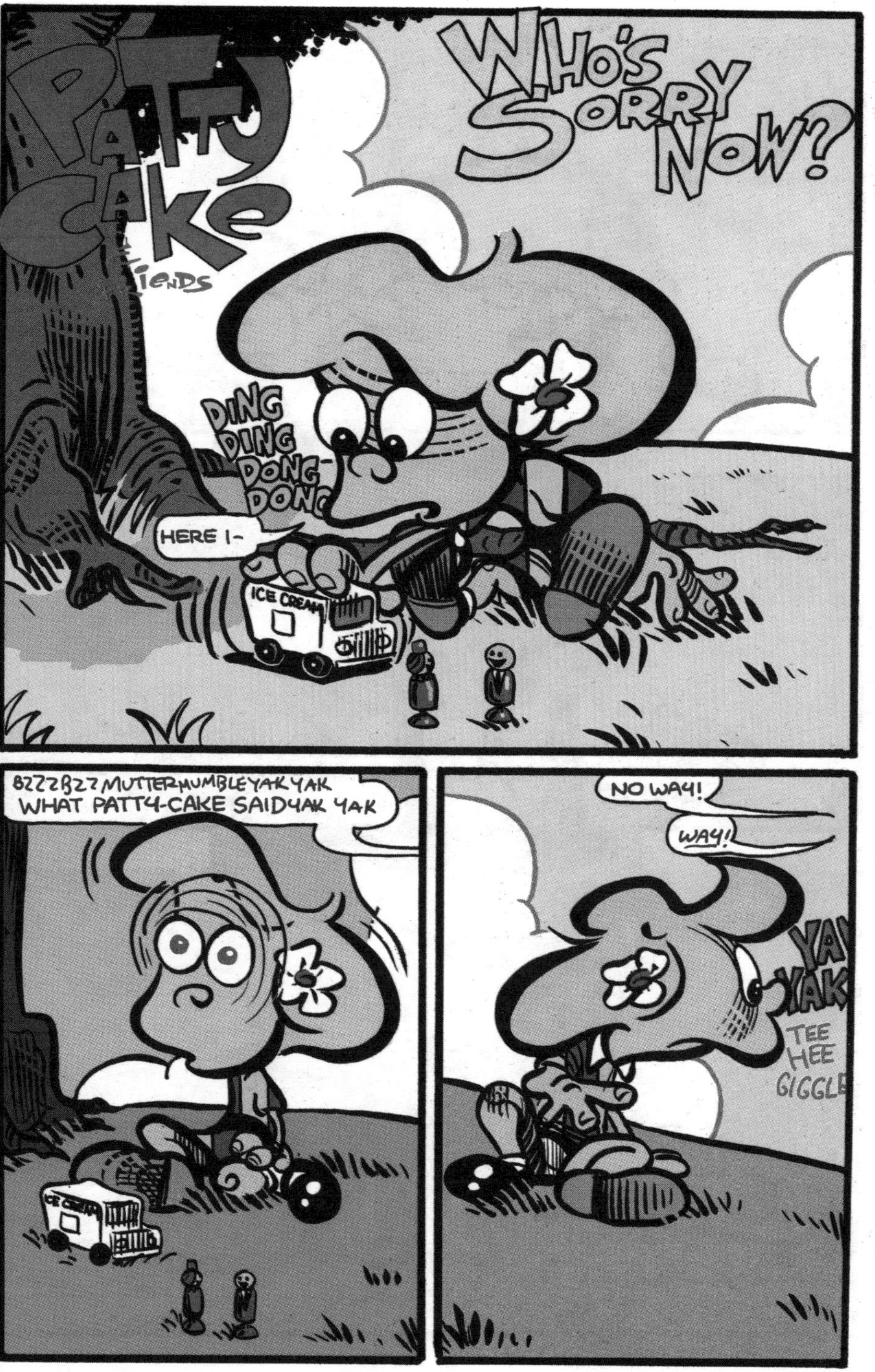
PATTY CAKE
WHO'S SORRY NOW?
DING DING DONG-DONG
HERE I-
ICE CREAM
BZZZBZZ MUTTERMUMBLEYAKYAK
WHAT PATTY-CAKE SAIDYAK YAK
ICE CREAM
NO WAY!
WAY!
YAK
TEE HEE

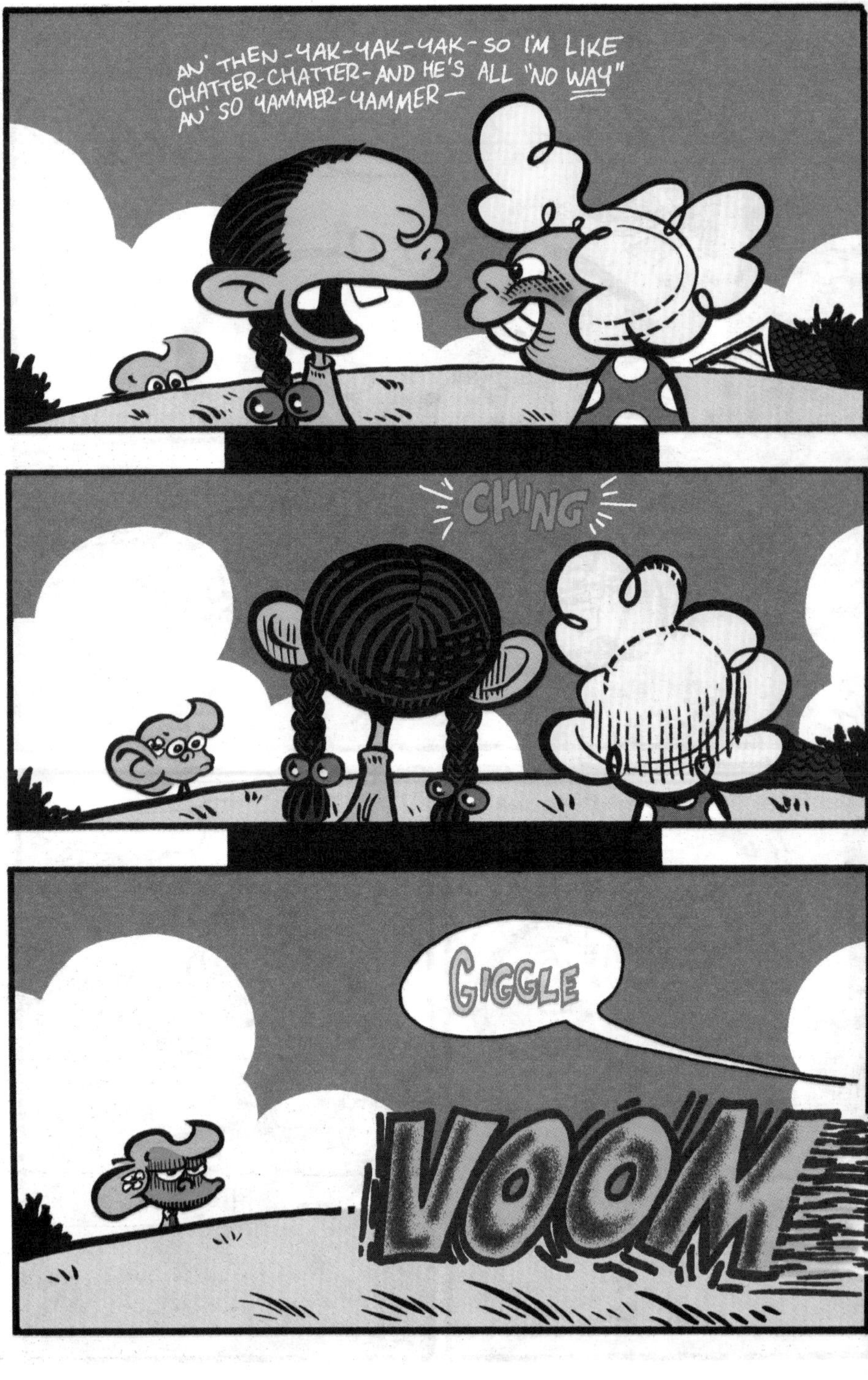
AN' THEN-YAK-YAK-YAK-SO I'M LIKE CHATTER-CHATTER-AND HE'S ALL "NO WAY" AN' SO YAMMER-YAMMER—
CHING
GIGGLE
VOOM

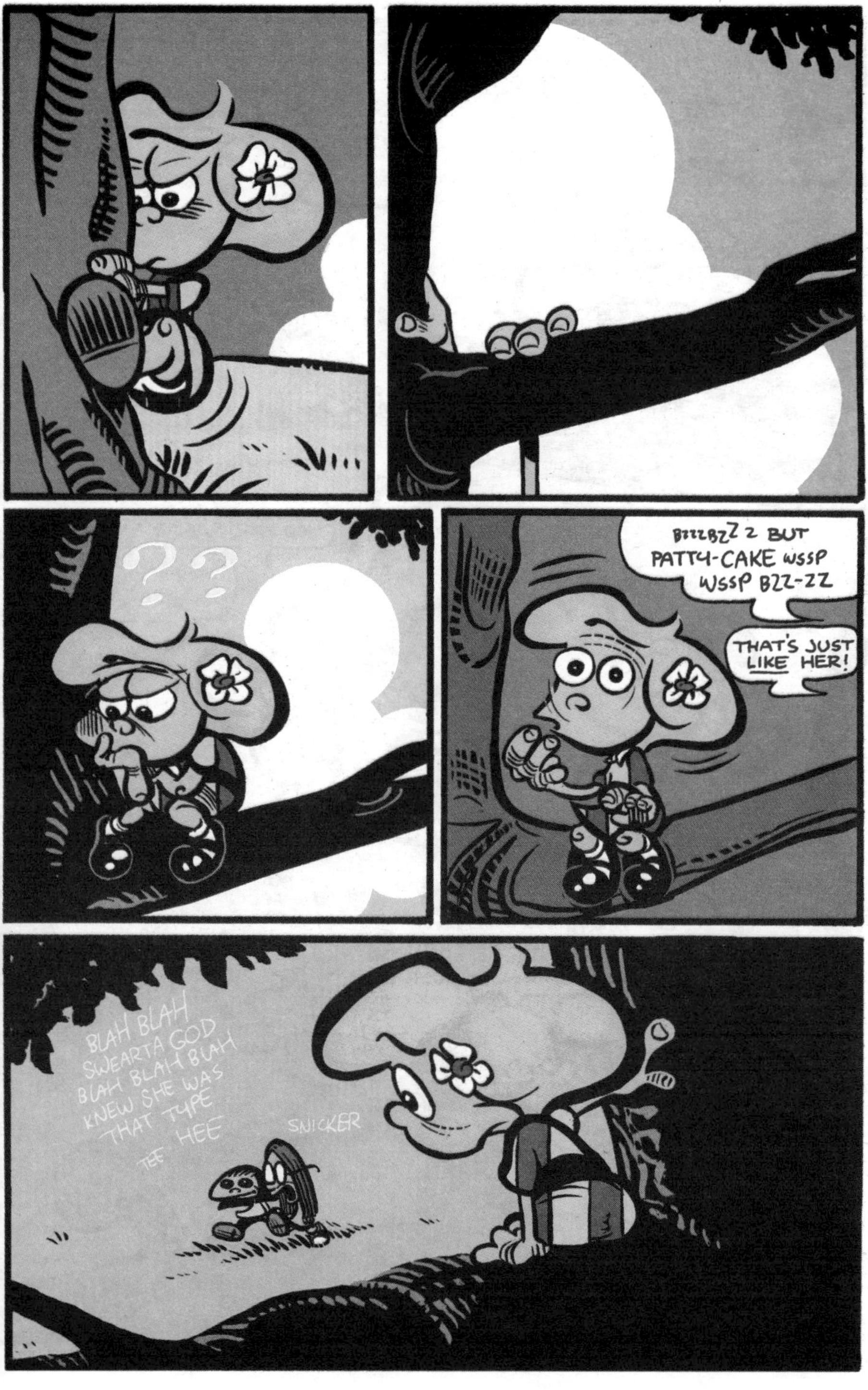
BZZZBZZ Z BUT PATTY-CAKE WSSP WSSP BZZ-ZZ
THAT'S JUST LIKE HER!
BLAH BLAH SWEARTA GOD BLAH BLAH BLAH KNEW SHE WAS THAT TYPE
HEE
TEE
SNICKER

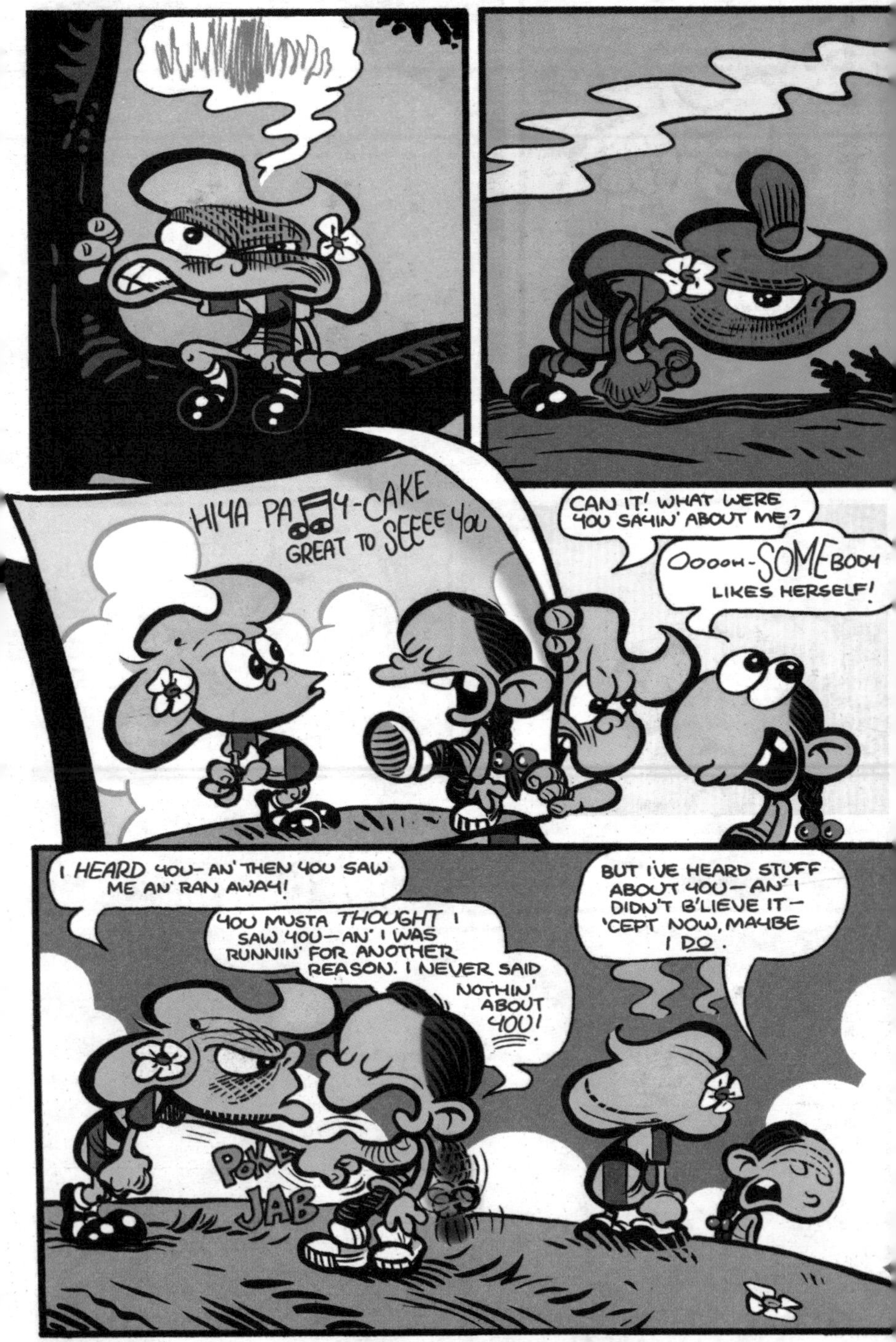
HIYA PA♫Y-CAKE
GREAT TO SEEEE YOU
CAN IT! WHAT WERE YOU SAYIN' ABOUT ME?
Ooooh-SOMEBODY LIKES HERSELF!
I HEARD YOU- AN' THEN YOU SAW ME AN' RAN AWAY!
YOU MUSTA THOUGHT I SAW YOU- AN' I WAS RUNNIN' FOR ANOTHER REASON. I NEVER SAID NOTHIN' ABOUT YOU!
POKE
JAB
BUT I'VE HEARD STUFF ABOUT YOU- AN' I DIDN'T B'LIEVE IT- 'CEPT NOW, MAYBE I DO.

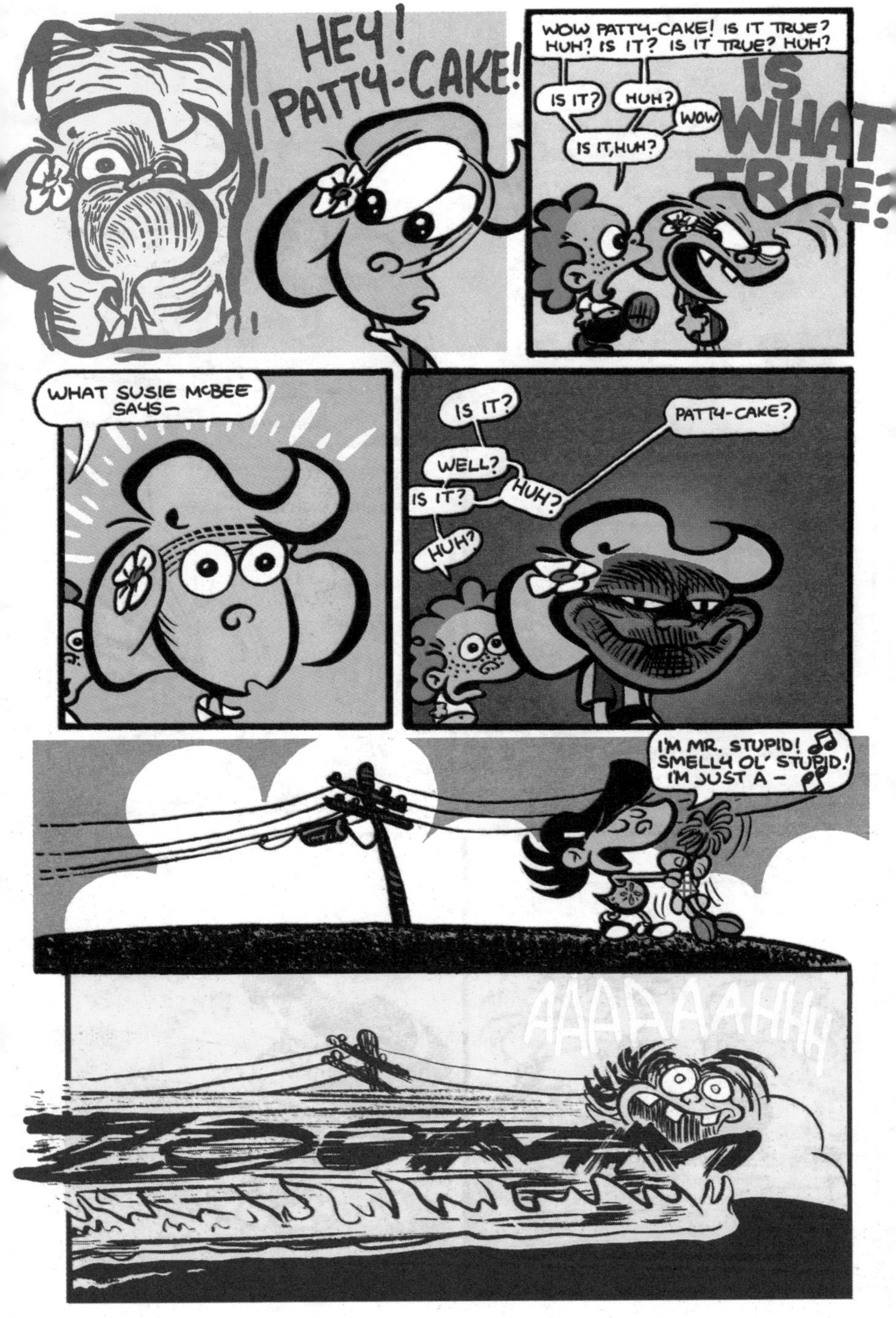
HEY! PATTY-CAKE!
WOW PATTY-CAKE! IS IT TRUE? HUH? IS IT? IS IT TRUE? HUH?
IS IT?
HUH?
WOW
IS IT, HUH?
IS WHAT TRUE?
WHAT SUSIE McBEE SAYS—
IS IT?
PATTY-CAKE?
WELL?
IS IT?
HUH?
HUH?
I'M MR. STUPID! SMELLY OL' STUPID! I'M JUST A—
AAAAAAHHH

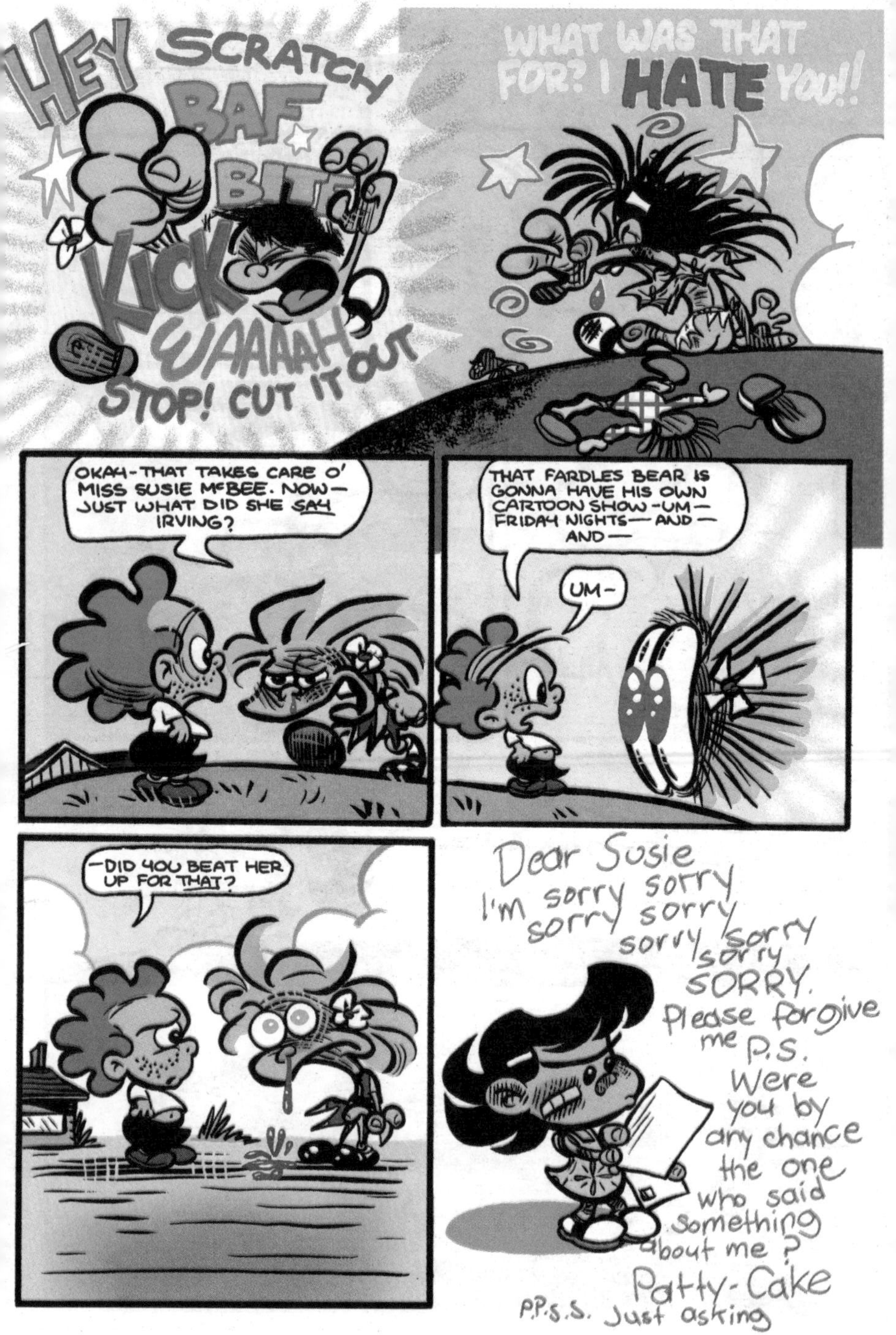
HEY SCRATCH
BAF
BITE
KICK
WAAAAH
STOP! CUT IT OUT
WHAT WAS THAT FOR? I HATE YOU!!
OKAY-THAT TAKES CARE O' MISS SUSIE McBEE. NOW— JUST WHAT DID SHE SAY IRVING?
THAT FARDLES BEAR IS GONNA HAVE HIS OWN CARTOON SHOW-UM— FRIDAY NIGHTS— AND— AND—
UM-
—DID YOU BEAT HER UP FOR THAT?
Dear Susie
I'm sorry sorry sorry sorry sorry sorry sorry SORRY. Please forgive me
P.S. Were you by any chance the one who said something about me?
Patty-Cake
P.P.S.S. Just asking

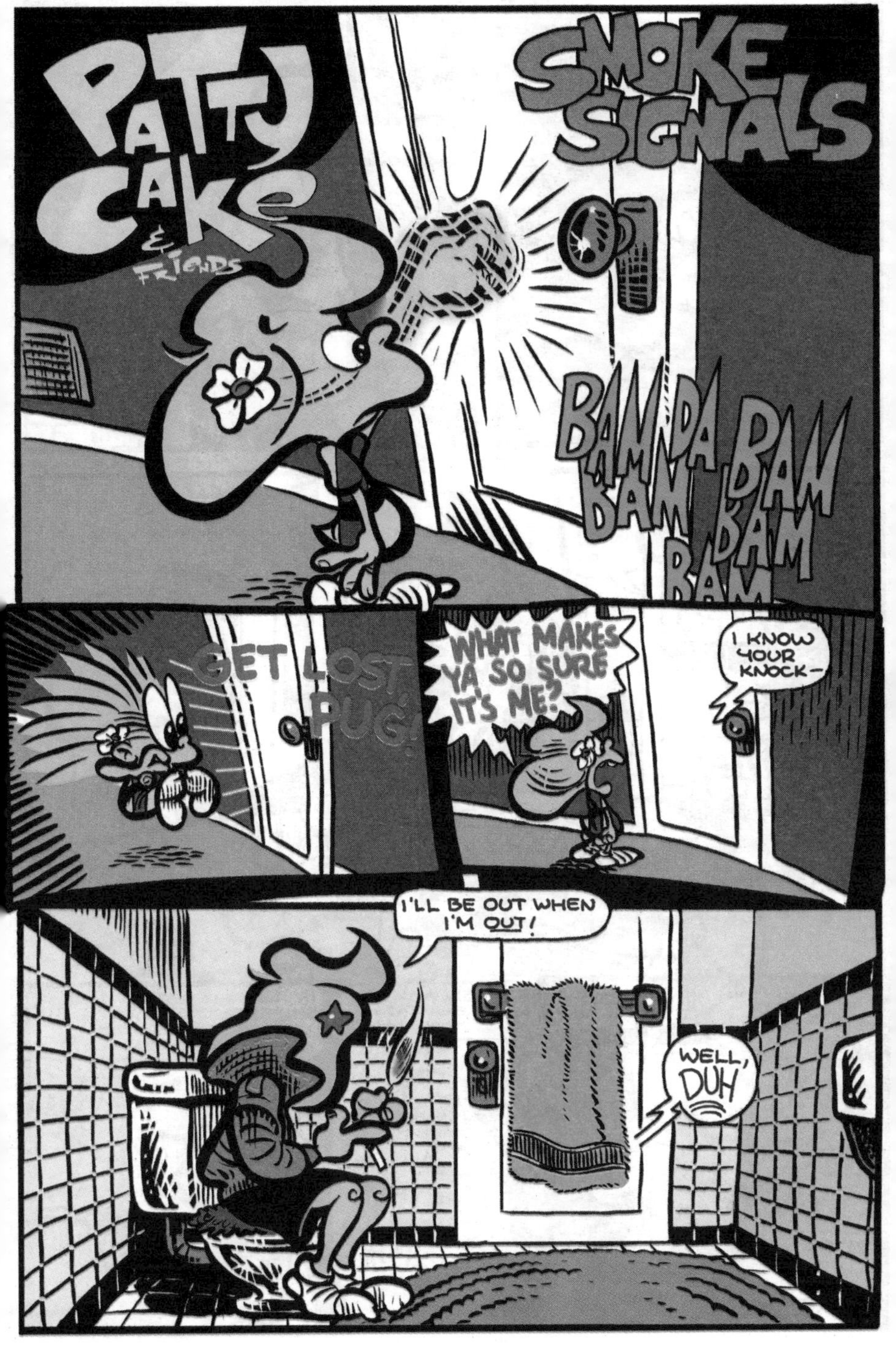
PATTY CAKE & FRIENDS
SMOKE SIGNALS
BAM DA BAM BAM BAM BAM BAM
GET LOST, PUG!
WHAT MAKES YA SO SURE IT'S ME?
I KNOW YOUR KNOCK—
I'LL BE OUT WHEN I'M OUT!
WELL, DUH

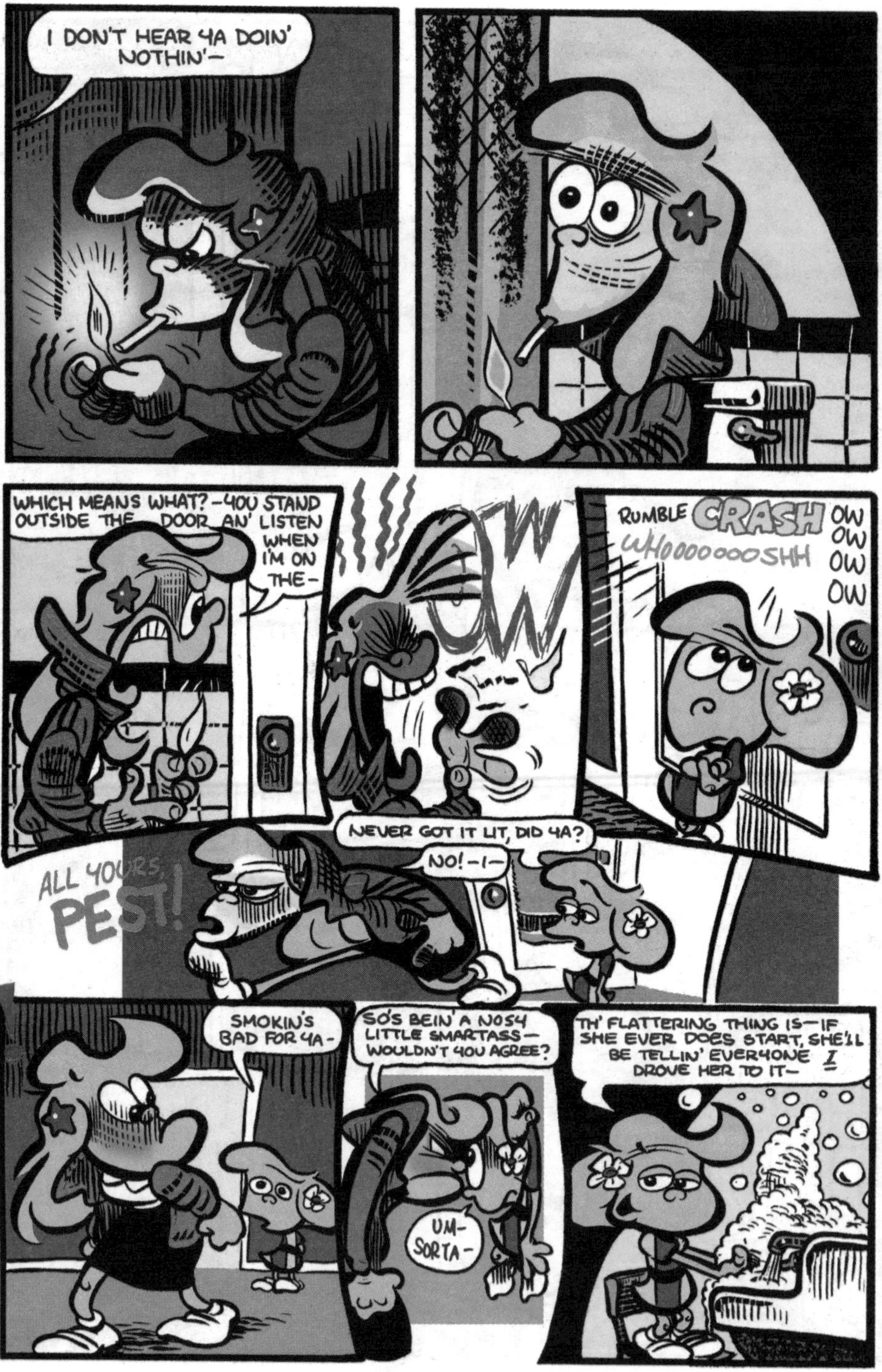

I DON'T HEAR YA DOIN' NOTHIN'—
WHICH MEANS WHAT?—YOU STAND OUTSIDE THE DOOR AN' LISTEN WHEN I'M ON THE—
OW
RUMBLE CRASH
WHOOOOOOOSHH
OW OW OW OW
NEVER GOT IT LIT, DID YA?
NO!—I—
ALL YOURS, PEST!
SMOKIN'S BAD FOR YA—
SO'S BEIN' A NOSY LITTLE SMARTASS—WOULDN'T YOU AGREE?
UM—SORTA—
TH' FLATTERING THING IS—IF SHE EVER DOES START, SHE'LL BE TELLIN' EVERYONE I DROVE HER TO IT—

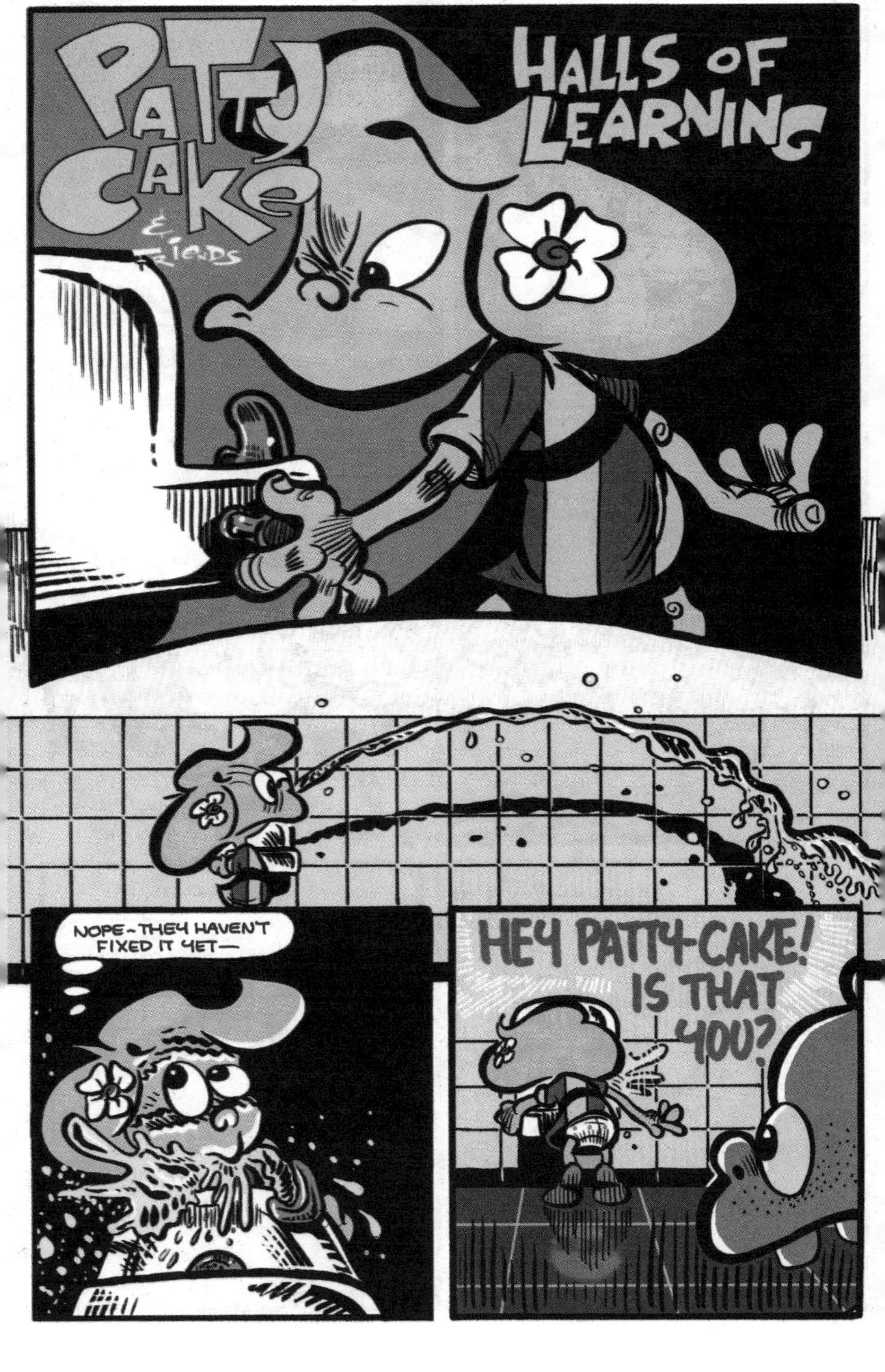
PATTY CAKE
& FRIENDS
HALLS OF LEARNING
NOPE–THEY HAVEN'T FIXED IT YET—
HEY PATTY-CAKE! IS THAT YOU?

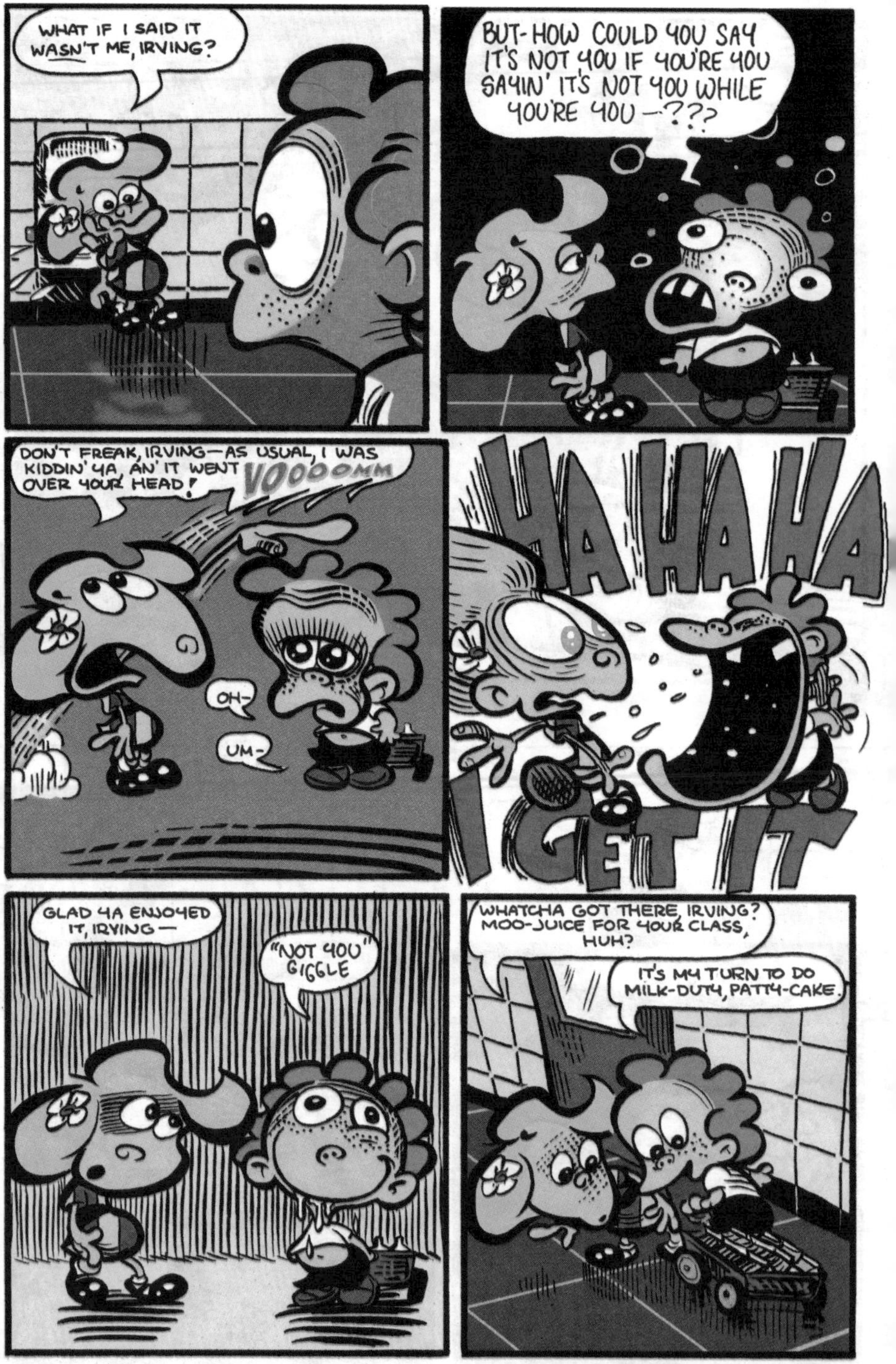
WHAT IF I SAID IT WASN'T ME, IRVING?
BUT-HOW COULD YOU SAY IT'S NOT YOU IF YOU'RE YOU SAYIN' IT'S NOT YOU WHILE YOU'RE YOU—???
DON'T FREAK, IRVING—AS USUAL, I WAS KIDDIN' YA, AN' IT WENT OVER YOUR HEAD!
VOOOOOMM
OH-
UM-
HAHAHA
I GET IT
GLAD YA ENJOYED IT, IRVING—
"NOT YOU" GIGGLE
WHATCHA GOT THERE, IRVING? MOO-JUICE FOR YOUR CLASS, HUH?
IT'S MY TURN TO DO MILK-DUTY, PATTY-CAKE.

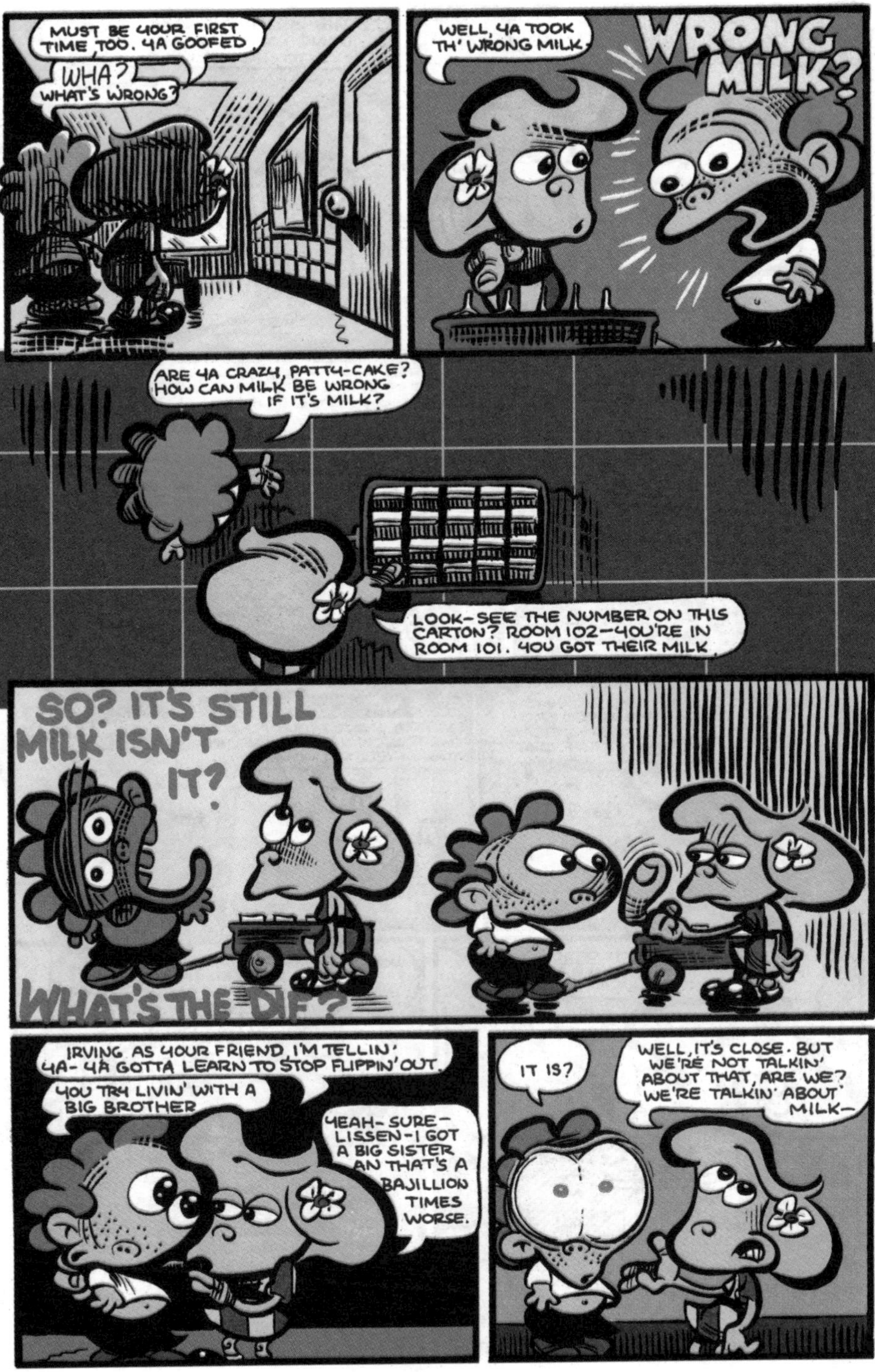
MUST BE YOUR FIRST TIME, TOO. YA GOOFED
WHA? WHAT'S WRONG?
WELL, YA TOOK TH' WRONG MILK
WRONG MILK?
ARE YA CRAZY, PATTY-CAKE? HOW CAN MILK BE WRONG IF IT'S MILK?
LOOK- SEE THE NUMBER ON THIS CARTON? ROOM 102—YOU'RE IN ROOM 101. YOU GOT THEIR MILK
SO? IT'S STILL MILK ISN'T IT?
WHAT'S THE DIF?
IRVING AS YOUR FRIEND I'M TELLIN' YA- YA GOTTA LEARN TO STOP FLIPPIN' OUT.
YOU TRY LIVIN' WITH A BIG BROTHER
YEAH- SURE- LISSEN- I GOT A BIG SISTER AN THAT'S A BAJILLION TIMES WORSE.
IT IS?
WELL, IT'S CLOSE. BUT WE'RE NOT TALKIN' ABOUT THAT, ARE WE? WE'RE TALKIN' ABOUT MILK—

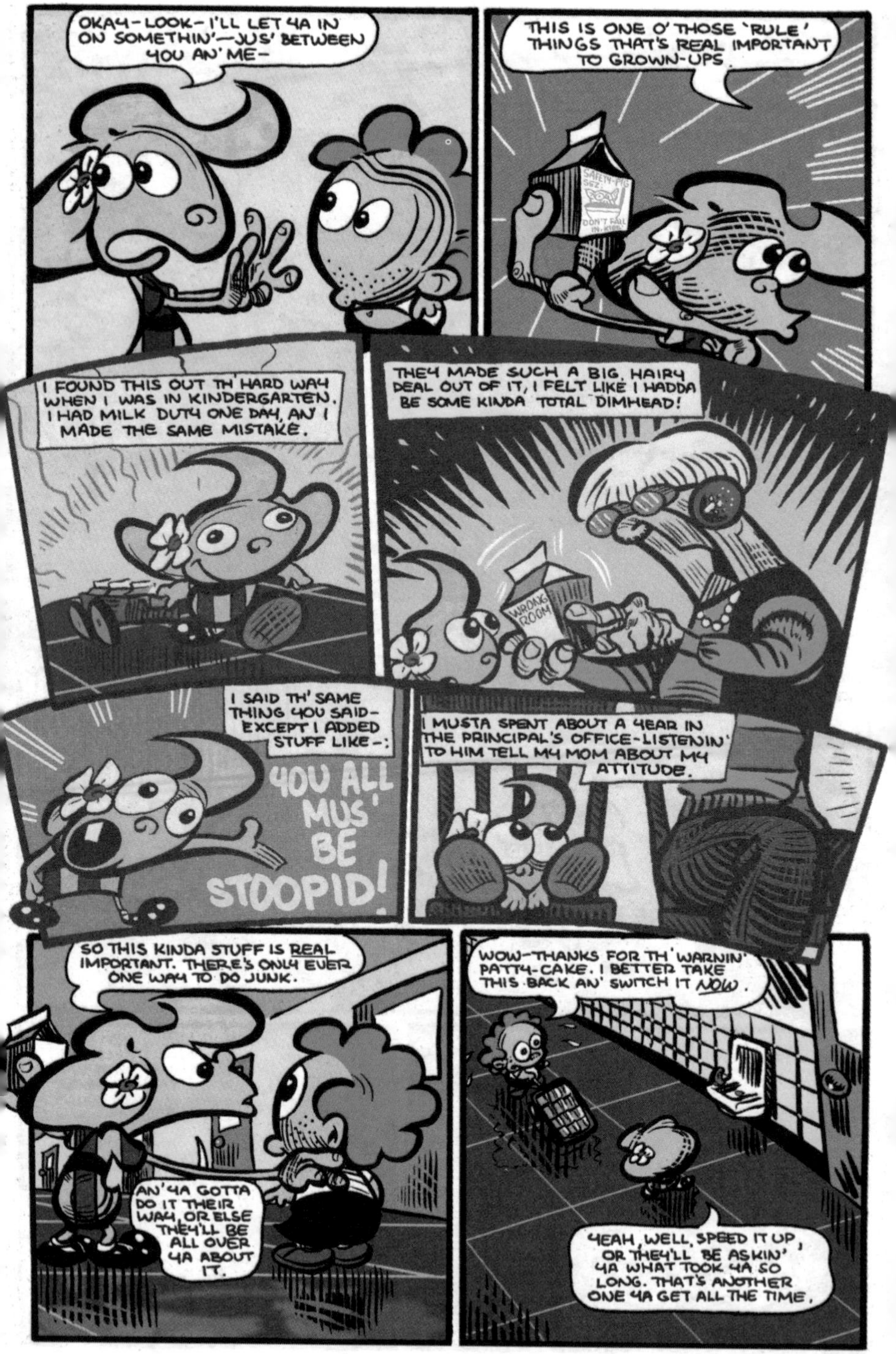
OKAY-LOOK-I'LL LET YA IN ON SOMETHIN'—JUS' BETWEEN YOU AN' ME-
THIS IS ONE O' THOSE 'RULE' THINGS THAT'S REAL IMPORTANT TO GROWN-UPS.
SAFETY-PIG SEZ: DON'T FALL IN KIDS
I FOUND THIS OUT TH' HARD WAY WHEN I WAS IN KINDERGARTEN. I HAD MILK DUTY ONE DAY, AN' I MADE THE SAME MISTAKE.
THEY MADE SUCH A BIG, HAIRY DEAL OUT OF IT, I FELT LIKE I HADDA BE SOME KINDA TOTAL DIMHEAD!
WRONG ROOM
I SAID TH' SAME THING YOU SAID-EXCEPT I ADDED STUFF LIKE-:
YOU ALL MUS' BE STOOPID!
I MUSTA SPENT ABOUT A YEAR IN THE PRINCIPAL'S OFFICE-LISTENIN' TO HIM TELL MY MOM ABOUT MY ATTITUDE.
SO THIS KINDA STUFF IS REAL IMPORTANT. THERE'S ONLY EVER ONE WAY TO DO JUNK.
AN' YA GOTTA DO IT THEIR WAY, OR ELSE THEY'LL BE ALL OVER YA ABOUT IT.
WOW-THANKS FOR TH' WARNIN' PATTY-CAKE. I BETTER TAKE THIS BACK AN' SWITCH IT NOW.
YEAH, WELL, SPEED IT UP, OR THEY'LL BE ASKIN' YA WHAT TOOK YA SO LONG. THAT'S ANOTHER ONE YA GET ALL THE TIME.

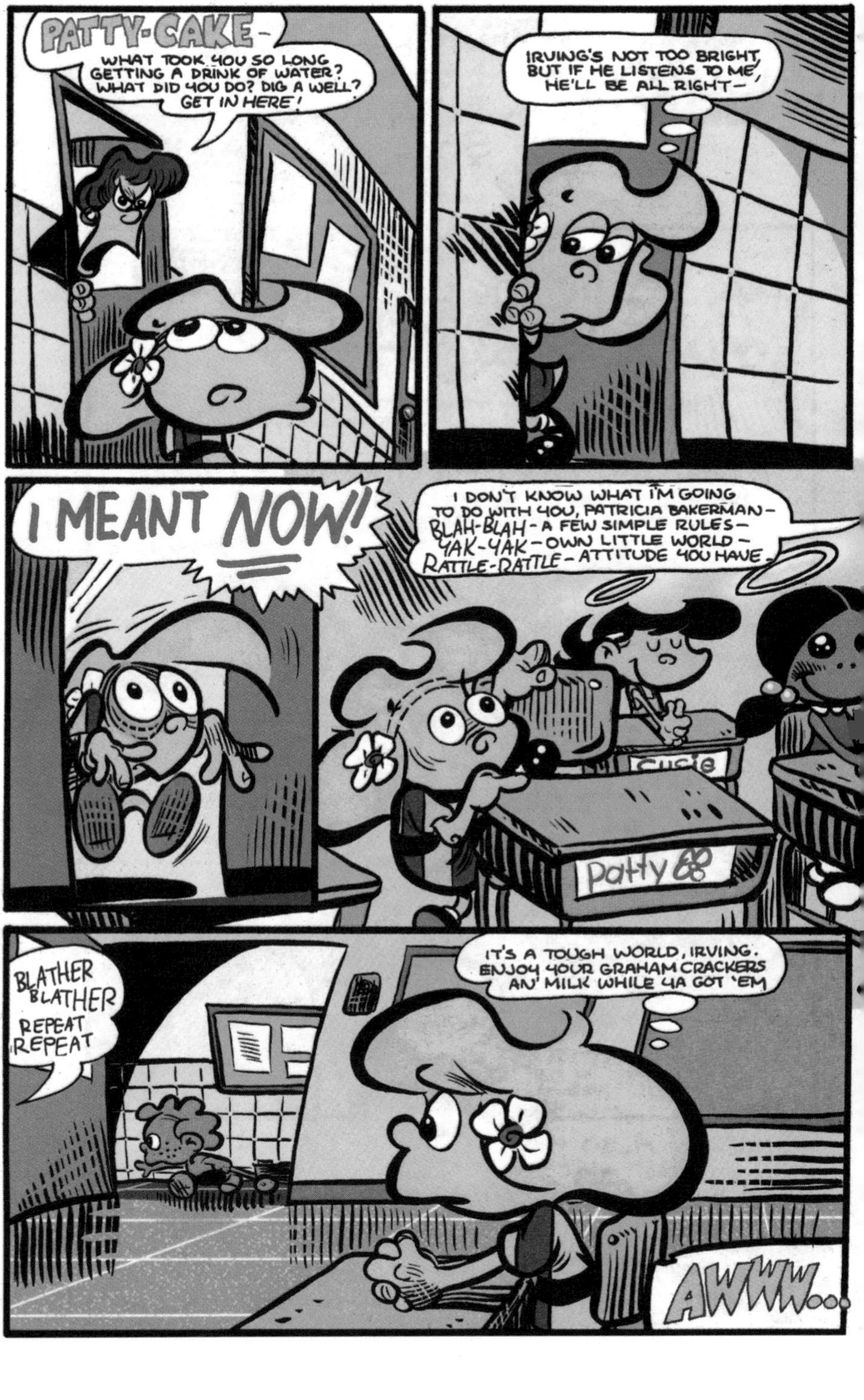
PATTY-CAKE—
WHAT TOOK YOU SO LONG GETTING A DRINK OF WATER? WHAT DID YOU DO? DIG A WELL? GET IN HERE!
IRVING'S NOT TOO BRIGHT, BUT IF HE LISTENS TO ME, HE'LL BE ALL RIGHT—
I MEANT NOW!
I DON'T KNOW WHAT I'M GOING TO DO WITH YOU, PATRICIA BAKERMAN—BLAH-BLAH—A FEW SIMPLE RULES—YAK-YAK—OWN LITTLE WORLD—RATTLE-RATTLE—ATTITUDE YOU HAVE
Susie
Patty
BLATHER BLATHER REPEAT REPEAT
IT'S A TOUGH WORLD, IRVING. ENJOY YOUR GRAHAM CRACKERS AN' MILK WHILE YA GOT 'EM
AWWW...

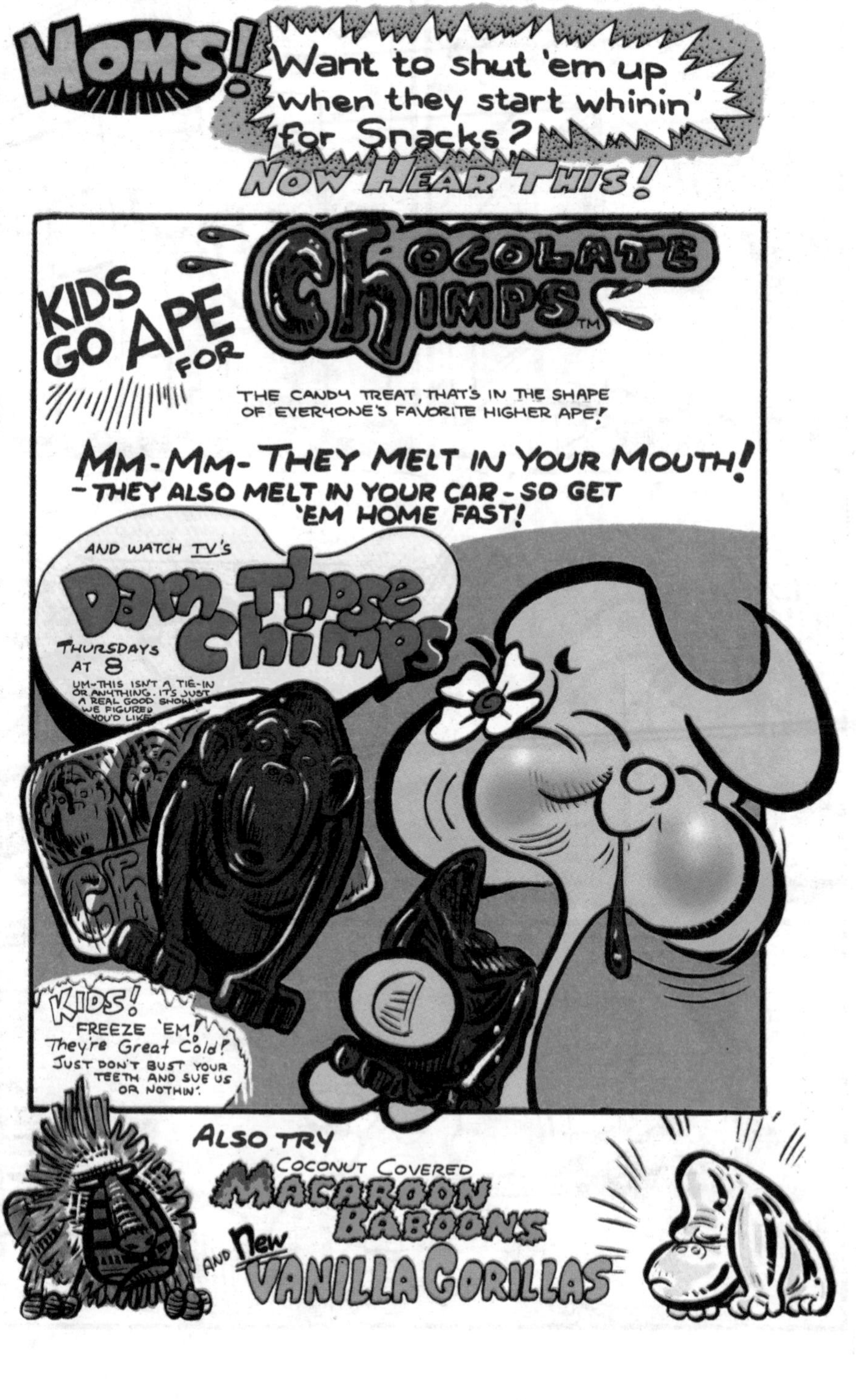
MOMS!
Want to shut 'em up when they start whinin' for Snacks?
NOW HEAR THIS!
KIDS GO APE FOR
CHOCOLATE CHIMPS™
THE CANDY TREAT, THAT'S IN THE SHAPE OF EVERYONE'S FAVORITE HIGHER APE!
MM-MM- THEY MELT IN YOUR MOUTH!
- THEY ALSO MELT IN YOUR CAR - SO GET 'EM HOME FAST!
AND WATCH TV'S
Darn Those Chimps
THURSDAYS AT 8
KIDS!
FREEZE 'EM!
They're Great Cold!
JUST DON'T BUST YOUR TEETH AND SUE US OR NOTHIN'.
ALSO TRY
COCONUT COVERED
MACAROON BABOONS
AND New
VANILLA GORILLAS

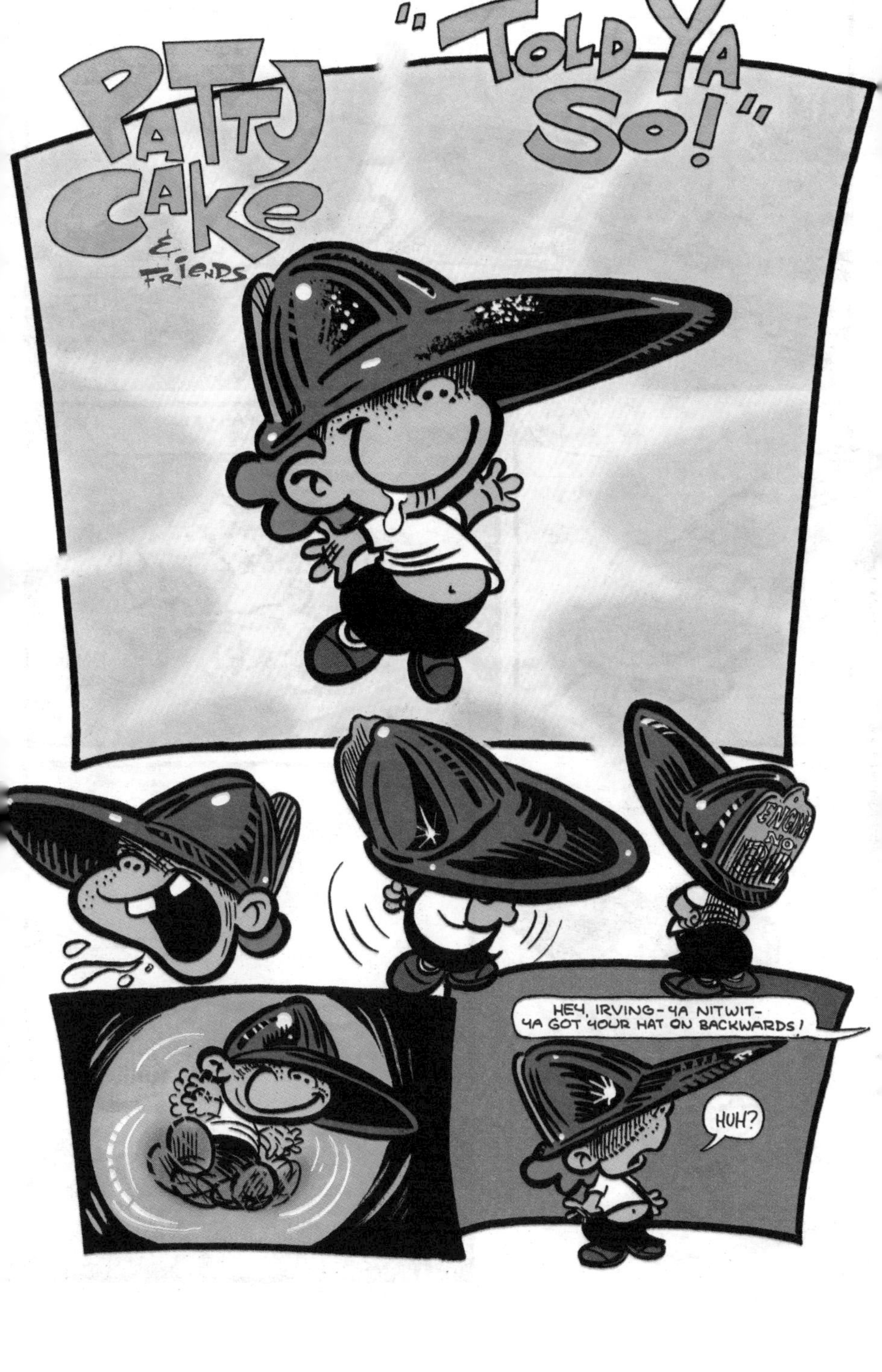
PATTY CAKE & FRIENDS
"TOLD YA SO!"
ENGINE NO
HEY, IRVING–YA NITWIT–
YA GOT YOUR HAT ON BACKWARDS!
HUH?

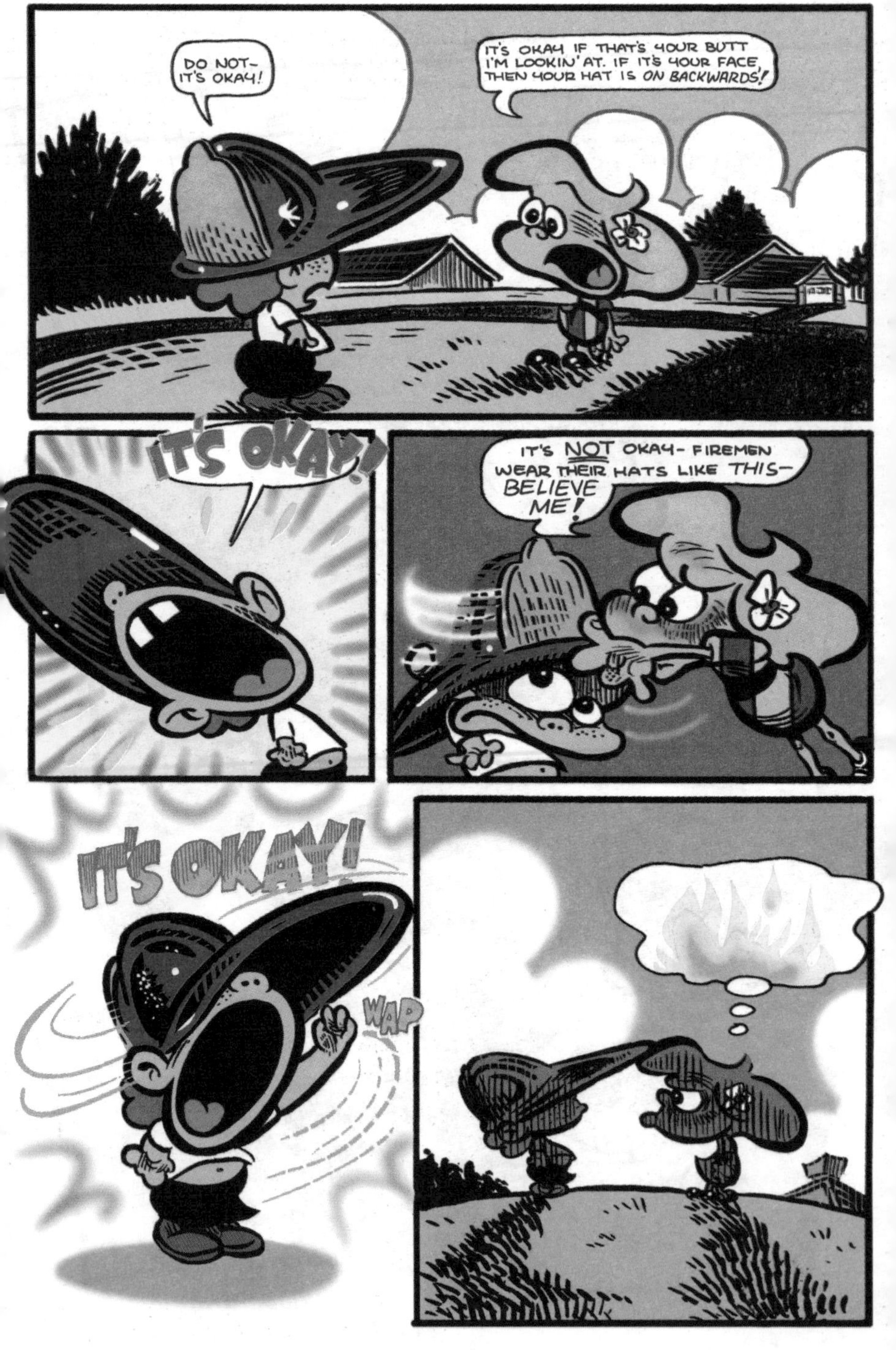
DO NOT-
IT'S OKAY!
IT'S OKAY IF THAT'S YOUR BUTT I'M LOOKIN' AT. IF IT'S YOUR FACE, THEN YOUR HAT IS ON BACKWARDS!
IT'S OKAY!!
IT'S NOT OKAY- FIREMEN WEAR THEIR HATS LIKE THIS- BELIEVE ME!
IT'S OKAY!
WAP

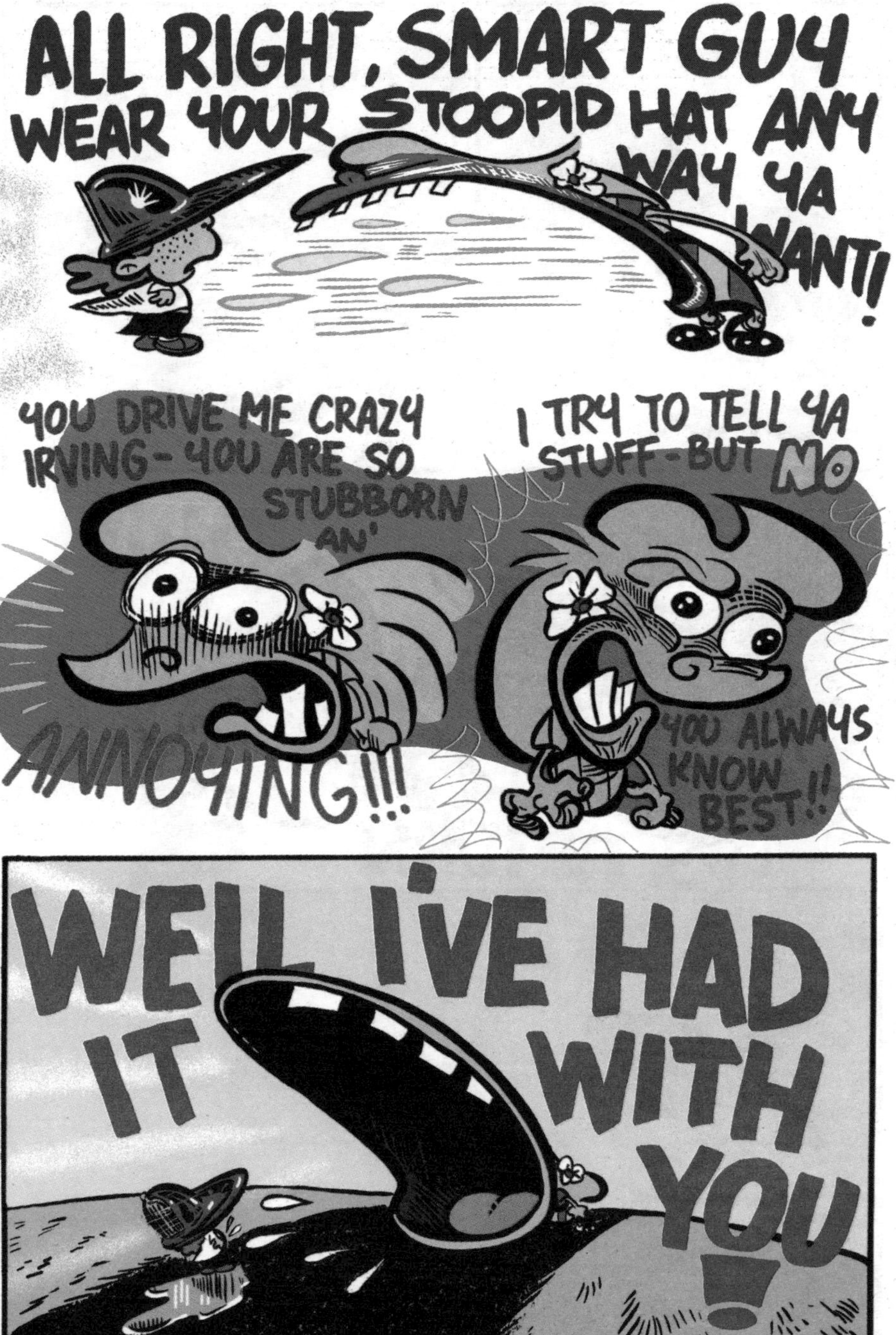
ALL RIGHT, SMART GUY
WEAR YOUR STOOPID HAT ANY WAY YA WANT!
YOU DRIVE ME CRAZY IRVING - YOU ARE SO STUBBORN AN' ANNOYING!!!
I TRY TO TELL YA STUFF - BUT NO
YOU ALWAYS KNOW BEST!!
WELL I'VE HAD IT WITH YOU!

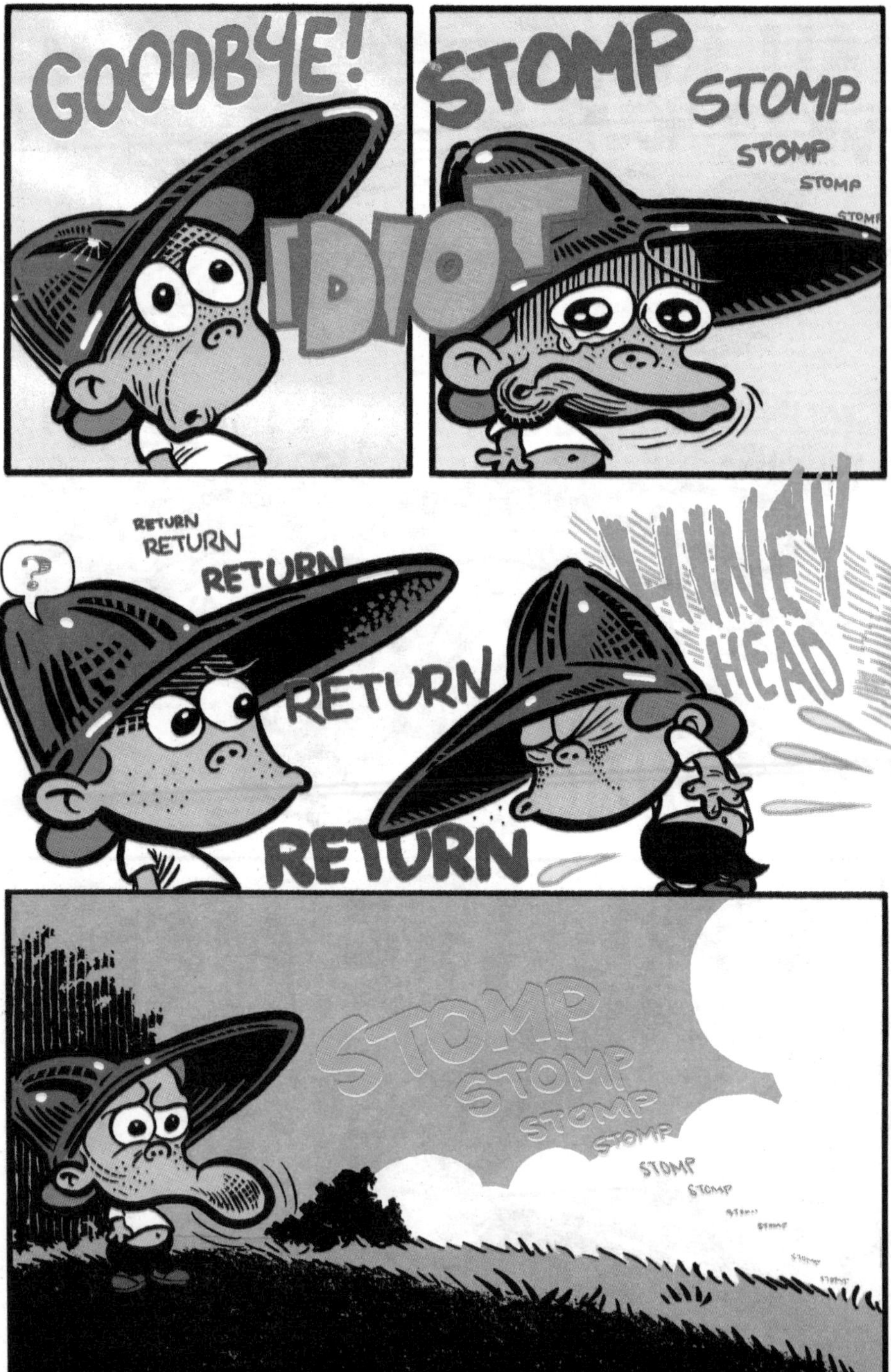
GOODBYE!
IDIOT
STOMP
STOMP
STOMP
STOMP
RETURN
RETURN
RETURN
?
RETURN
RETURN
HINEY HEAD
STOMP
STOMP
STOMP
STOMP
STOMP
STOMP

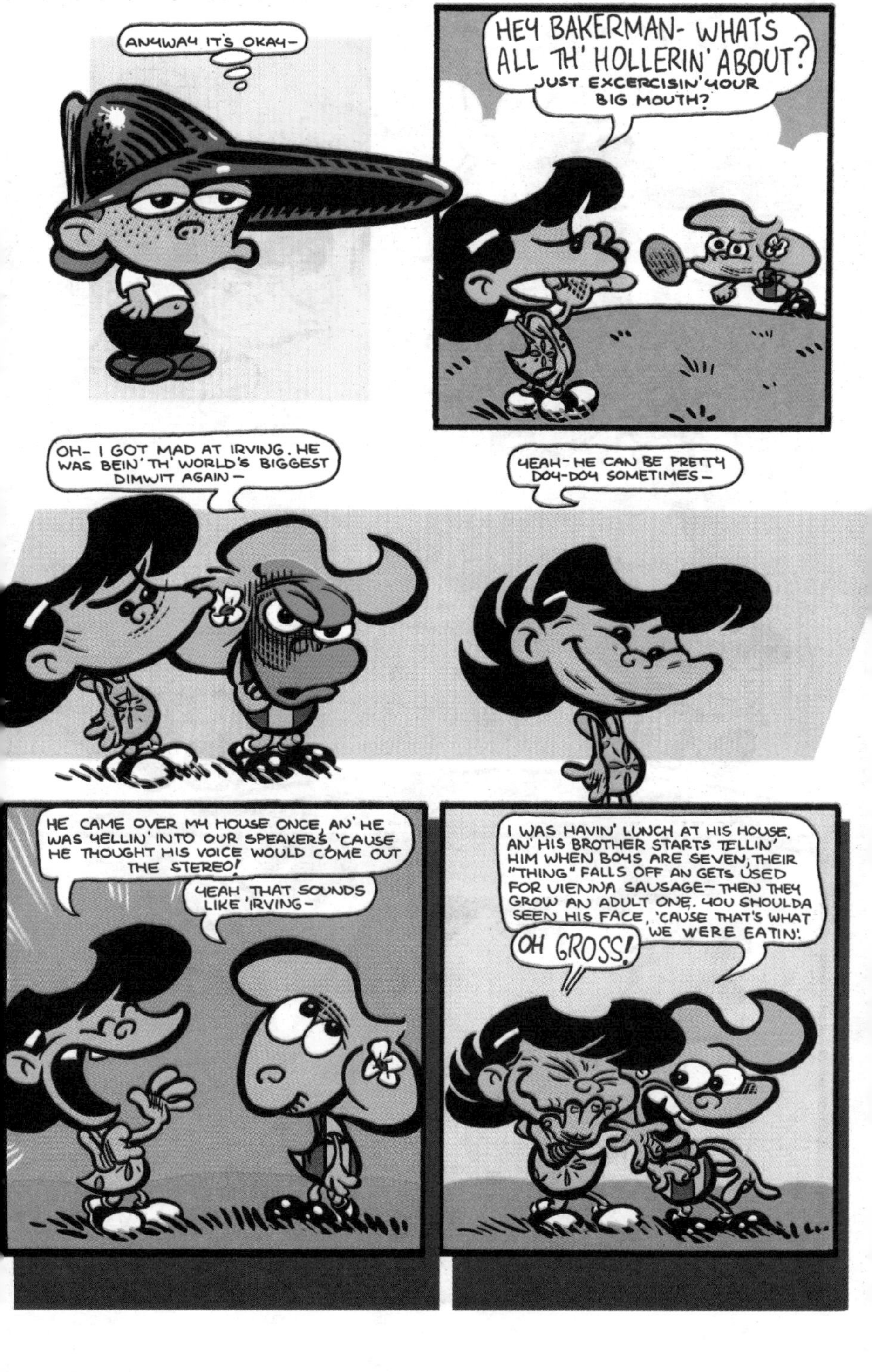
ANYWAY IT'S OKAY-
HEY BAKERMAN- WHAT'S ALL TH' HOLLERIN' ABOUT? JUST EXCERCISIN' YOUR BIG MOUTH?
OH- I GOT MAD AT IRVING. HE WAS BEIN' TH' WORLD'S BIGGEST DIMWIT AGAIN-
YEAH- HE CAN BE PRETTY DOY-DOY SOMETIMES-
HE CAME OVER MY HOUSE ONCE, AN' HE WAS YELLIN' INTO OUR SPEAKERS 'CAUSE HE THOUGHT HIS VOICE WOULD COME OUT THE STEREO!
YEAH THAT SOUNDS LIKE IRVING-
I WAS HAVIN' LUNCH AT HIS HOUSE, AN' HIS BROTHER STARTS TELLIN' HIM WHEN BOYS ARE SEVEN, THEIR "THING" FALLS OFF AN GETS USED FOR VIENNA SAUSAGE- THEN THEY GROW AN ADULT ONE. YOU SHOULDA SEEN HIS FACE, 'CAUSE THAT'S WHAT WE WERE EATIN'.
OH GROSS!

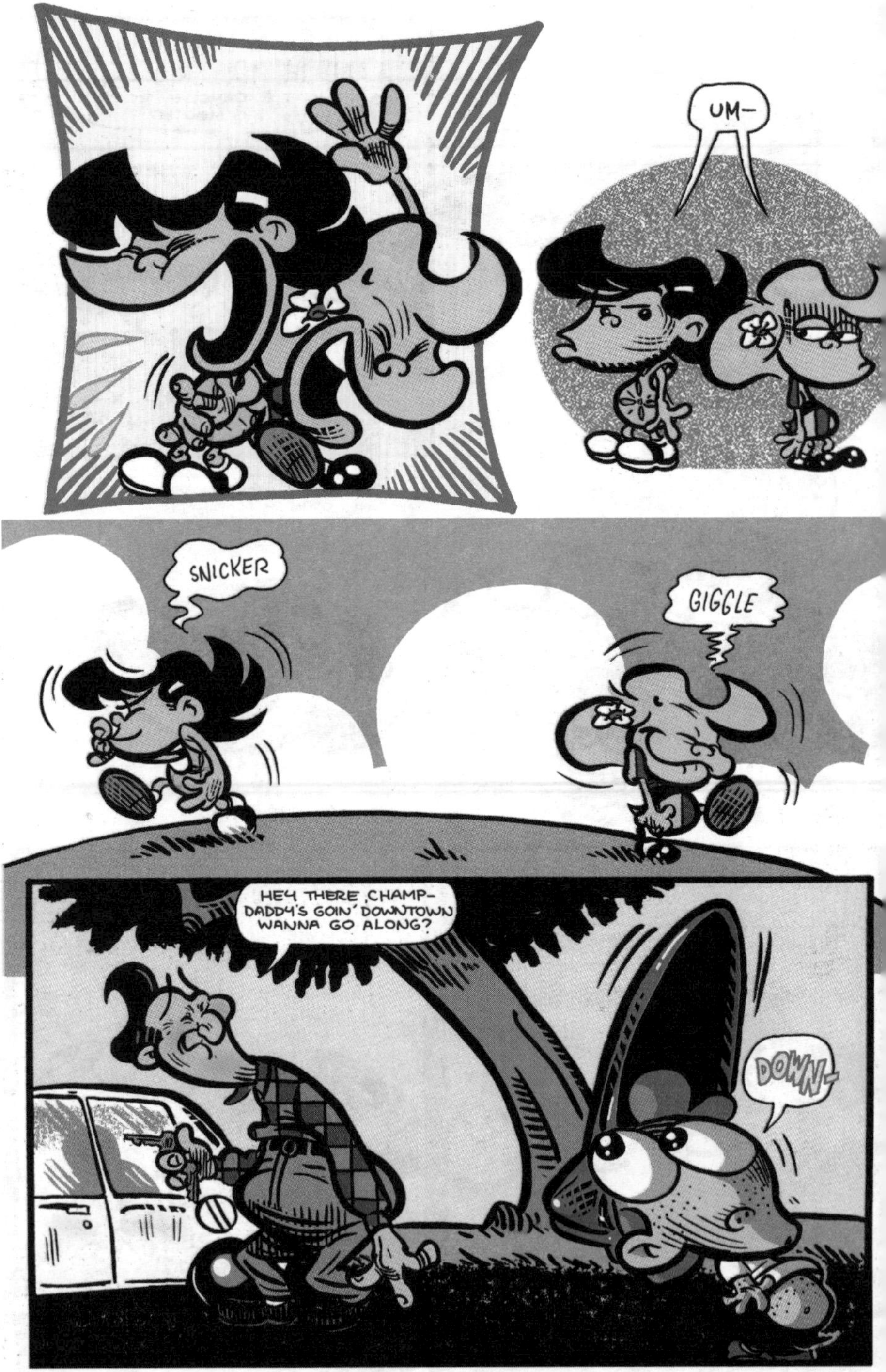
UM–
SNICKER
GIGGLE
HEY THERE, CHAMP-
DADDY'S GOIN' DOWNTOWN
WANNA GO ALONG?
DOWN-

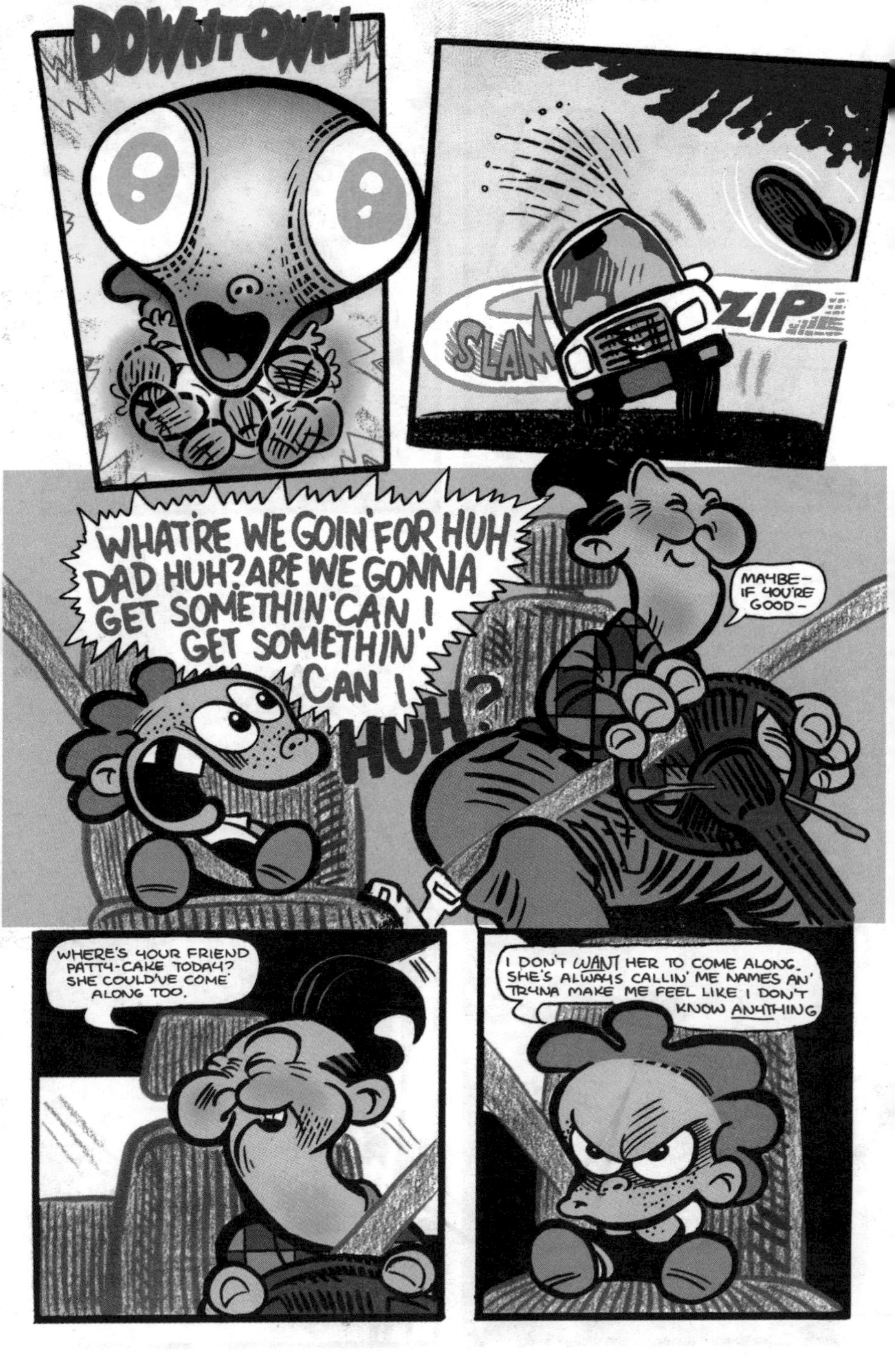
DOWNTOWN
SLAM
ZIP
WHATRE WE GOIN' FOR HUH DAD HUH? ARE WE GONNA GET SOMETHIN' CAN I GET SOMETHIN' CAN I
HUH?
MAYBE— IF YOU'RE GOOD—
WHERE'S YOUR FRIEND PATTY-CAKE TODAY? SHE COULD'VE COME ALONG TOO.
I DON'T WANT HER TO COME ALONG. SHE'S ALWAYS CALLIN' ME NAMES AN' TRYNA MAKE ME FEEL LIKE I DON'T KNOW ANYTHING

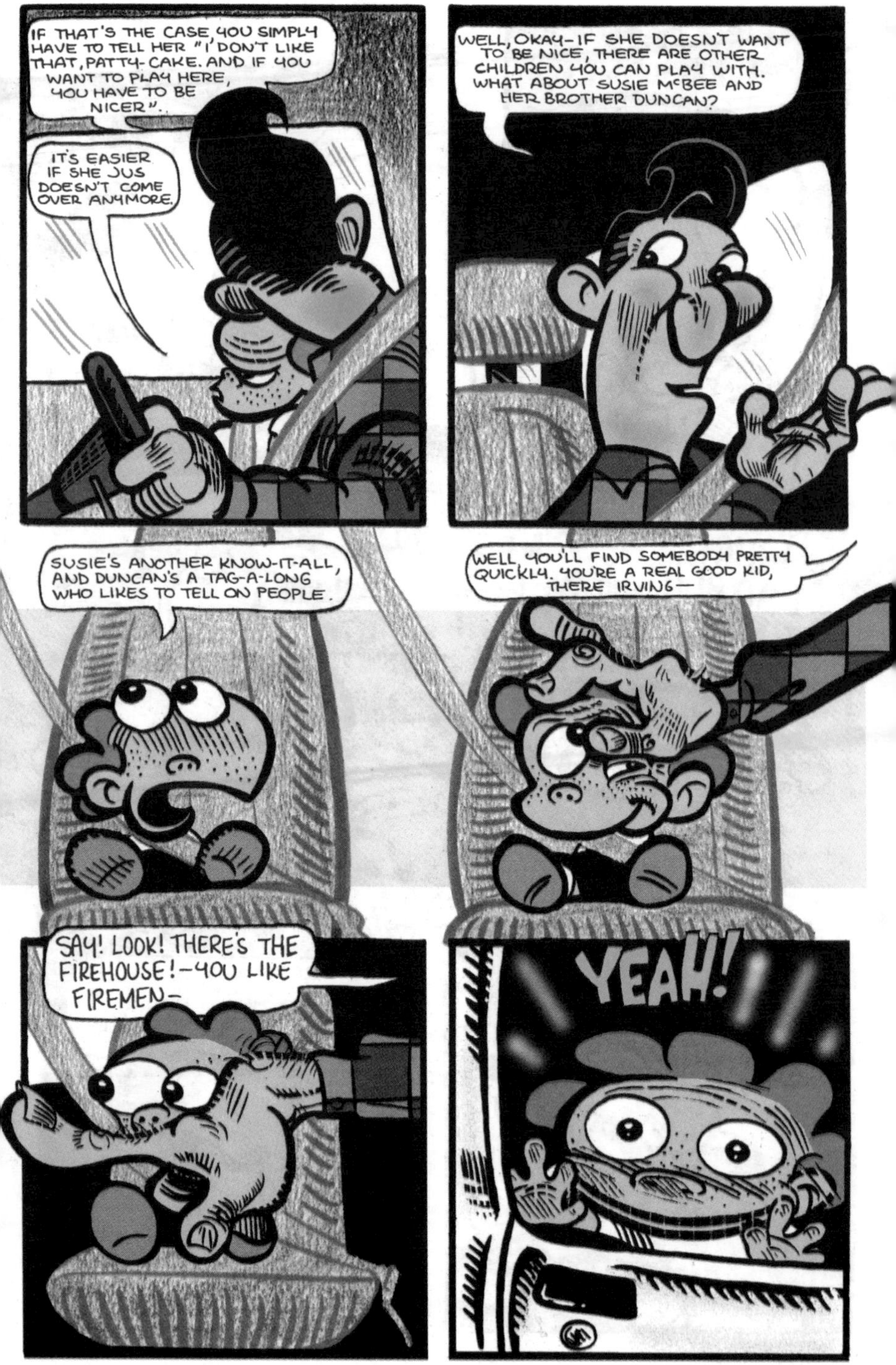
IF THAT'S THE CASE, YOU SIMPLY HAVE TO TELL HER "I DON'T LIKE THAT, PATTY-CAKE. AND IF YOU WANT TO PLAY HERE, YOU HAVE TO BE NICER".
IT'S EASIER IF SHE JUS DOESN'T COME OVER ANYMORE.
WELL, OKAY- IF SHE DOESN'T WANT TO BE NICE, THERE ARE OTHER CHILDREN YOU CAN PLAY WITH. WHAT ABOUT SUSIE McBEE AND HER BROTHER DUNCAN?
SUSIE'S ANOTHER KNOW-IT-ALL, AND DUNCAN'S A TAG-A-LONG WHO LIKES TO TELL ON PEOPLE.
WELL, YOU'LL FIND SOMEBODY PRETTY QUICKLY. YOU'RE A REAL GOOD KID, THERE IRVING—
SAY! LOOK! THERE'S THE FIREHOUSE! —YOU LIKE FIREMEN—
YEAH!

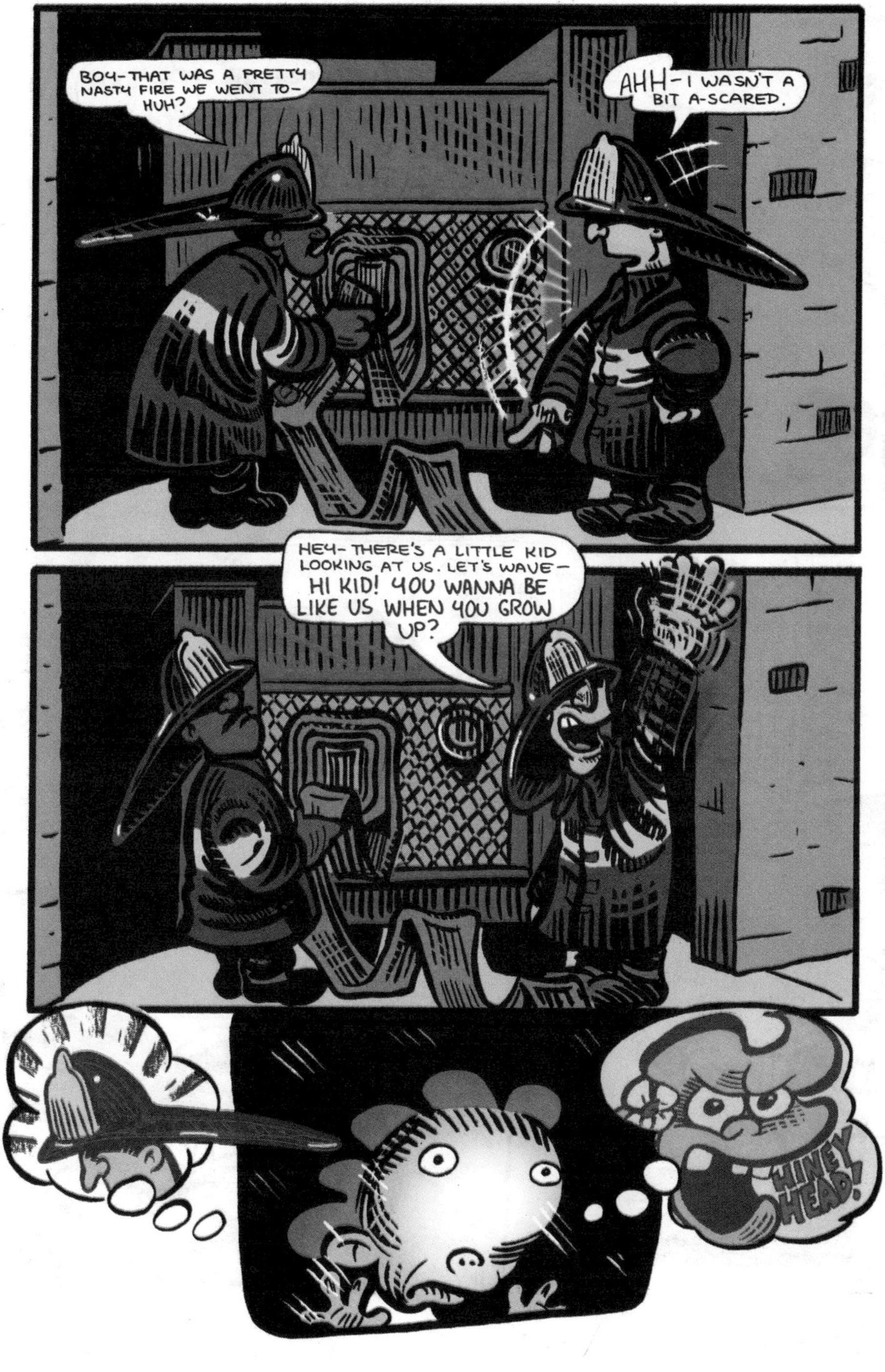
BOY-THAT WAS A PRETTY NASTY FIRE WE WENT TO-HUH?
AHH-I WASN'T A BIT A-SCARED.
HEY-THERE'S A LITTLE KID LOOKING AT US. LET'S WAVE-
HI KID! YOU WANNA BE LIKE US WHEN YOU GROW UP?
HINEY HEAD!

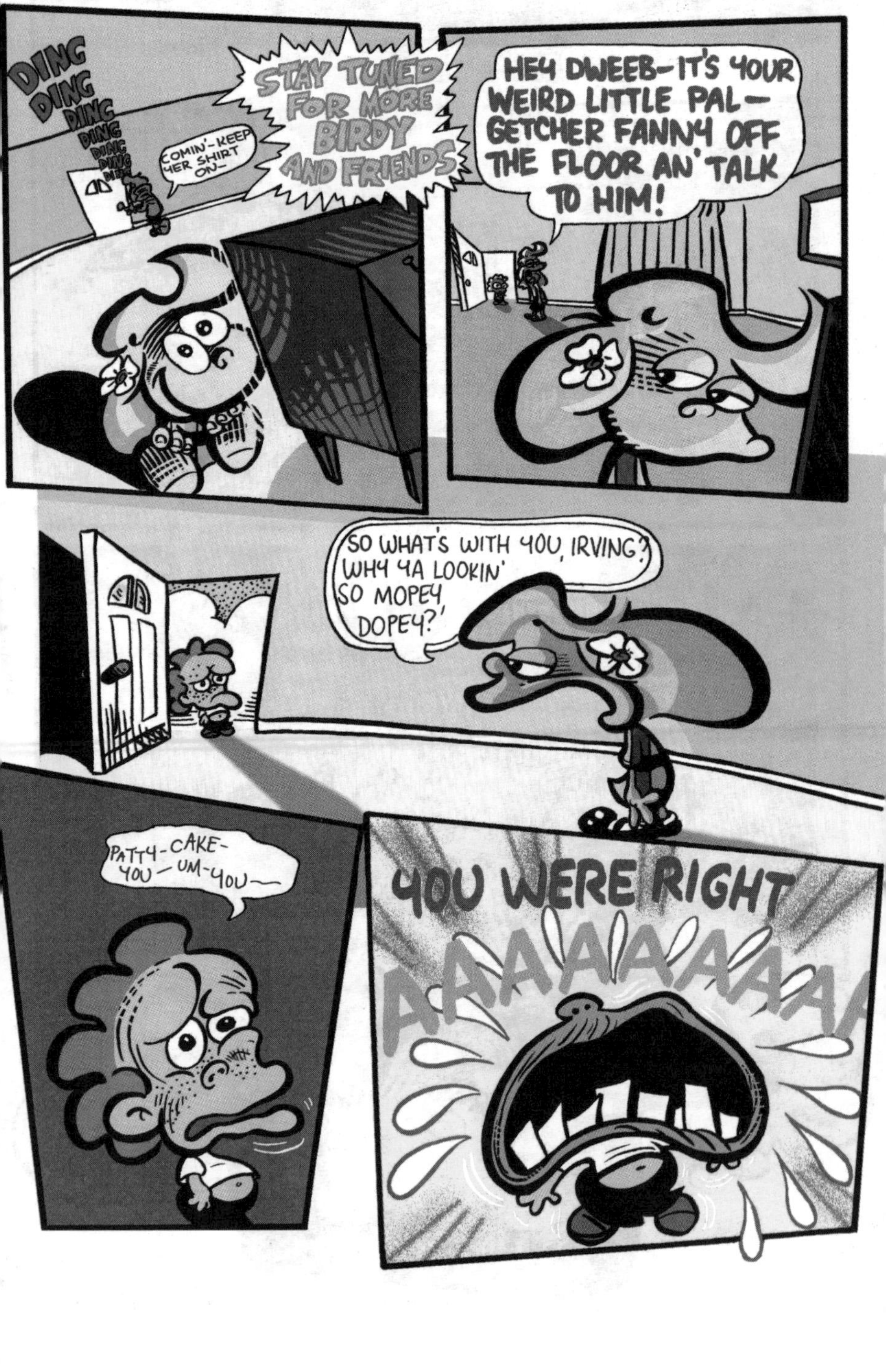
DING DING DING DING DING DING DING
COMIN'-KEEP YER SHIRT ON-
STAY TUNED FOR MORE BIRDY AND FRIENDS
HEY DWEEB-IT'S YOUR WEIRD LITTLE PAL-GETCHER FANNY OFF THE FLOOR AN' TALK TO HIM!
SO WHAT'S WITH YOU, IRVING? WHY YA LOOKIN' SO MOPEY, DOPEY?
PATTY-CAKE-YOU-UM-YOU-
YOU WERE RIGHT
AAAAAAAA

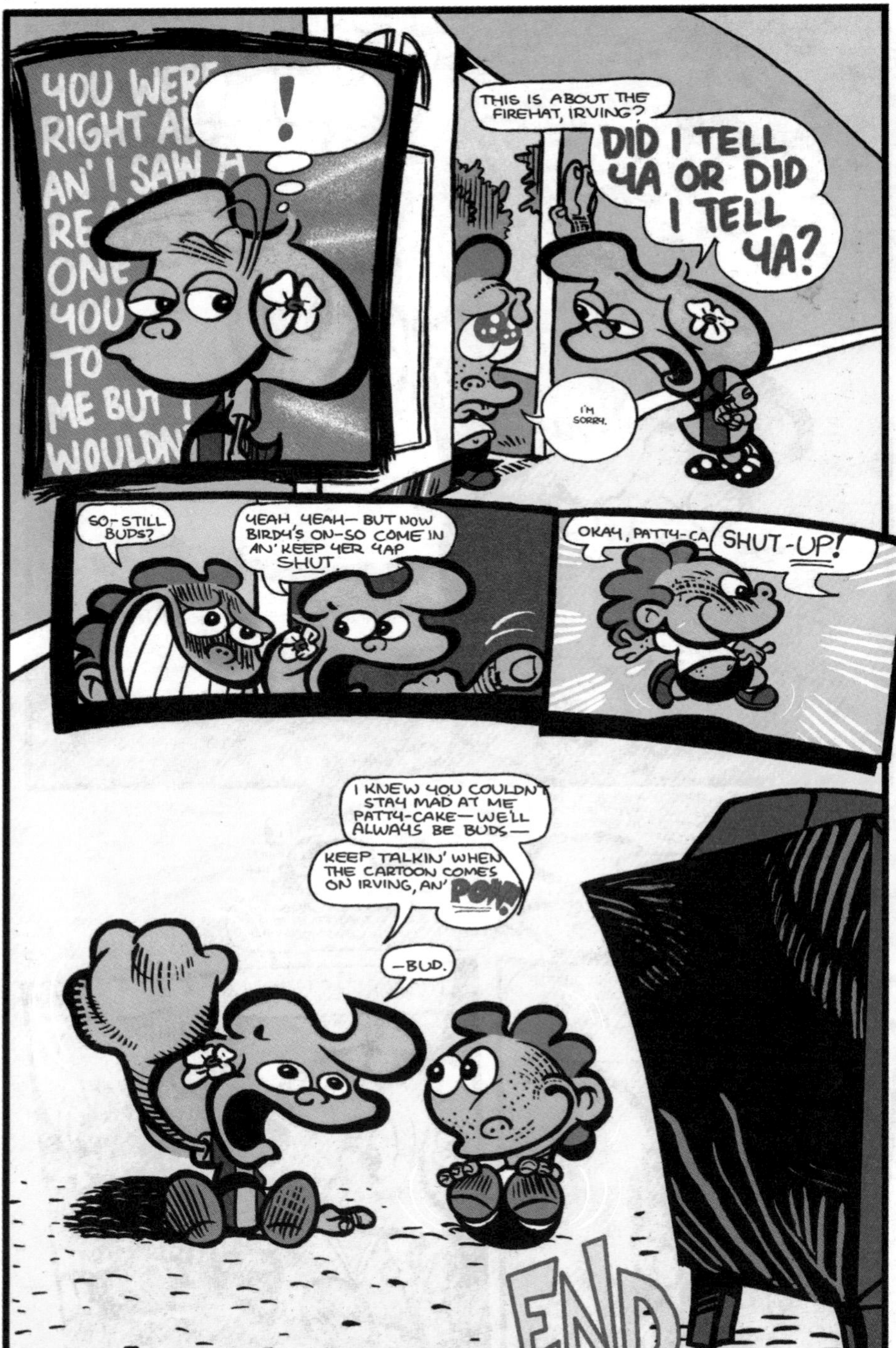

YOU WERE
RIGHT AL
AN' I SAW A
RE
ONE
YOU
TO
ME BUT I
WOULDN'
!
THIS IS ABOUT THE FIREHAT, IRVING?
DID I TELL YA OR DID I TELL YA?
I'M SORRY.
SO- STILL BUDS?
YEAH YEAH- BUT NOW BIRDY'S ON- SO COME IN AN' KEEP YER YAP SHUT.
OKAY, PATTY-CA
SHUT-UP!
I KNEW YOU COULDN'T STAY MAD AT ME PATTY-CAKE- WE'LL ALWAYS BE BUDS-
KEEP TALKIN' WHEN THE CARTOON COMES ON IRVING, AN' POW!
-BUD.
END

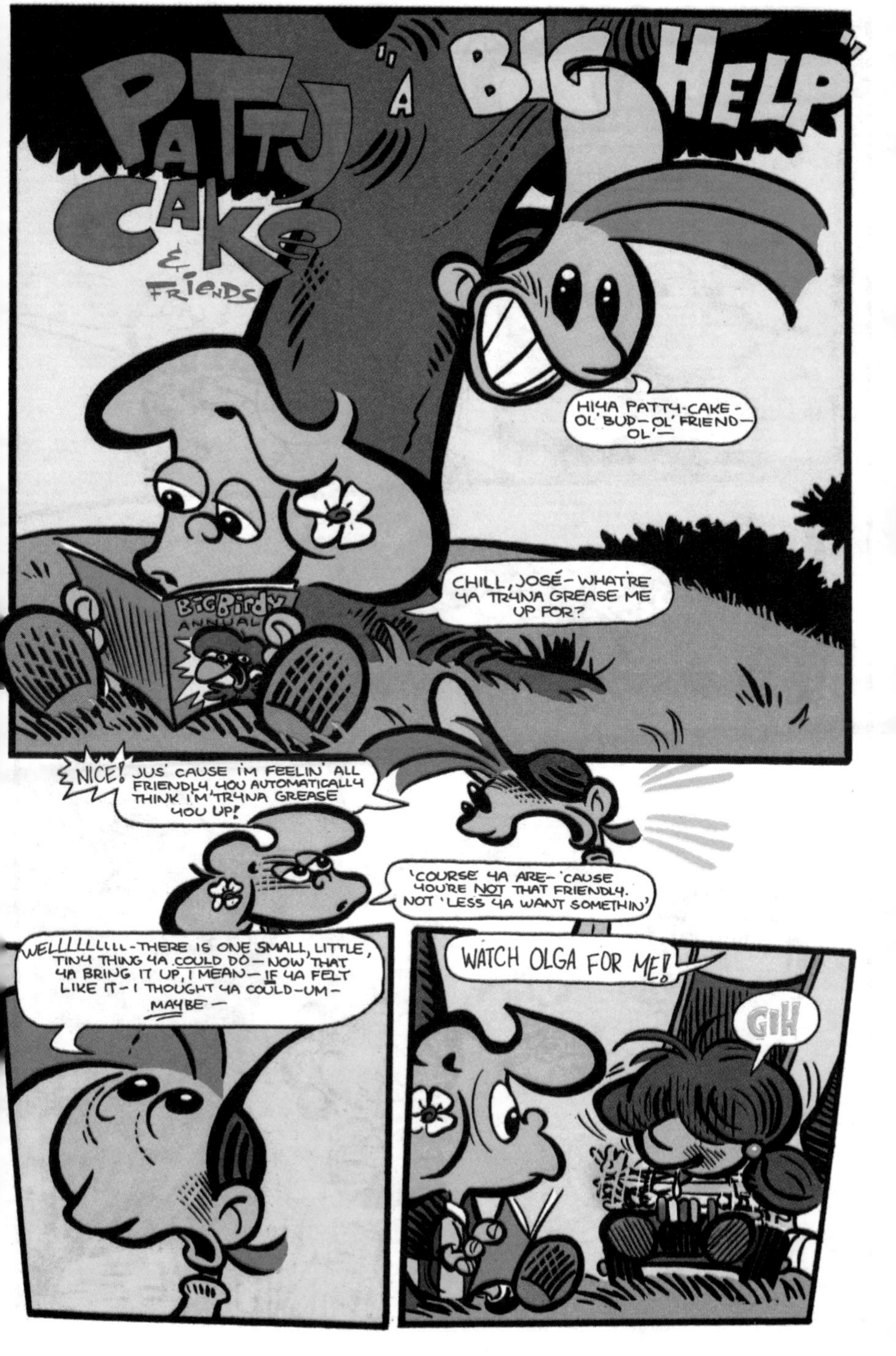

PATTY CAKE & FRIENDS
"A BIG HELP"
HIYA PATTY-CAKE - OL' BUD - OL' FRIEND - OL' —
CHILL, JOSÉ - WHAT'RE YA TRYNA GREASE ME UP FOR?
BIG BIRDY ANNUAL
NICE! JUS' CAUSE I'M FEELIN' ALL FRIENDLY YOU AUTOMATICALLY THINK I'M TRYNA GREASE YOU UP!
'COURSE YA ARE - 'CAUSE YOU'RE NOT THAT FRIENDLY. NOT 'LESS YA WANT SOMETHIN'
WELLLLLLLLL - THERE IS ONE SMALL, LITTLE, TINY THING YA COULD DO — NOW THAT YA BRING IT UP, I MEAN — IF YA FELT LIKE IT - I THOUGHT YA COULD - UM - MAYBE —
WATCH OLGA FOR ME!
GIH

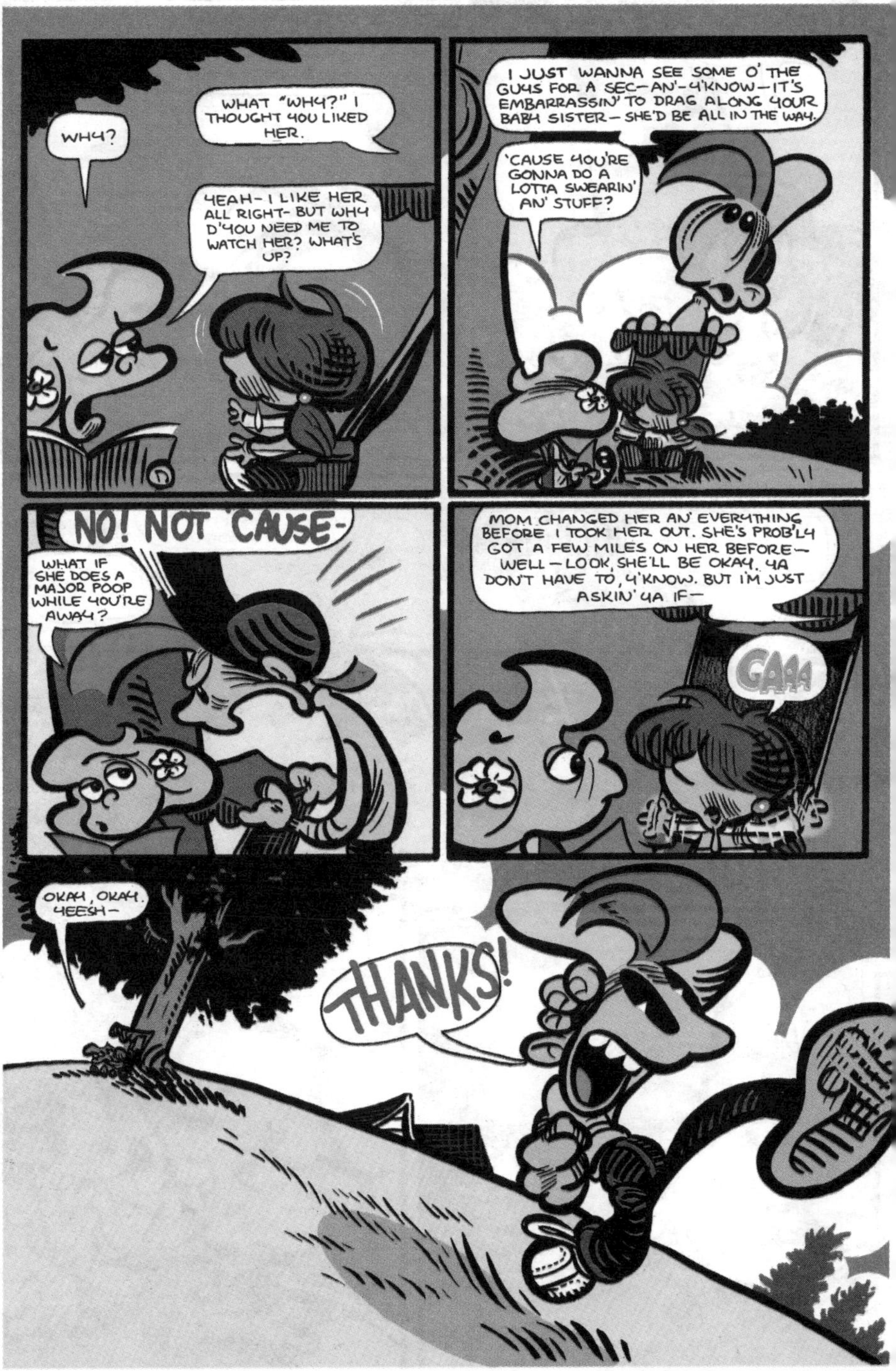
WHY?
WHAT "WHY?" I THOUGHT YOU LIKED HER.
YEAH- I LIKE HER ALL RIGHT- BUT WHY D'YOU NEED ME TO WATCH HER? WHAT'S UP?
I JUST WANNA SEE SOME O' THE GUYS FOR A SEC—AN'—Y'KNOW—IT'S EMBARRASSIN' TO DRAG ALONG YOUR BABY SISTER—SHE'D BE ALL IN THE WAY.
'CAUSE YOU'RE GONNA DO A LOTTA SWEARIN' AN' STUFF?
NO! NOT 'CAUSE-
WHAT IF SHE DOES A MAJOR POOP WHILE YOU'RE AWAY?
MOM CHANGED HER AN' EVERYTHING BEFORE I TOOK HER OUT. SHE'S PROB'LY GOT A FEW MILES ON HER BEFORE— WELL—LOOK, SHE'LL BE OKAY. YA DON'T HAVE TO, Y'KNOW. BUT I'M JUST ASKIN' YA IF—
GAAA
OKAY, OKAY. YEESH—
THANKS!

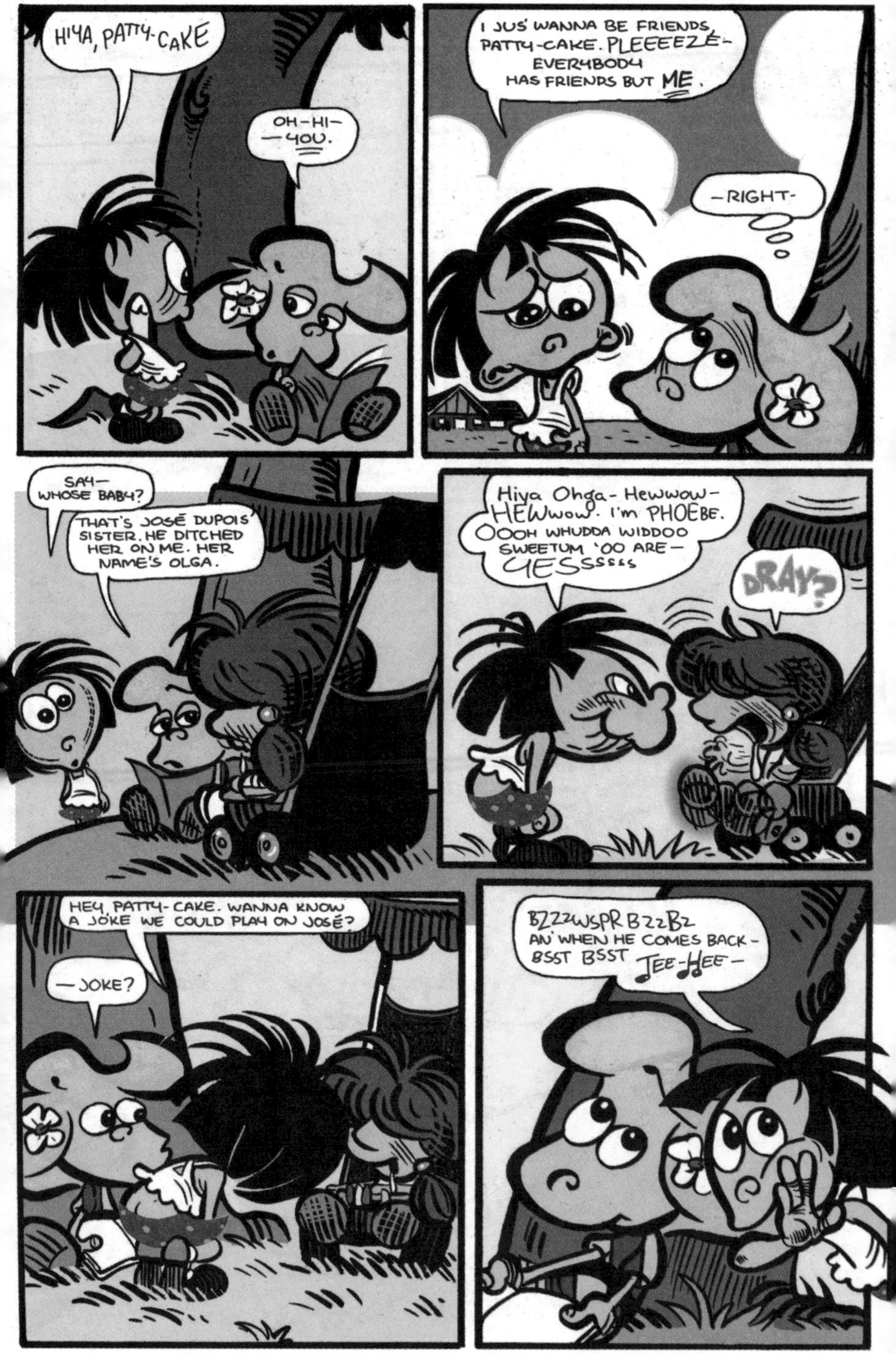
HIYA, PATTY-CAKE
OH-HI- —YOU.
I JUS' WANNA BE FRIENDS, PATTY-CAKE. PLEEEEZE— EVERYBODY HAS FRIENDS BUT ME.
—RIGHT—
SAY— WHOSE BABY?
THAT'S JOSÉ DUPOIS' SISTER. HE DITCHED HER ON ME. HER NAME'S OLGA.
Hiya Ohga- Hewwow- HEWwow. I'm PHOEBE. OOOH WHUDDA WIDDOO SWEETUM 'OO ARE— YESsssss
DRAY?
HEY, PATTY-CAKE. WANNA KNOW A JOKE WE COULD PLAY ON JOSÉ?
—JOKE?
BZZZWSPR BZZBZ AN' WHEN HE COMES BACK- BSST BSST JEE-HEE—

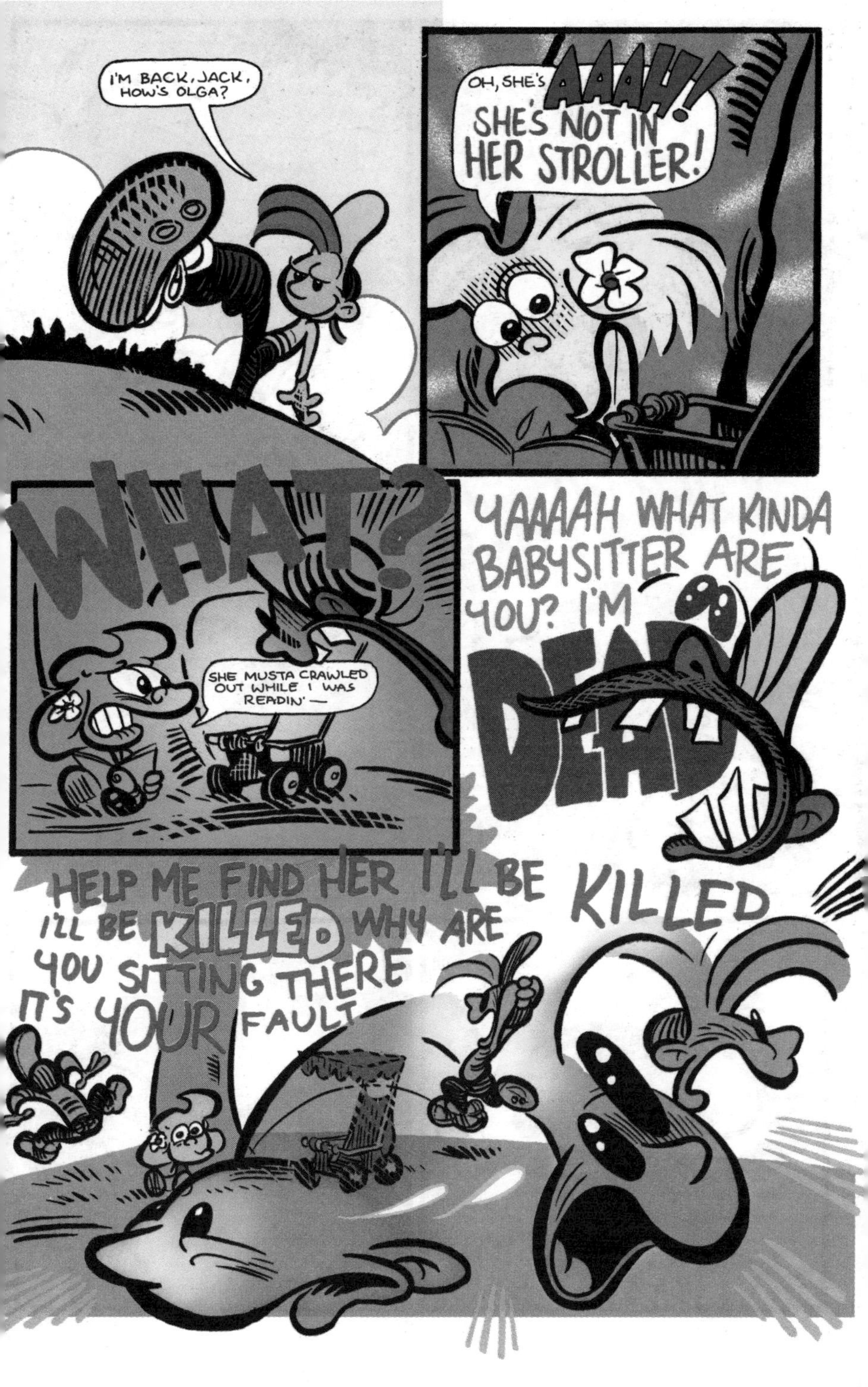
I'M BACK, JACK, HOW'S OLGA?
OH, SHE'S AAAH! SHE'S NOT IN HER STROLLER!
WHAT?
SHE MUSTA CRAWLED OUT WHILE I WAS READIN' —
YAAAAH WHAT KINDA BABYSITTER ARE YOU? I'M DEAD
HELP ME FIND HER I'LL BE KILLED I'LL BE KILLED WHY ARE YOU SITTING THERE IT'S YOUR FAULT

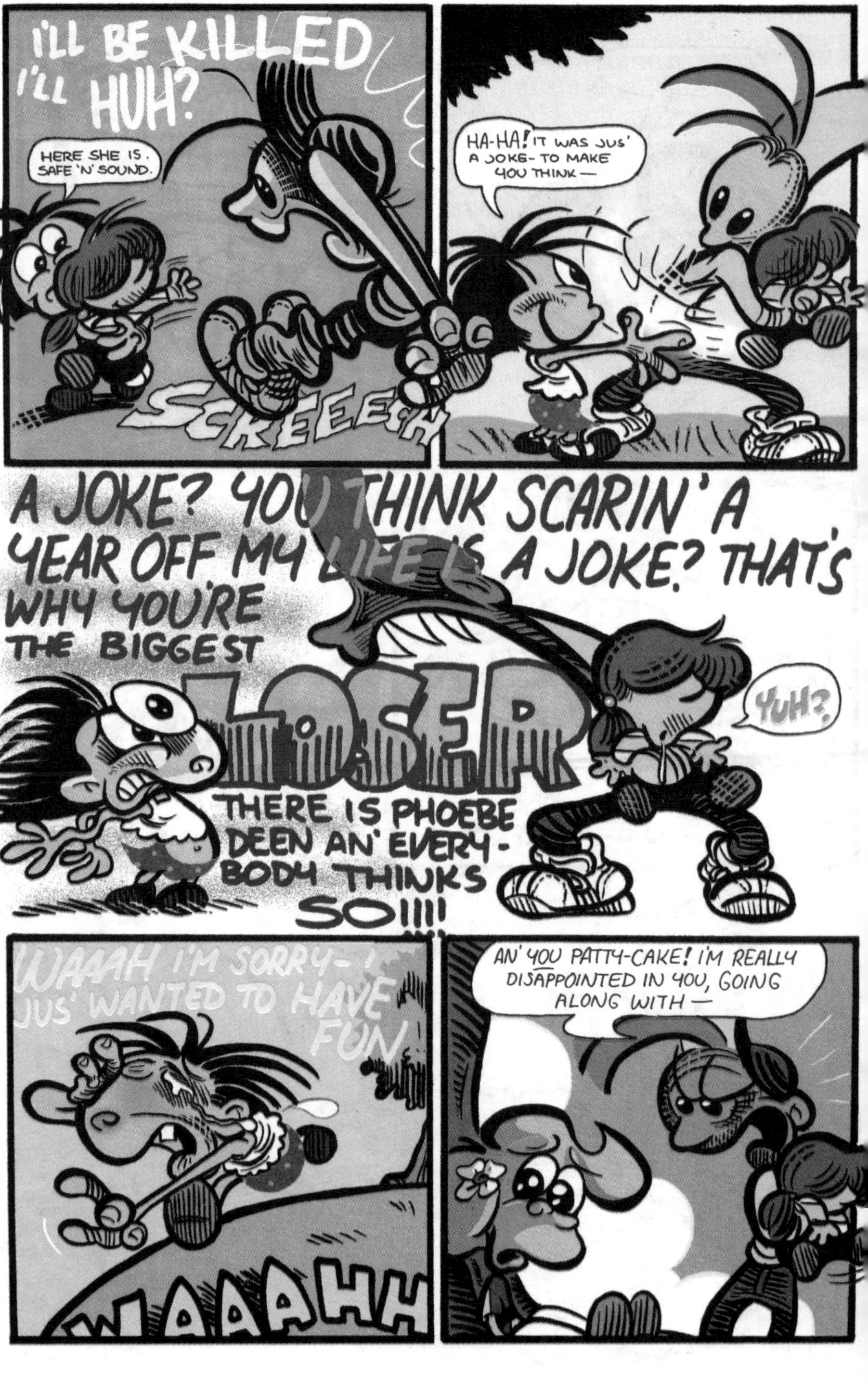
I'LL BE KILLED
I'LL HUH?
HERE SHE IS. SAFE 'N' SOUND.
SCREEECH
HA-HA! IT WAS JUS' A JOKE- TO MAKE YOU THINK—
A JOKE? YOU THINK SCARIN' A YEAR OFF MY LIFE IS A JOKE? THAT'S WHY YOU'RE THE BIGGEST LOSER THERE IS PHOEBE DEEN AN' EVERY-BODY THINKS SO!!!!
YUH?
WAAAH I'M SORRY- I JUS' WANTED TO HAVE FUN
WAAAHH
AN' YOU PATTY-CAKE! I'M REALLY DISAPPOINTED IN YOU, GOING ALONG WITH—

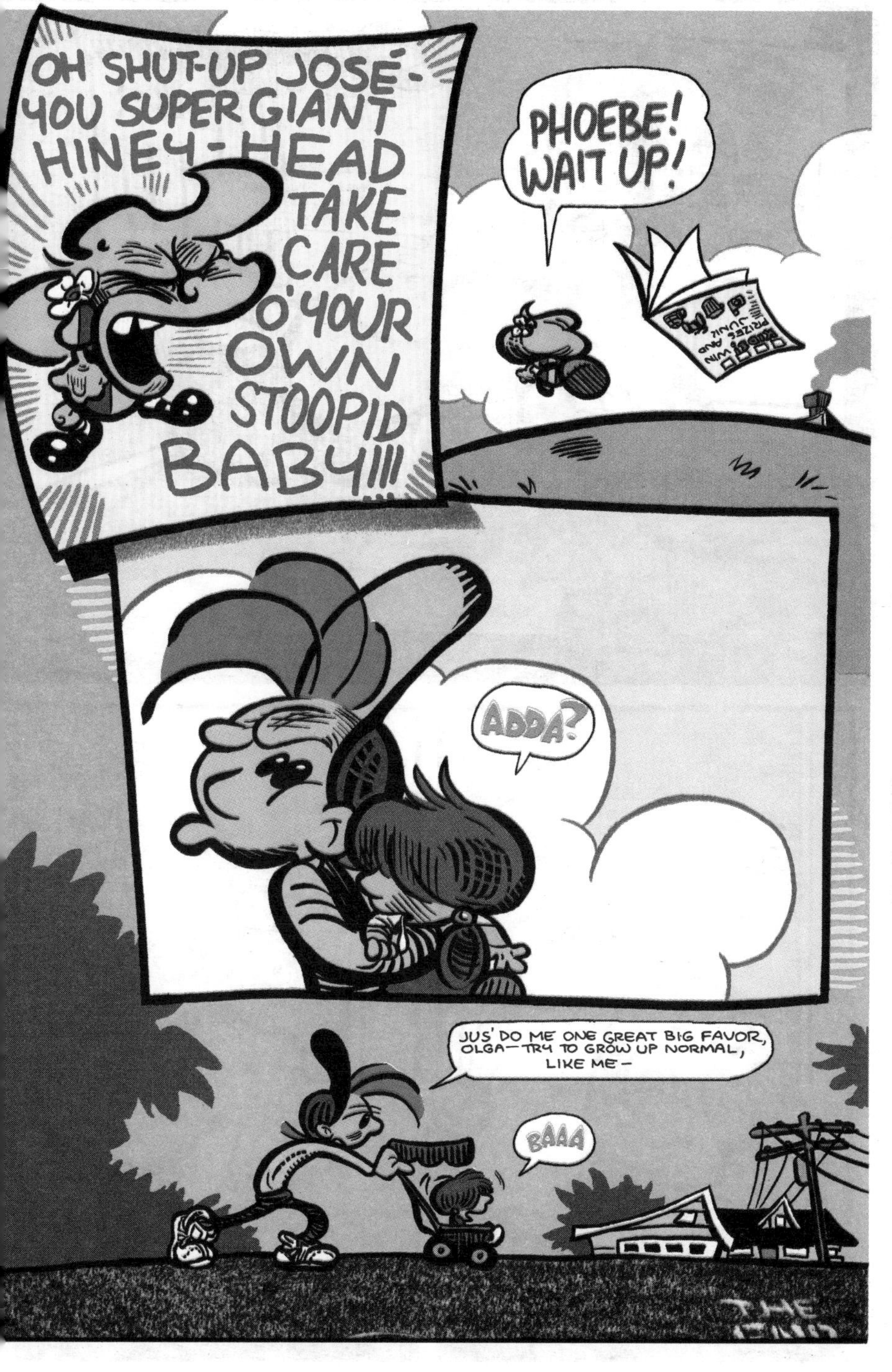
OH SHUT-UP JOSÉ-
YOU SUPER GIANT
HINEY-HEAD
TAKE
CARE
O' YOUR
OWN
STOOPID
BABY!!!!
PHOEBE! WAIT UP!
ADDA?
JUS' DO ME ONE GREAT BIG FAVOR, OLGA— TRY TO GROW UP NORMAL, LIKE ME—
BAAA
THE

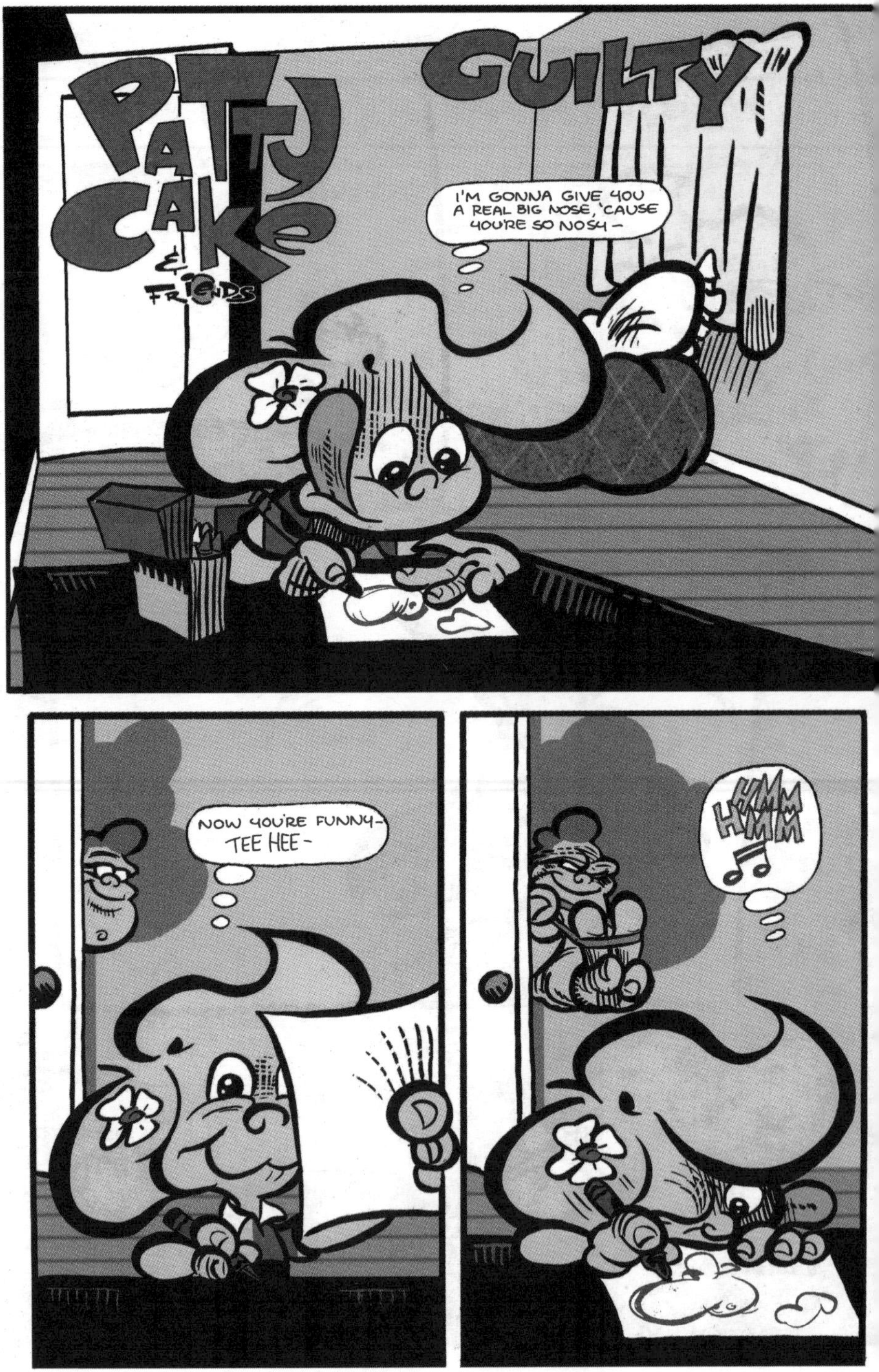
PATTY CAKE & FRIENDS
GUILTY
I'M GONNA GIVE YOU A REAL BIG NOSE, 'CAUSE YOU'RE SO NOSY -
NOW YOU'RE FUNNY- TEE HEE -
HMM HMM

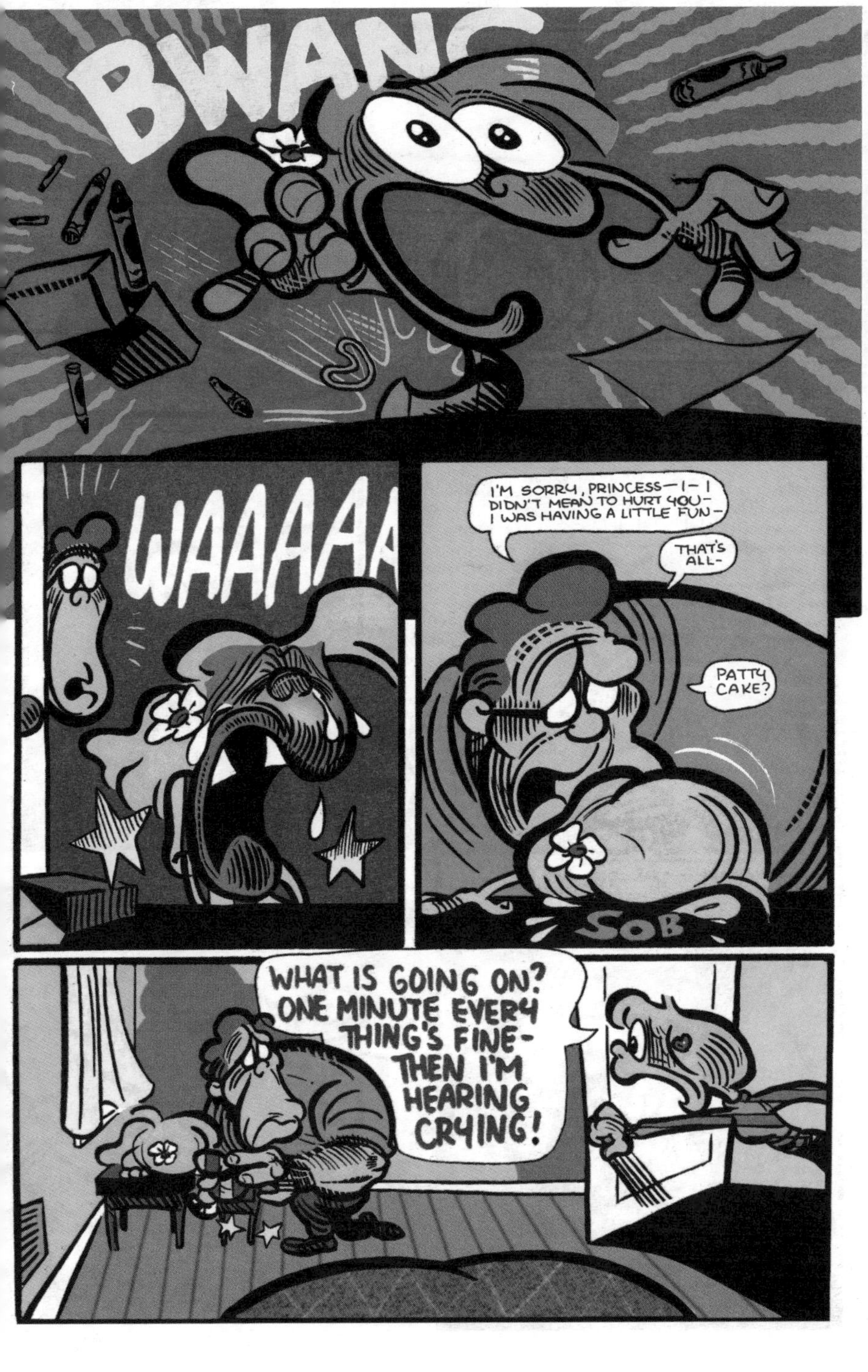
BWANG
WAAAAA
I'M SORRY, PRINCESS—I— I DIDN'T MEAN TO HURT YOU— I WAS HAVING A LITTLE FUN—
THAT'S ALL-
PATTY CAKE?
SOB
WHAT IS GOING ON? ONE MINUTE EVERY THING'S FINE- THEN I'M HEARING CRYING!

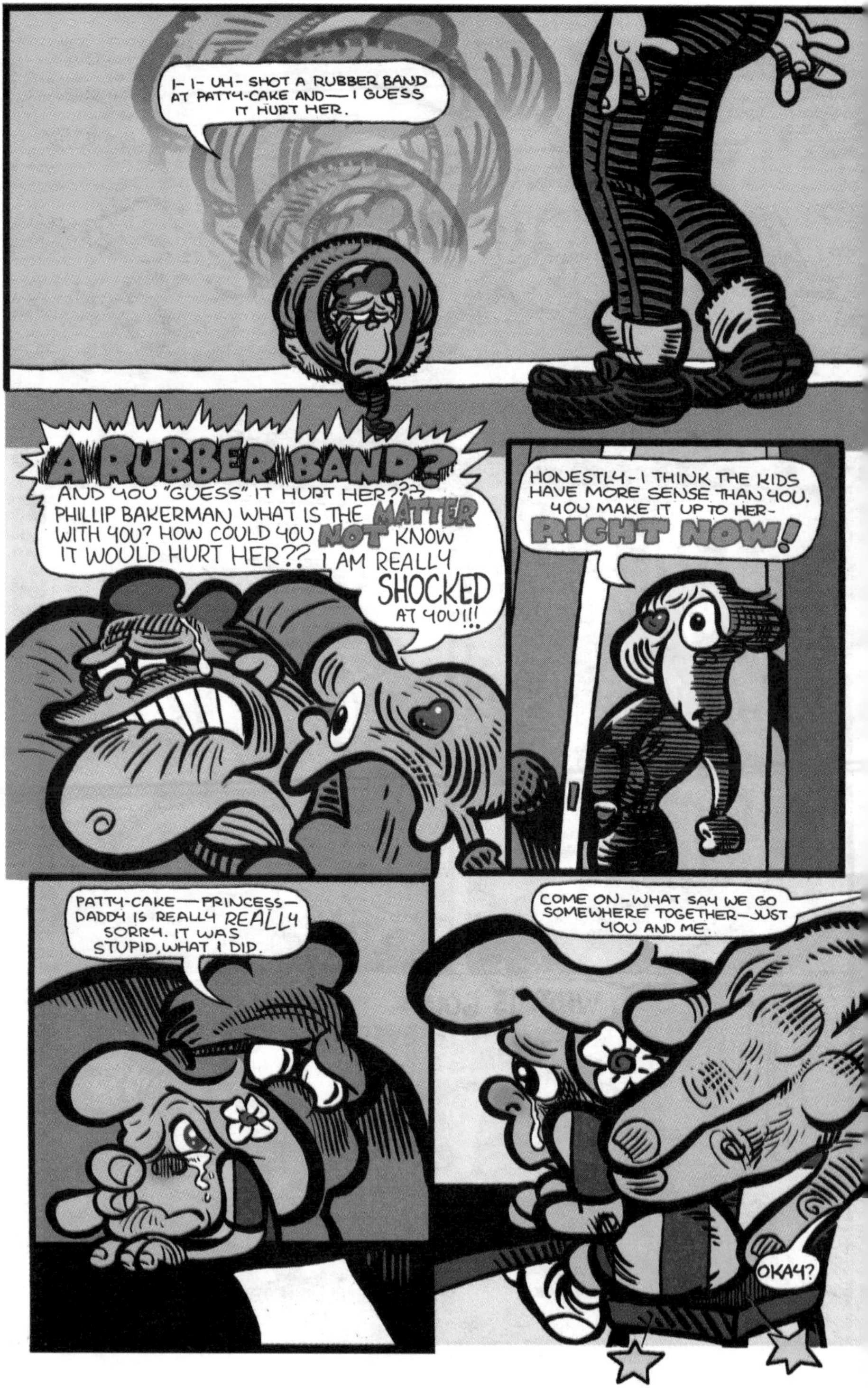
I- I- UH- SHOT A RUBBER BAND AT PATTY-CAKE AND— I GUESS IT HURT HER.
A RUBBER BAND? AND YOU "GUESS" IT HURT HER??? PHILLIP BAKERMAN WHAT IS THE MATTER WITH YOU? HOW COULD YOU NOT KNOW IT WOULD HURT HER?? I AM REALLY SHOCKED AT YOU!!!
HONESTLY- I THINK THE KIDS HAVE MORE SENSE THAN YOU. YOU MAKE IT UP TO HER- RIGHT NOW!
PATTY-CAKE— PRINCESS— DADDY IS REALLY REALLY SORRY. IT WAS STUPID, WHAT I DID.
COME ON- WHAT SAY WE GO SOMEWHERE TOGETHER- JUST YOU AND ME.
OKAY?

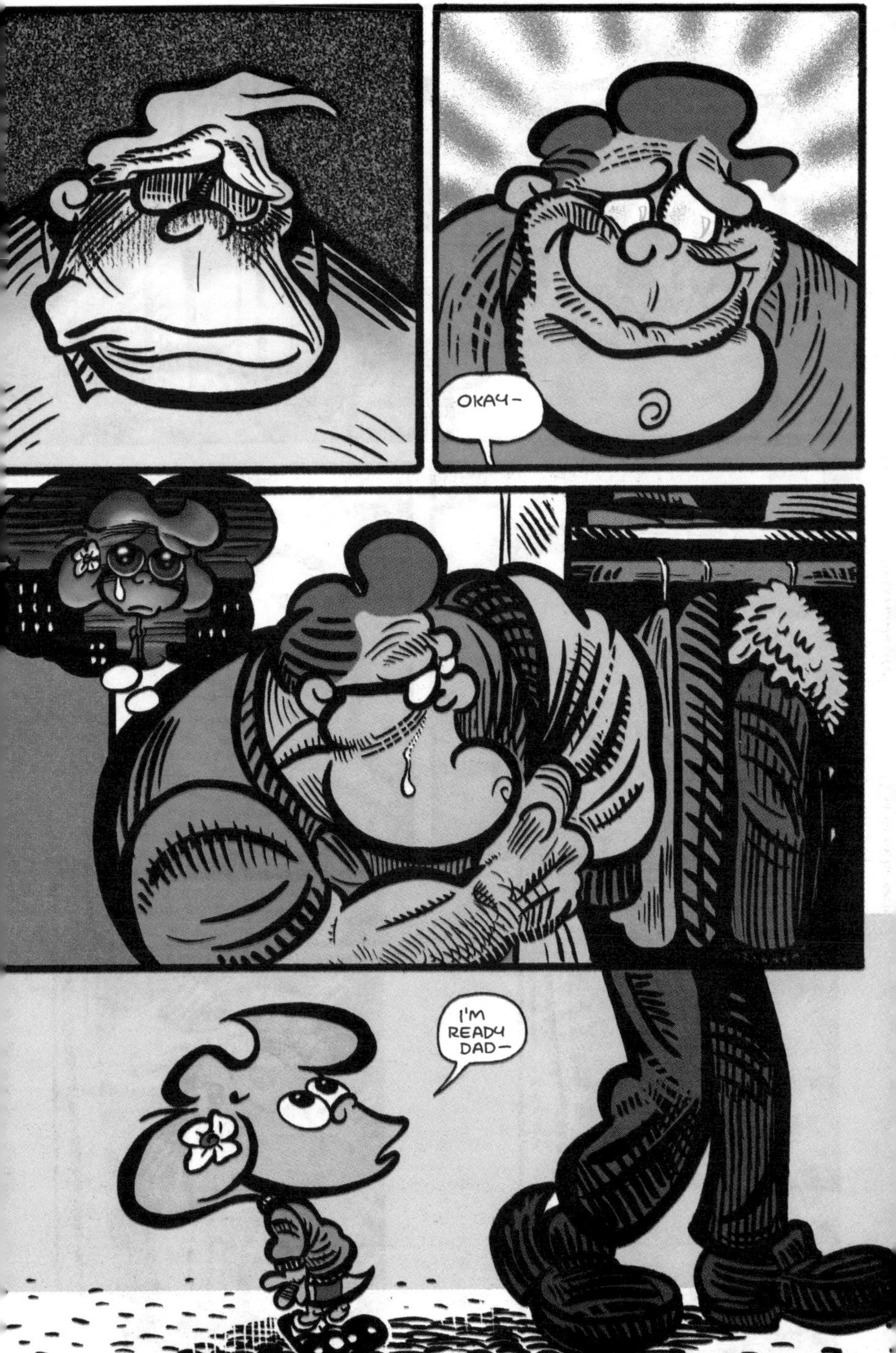
OKAY-
I'M READY DAD-

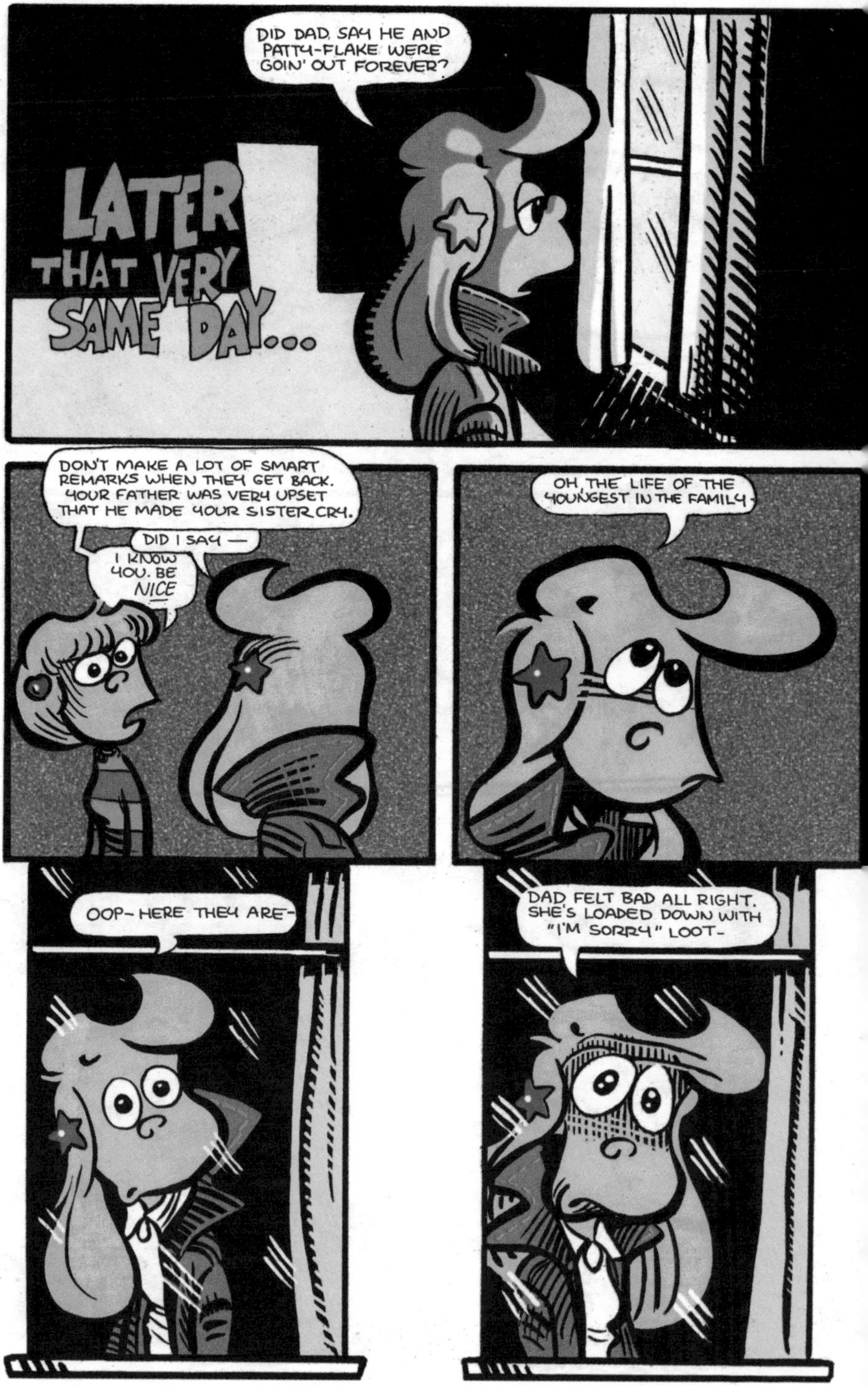
DID DAD SAY HE AND PATTY-FLAKE WERE GOIN' OUT FOREVER?
LATER THAT VERY SAME DAY...
DON'T MAKE A LOT OF SMART REMARKS WHEN THEY GET BACK. YOUR FATHER WAS VERY UPSET THAT HE MADE YOUR SISTER CRY.
DID I SAY —
I KNOW YOU. BE NICE
OH THE LIFE OF THE YOUNGEST IN THE FAMILY-
OOP- HERE THEY ARE-
DAD FELT BAD ALL RIGHT. SHE'S LOADED DOWN WITH "I'M SORRY" LOOT-

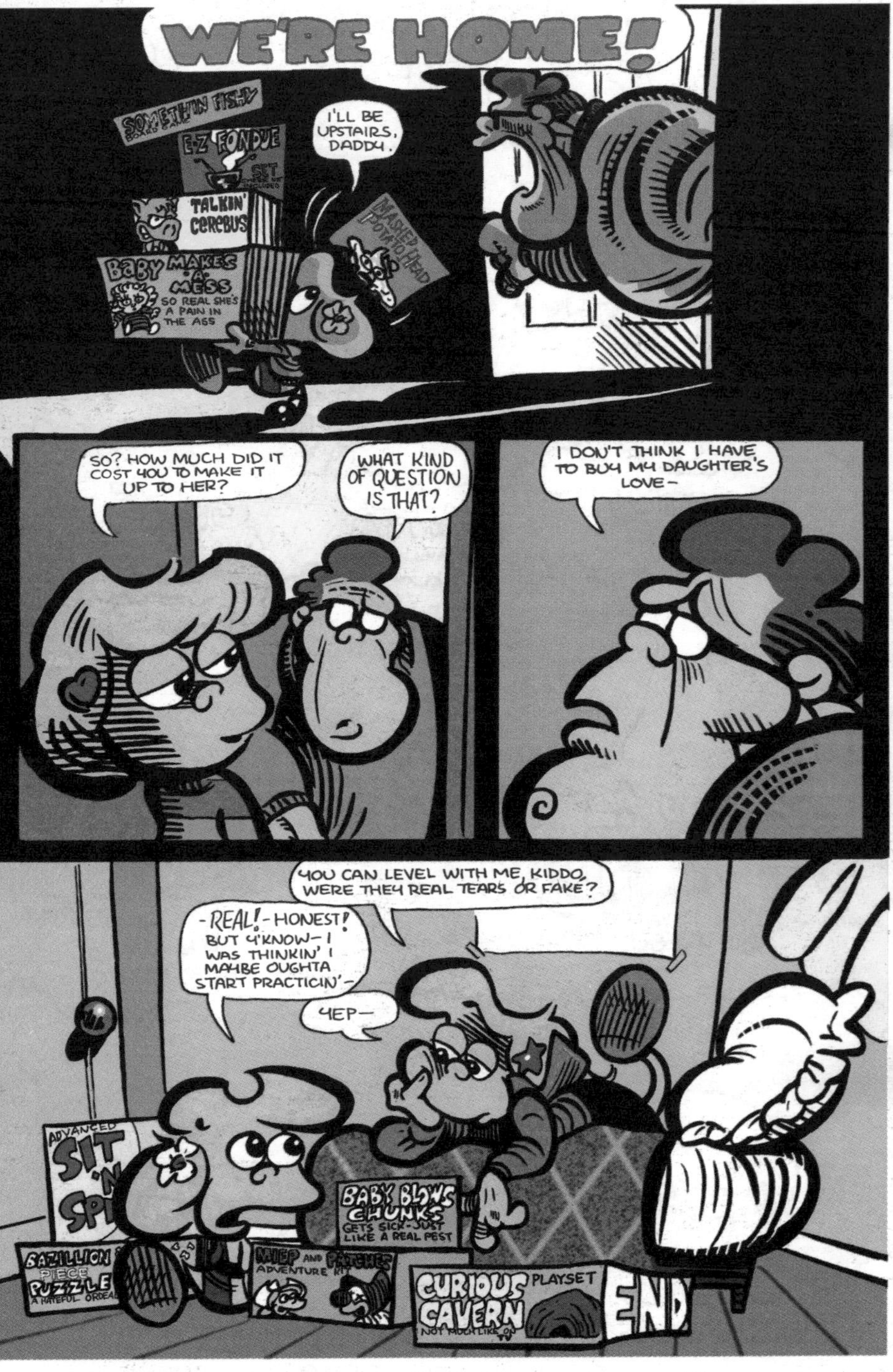
WE'RE HOME!
SOMETHIN' FISHY
E-Z FONDUE SET
'TALKIN' CEREBUS
BABY MAKES A MESS SO REAL SHE'S A PAIN IN THE ASS
MASHED POTATO HEAD
I'LL BE UPSTAIRS, DADDY.
SO? HOW MUCH DID IT COST YOU TO MAKE IT UP TO HER?
WHAT KIND OF QUESTION IS THAT?
I DON'T THINK I HAVE TO BUY MY DAUGHTER'S LOVE—
YOU CAN LEVEL WITH ME, KIDDO, WERE THEY REAL TEARS OR FAKE?
-REAL!-HONEST! BUT Y'KNOW—I WAS THINKIN' I MAYBE OUGHTA START PRACTICIN'—
YEP—
ADVANCED
BABY BLOWS CHUNKS GETS SICK-JUST LIKE A REAL PEST
BAZILLION PIECE PUZZLE A HATEFUL ORDEAL
MIEP AND PATCHES ADVENTURE KIT
CURIOUS CAVERN PLAYSET
END

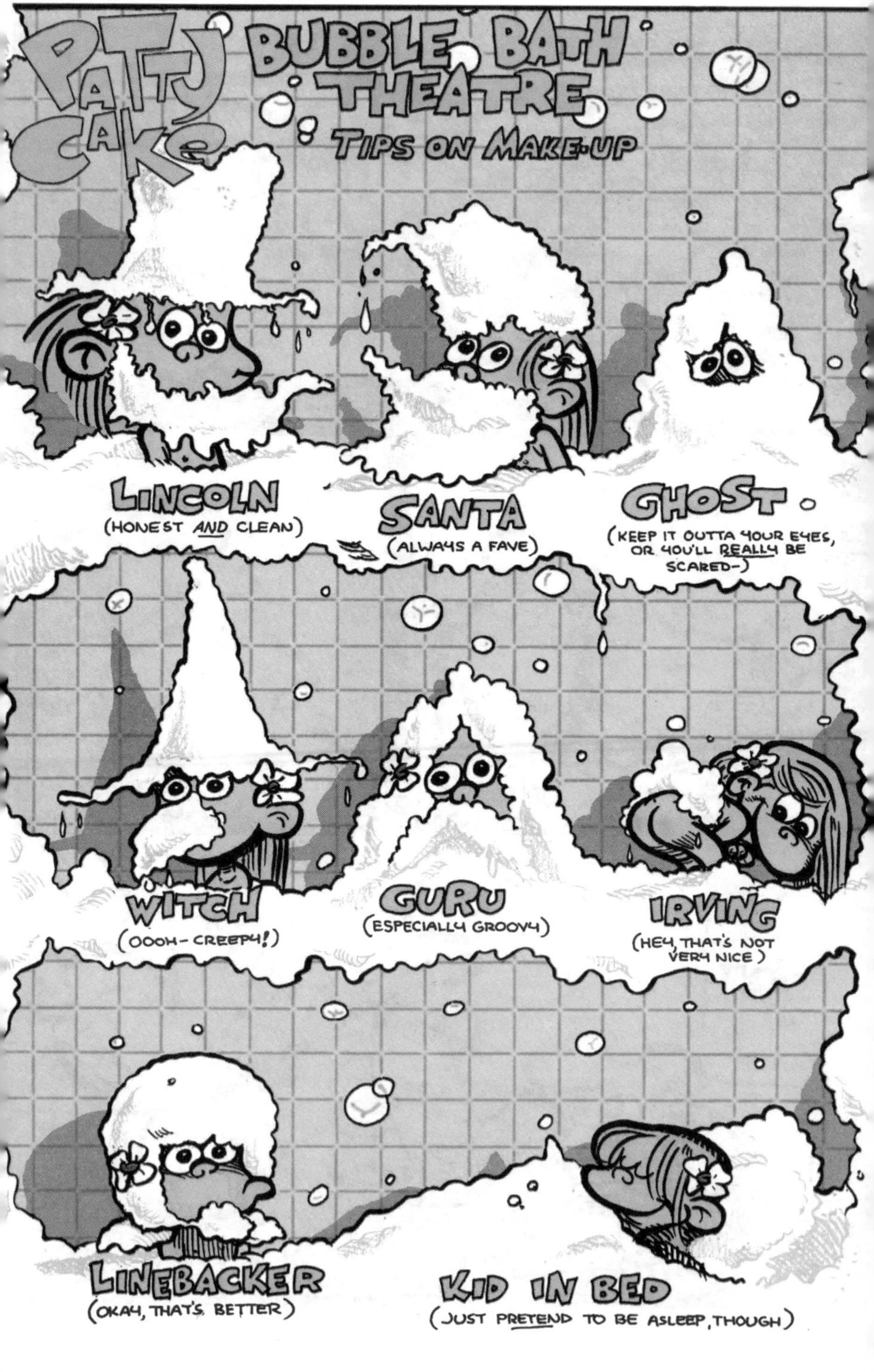
Patty Cake
Bubble Bath Theatre
Tips on Make-up
Lincoln
(Honest AND clean)
Santa
(Always a fave)
Ghost
(Keep it outta your eyes, or you'll REALLY be scared-)
Witch
(Oooh- creepy!)
Guru
(Especially groovy)
Irving
(Hey, that's not very nice)
Linebacker
(Okay, that's better)
Kid in Bed
(Just PRETEND to be asleep, though)

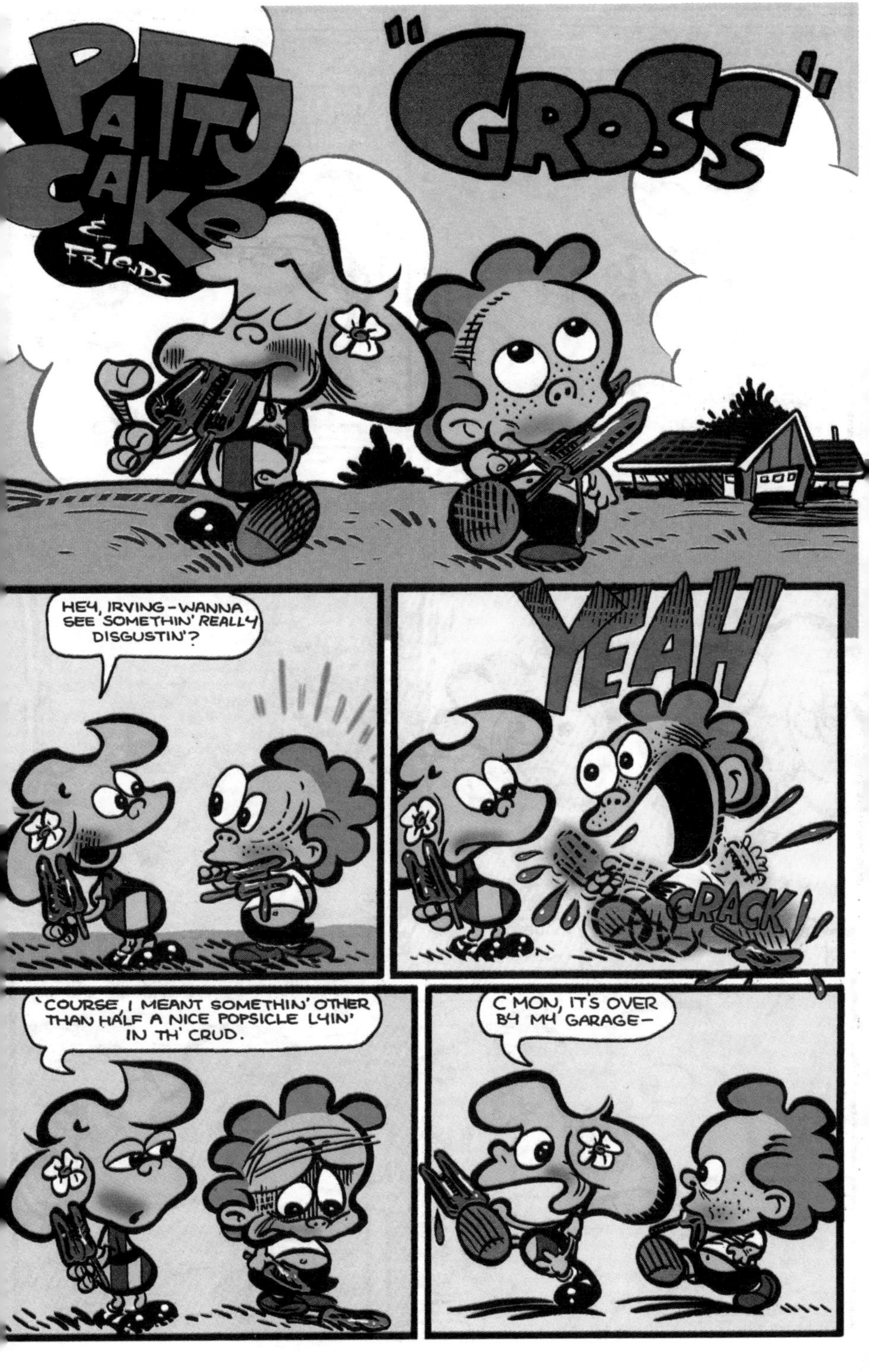
PATTY CAKE & FRIENDS
"GROSS"
HEY, IRVING—WANNA SEE SOMETHIN' REALLY DISGUSTIN'?
YEAH
CRACK!
'COURSE, I MEANT SOMETHIN' OTHER THAN HALF A NICE POPSICLE LYIN' IN TH' CRUD.
C'MON, IT'S OVER BY MY GARAGE—

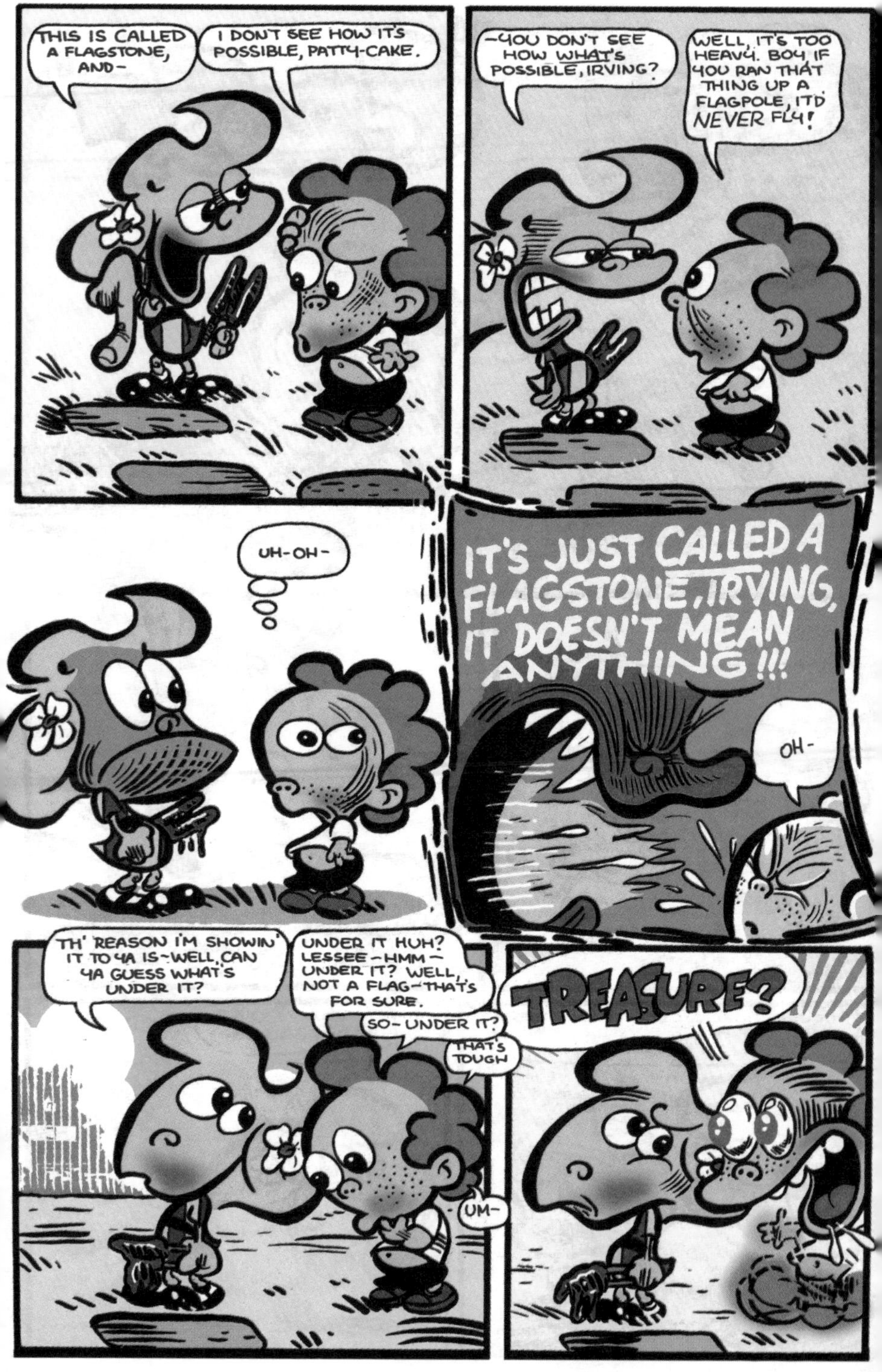
THIS IS CALLED A FLAGSTONE, AND–
I DON'T SEE HOW IT'S POSSIBLE, PATTY-CAKE.
–YOU DON'T SEE HOW WHAT'S POSSIBLE, IRVING?
WELL, IT'S TOO HEAVY. BOY IF YOU RAN THAT THING UP A FLAGPOLE, IT'D NEVER FLY!
UH-OH–
IT'S JUST CALLED A FLAGSTONE, IRVING, IT DOESN'T MEAN ANYTHING!!!
OH–
TH' REASON I'M SHOWIN' IT TO YA IS–WELL, CAN YA GUESS WHAT'S UNDER IT?
UNDER IT HUH? LESSEE–HMM–UNDER IT? WELL, NOT A FLAG–THAT'S FOR SURE.
SO–UNDER IT?
THAT'S TOUGH
UM–
TREASURE?

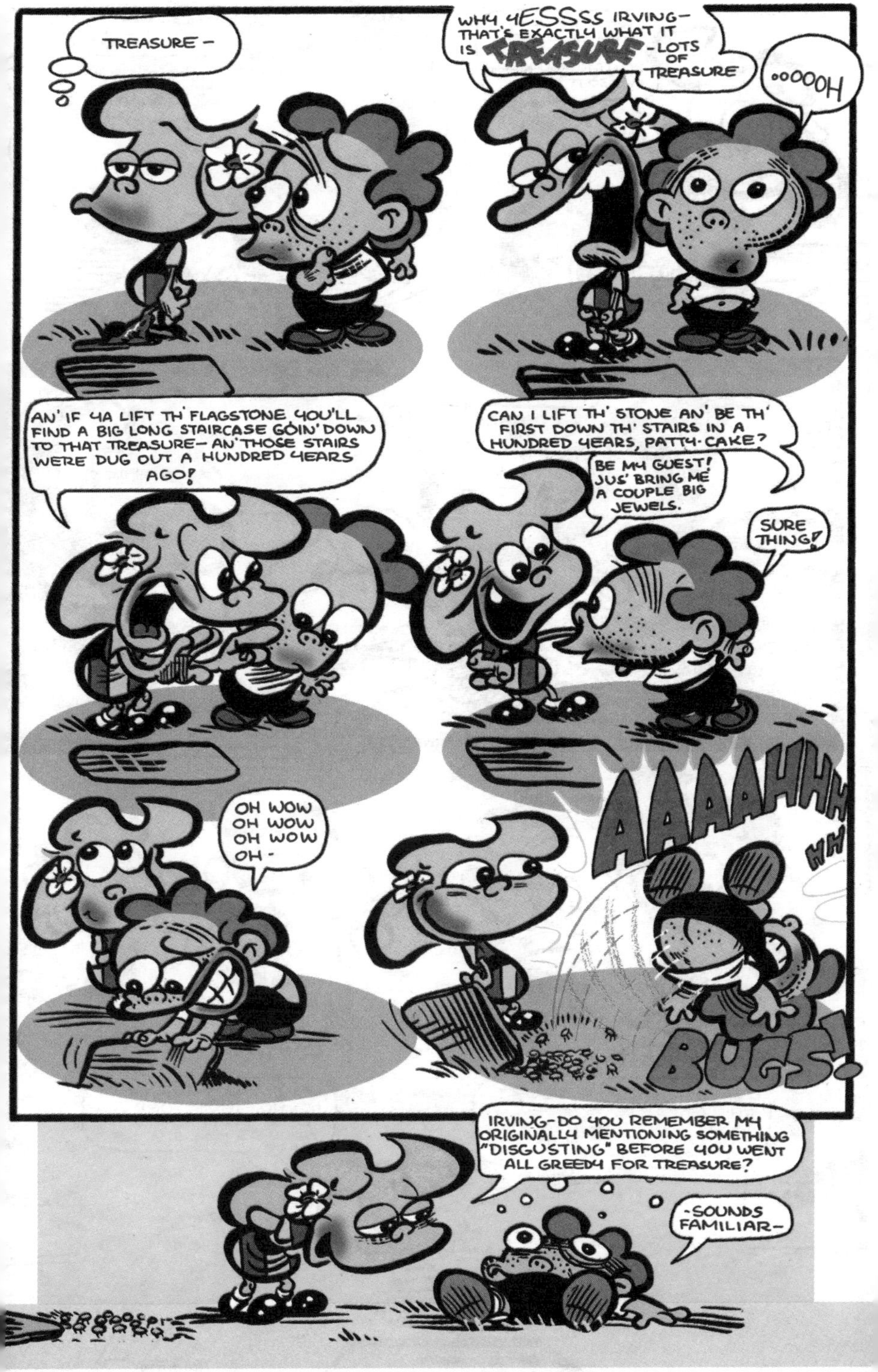
TREASURE -
WHY YESSSS IRVING- THAT'S EXACTLY WHAT IT IS TREASURE - LOTS OF TREASURE
ooOOOH
AN' IF YA LIFT TH' FLAGSTONE YOU'LL FIND A BIG LONG STAIRCASE GOIN' DOWN TO THAT TREASURE- AN' THOSE STAIRS WERE DUG OUT A HUNDRED YEARS AGO!
CAN I LIFT TH' STONE AN' BE TH' FIRST DOWN TH' STAIRS IN A HUNDRED YEARS, PATTY-CAKE?
BE MY GUEST! JUS' BRING ME A COUPLE BIG JEWELS.
SURE THING!
OH WOW OH WOW OH WOW OH -
AAAAHHHHH
BUGS!
IRVING-DO YOU REMEMBER MY ORIGINALLY MENTIONING SOMETHING "DISGUSTING" BEFORE YOU WENT ALL GREEDY FOR TREASURE?
-SOUNDS FAMILIAR-

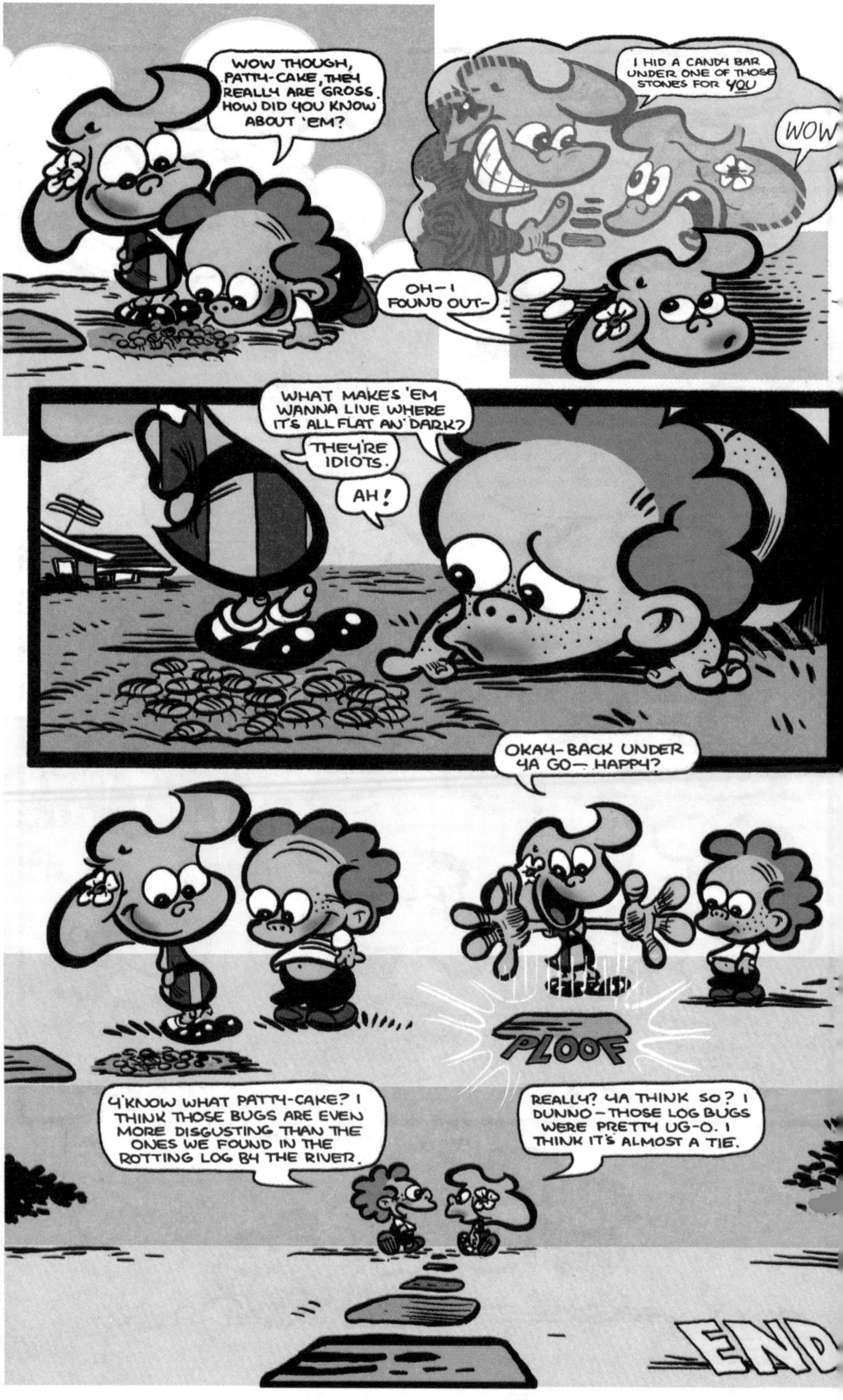

WOW THOUGH, PATTY-CAKE, THEY REALLY ARE GROSS. HOW DID YOU KNOW ABOUT 'EM?
I HID A CANDY BAR UNDER ONE OF THOSE STONES FOR YOU
WOW
OH-I FOUND OUT-
WHAT MAKES 'EM WANNA LIVE WHERE IT'S ALL FLAT AN' DARK?
THEY'RE IDIOTS.
AH!
OKAY-BACK UNDER YA GO— HAPPY?
PLOOF
Y'KNOW WHAT PATTY-CAKE? I THINK THOSE BUGS ARE EVEN MORE DISGUSTING THAN THE ONES WE FOUND IN THE ROTTING LOG BY THE RIVER.
REALLY? YA THINK SO? I DUNNO-THOSE LOG BUGS WERE PRETTY UG-O. I THINK IT'S ALMOST A TIE.
END

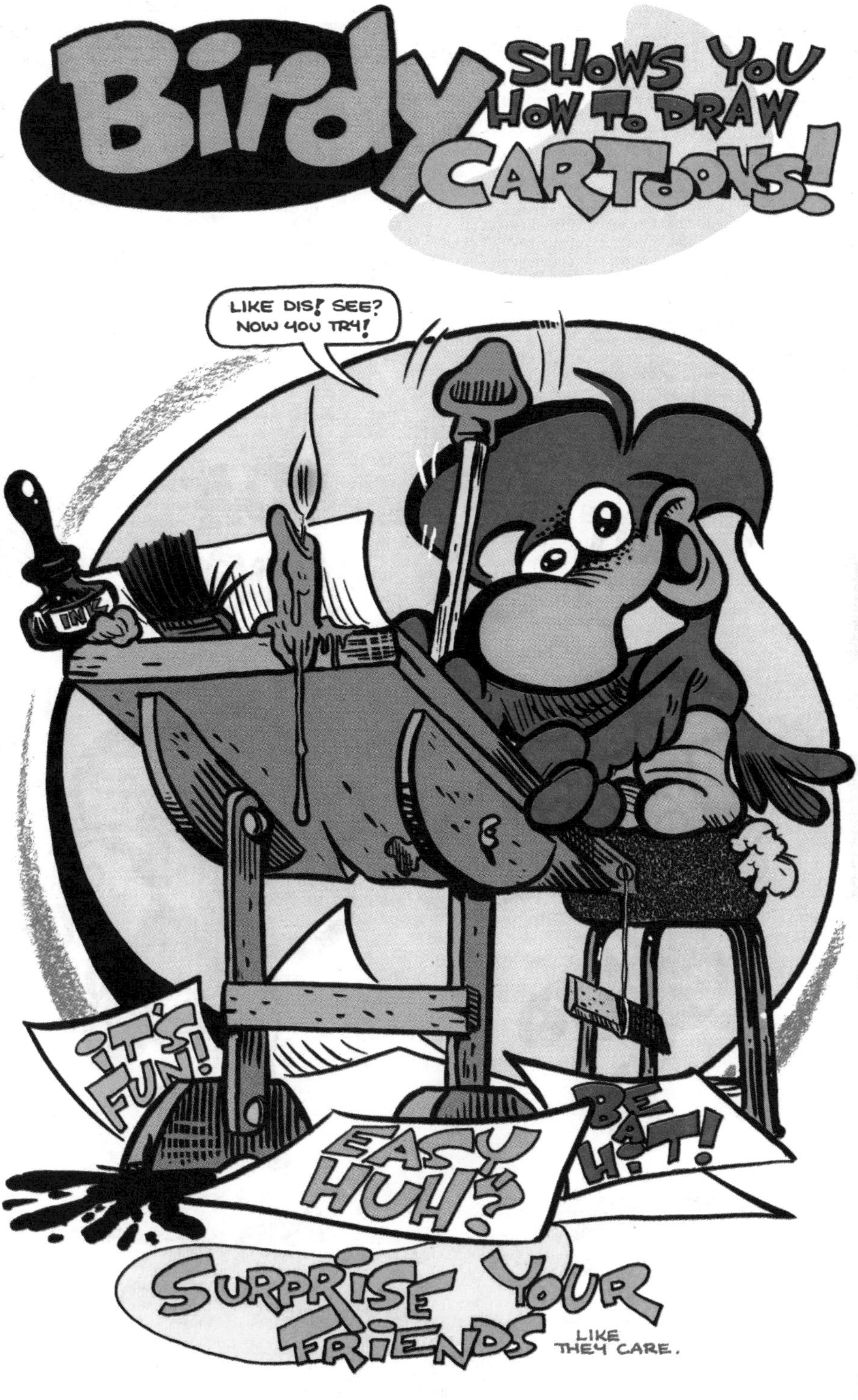
Birdy SHOWS YOU HOW TO DRAW CARTOONS!
LIKE DIS! SEE? NOW YOU TRY!
INK
IT'S FUN!
EASY HUH?
BE AT U. T!
SURPRISE YOUR FRIENDS
LIKE THEY CARE.

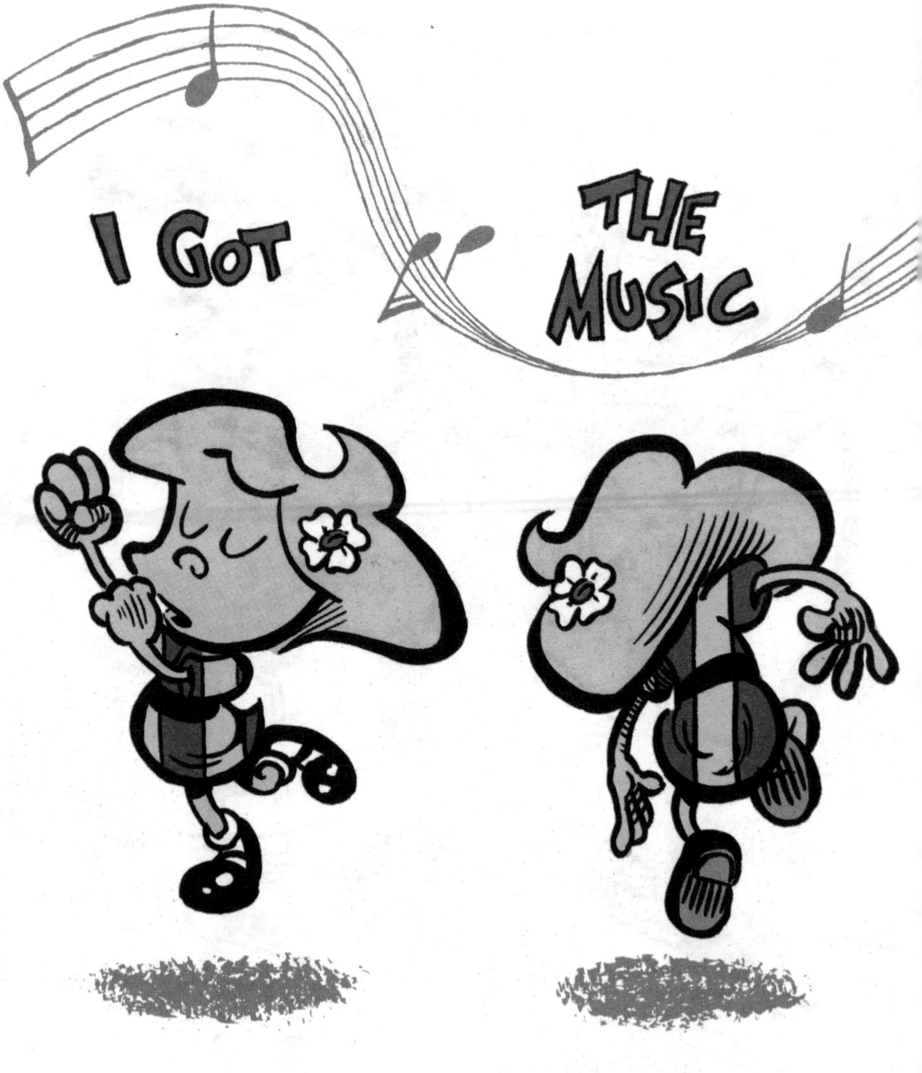
I GOT
THE MUSIC

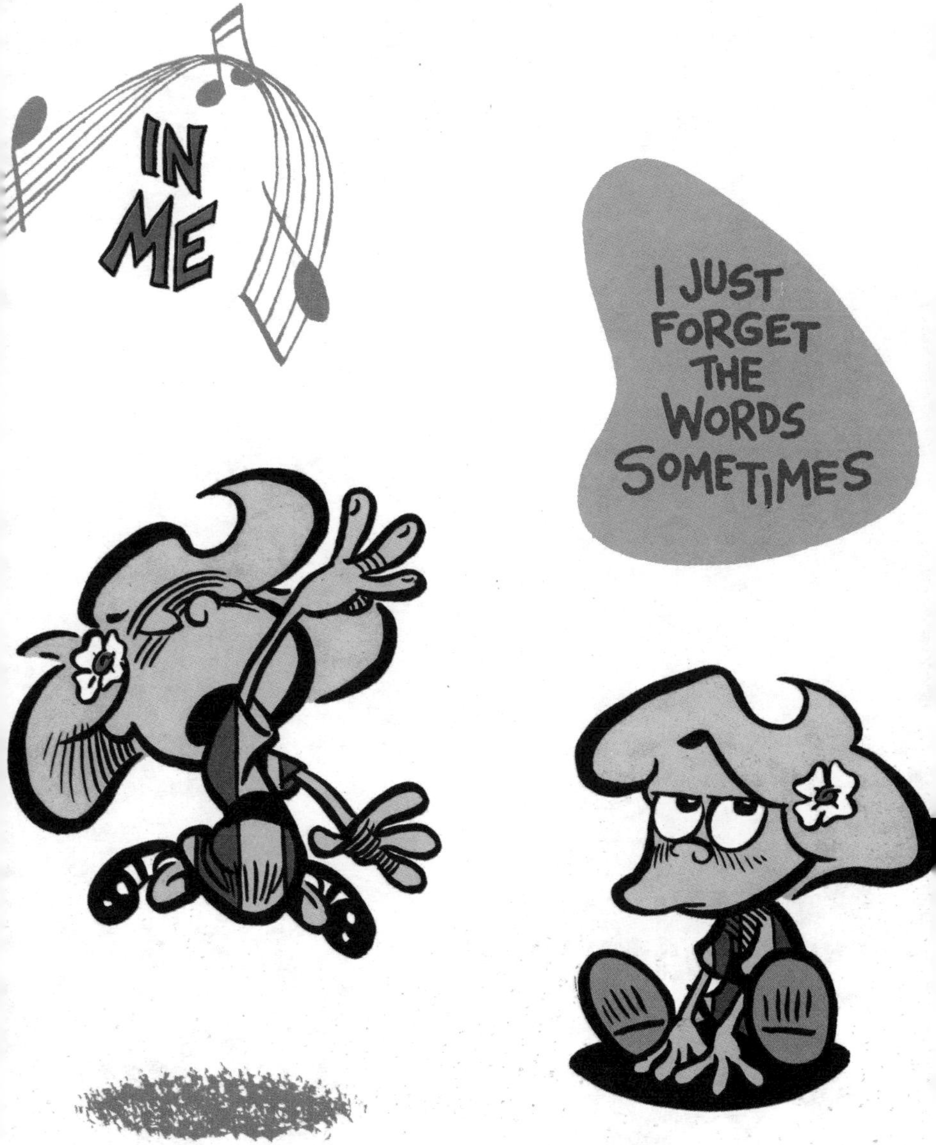
IN
ME
I JUST FORGET THE WORDS SOMETIMES

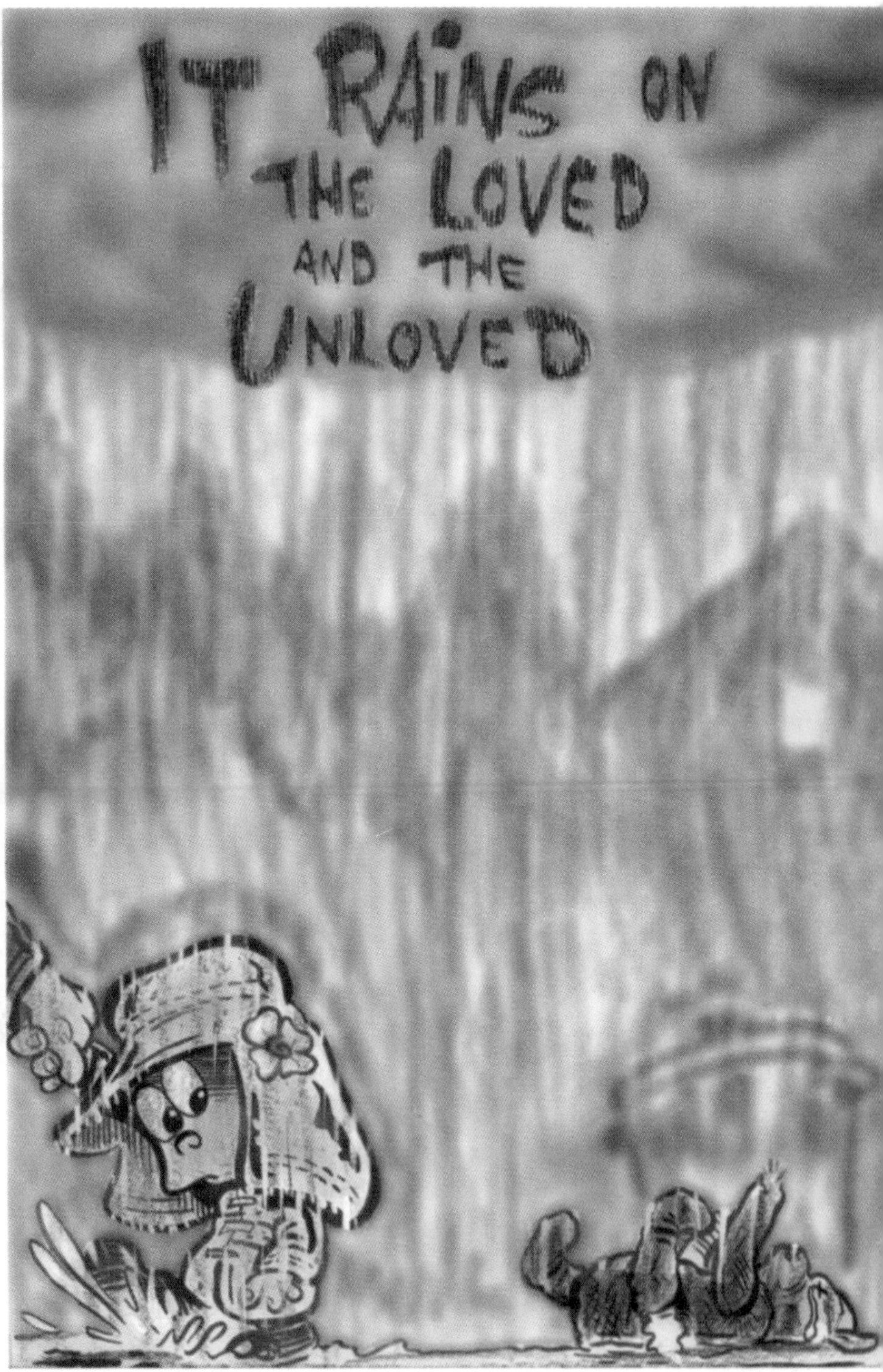
IT RAINS ON THE LOVED AND THE UNLOVED

LIFE-SIZE MONSTER

IS A R.I.P. OFF

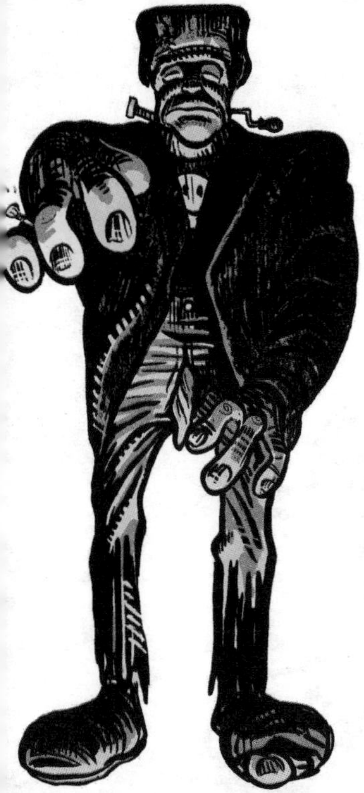

6 ft. tall-in full, lurid color- you'll be building this thing up in your imagination for weeks, until the big disappointment - when you get a load of what you blew your money on! Forget walking down the street and scaring lotsa strangers with your ghoulish bodyguard at your side. It ain't gonna happen. But hey, what'd you expect for one lousy dollar-a robot? Wise up.

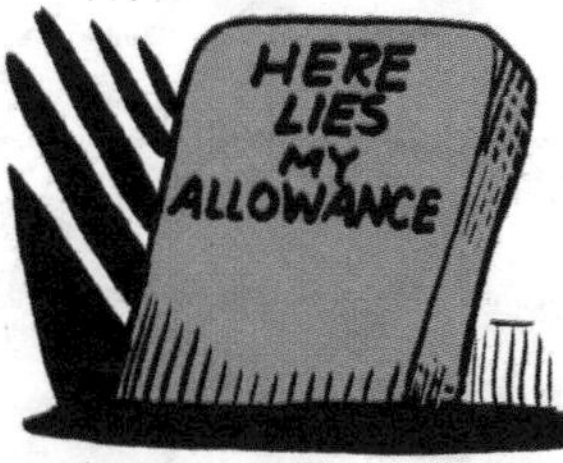
HERE LIES MY ALLOWANCE

$1.00

AMAZING SEA-MONKEYS!

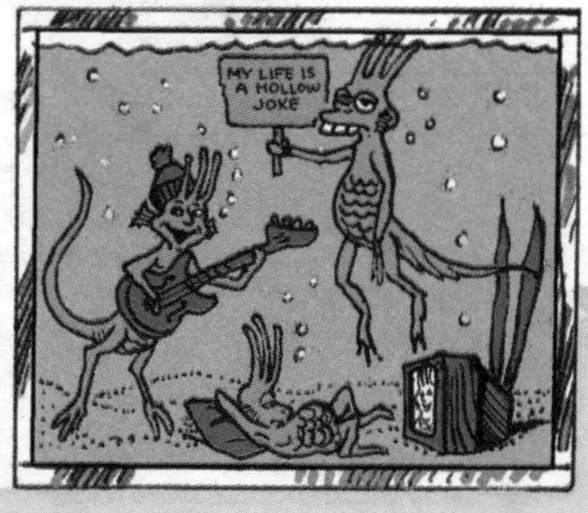
MY LIFE IS A HOLLOW JOKE

Yes, it'll be amazing if you see anything that even looks like monkeys! What is this crap - shrimp? Algae? One thing's for darn sure, it ain't loveable critters that play instruments. In fact, they pretty much do squat!

HOURS OF REGRET!

The fun never starts. Just empty the package of crystals into a bowl of water and you will immediately walk away in disgust. It's your money, pal.

THEY OBEY YOUR COMMANDS

As long as you keep 'em reasonable. "Smite my enemies" is out of the question, but easy stuff like "Float in the bowl like a whole lotta nothing" keeps 'em busy for hours!

DON'T DELAY!

Or they'll be dead.

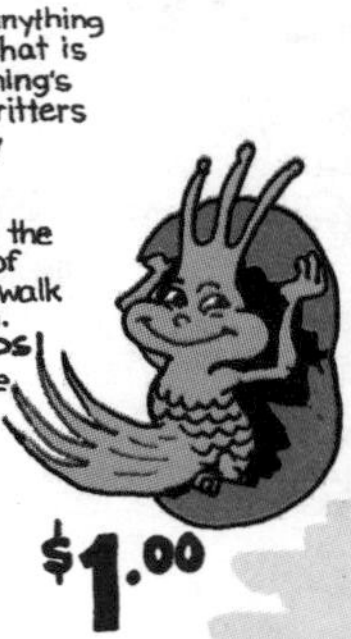

$1.00

THIS OFFER IS VOID WHERE YOU LIVE.

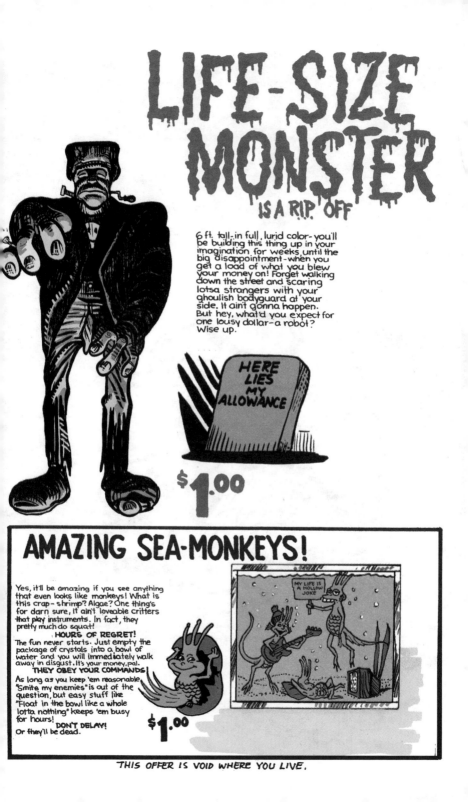

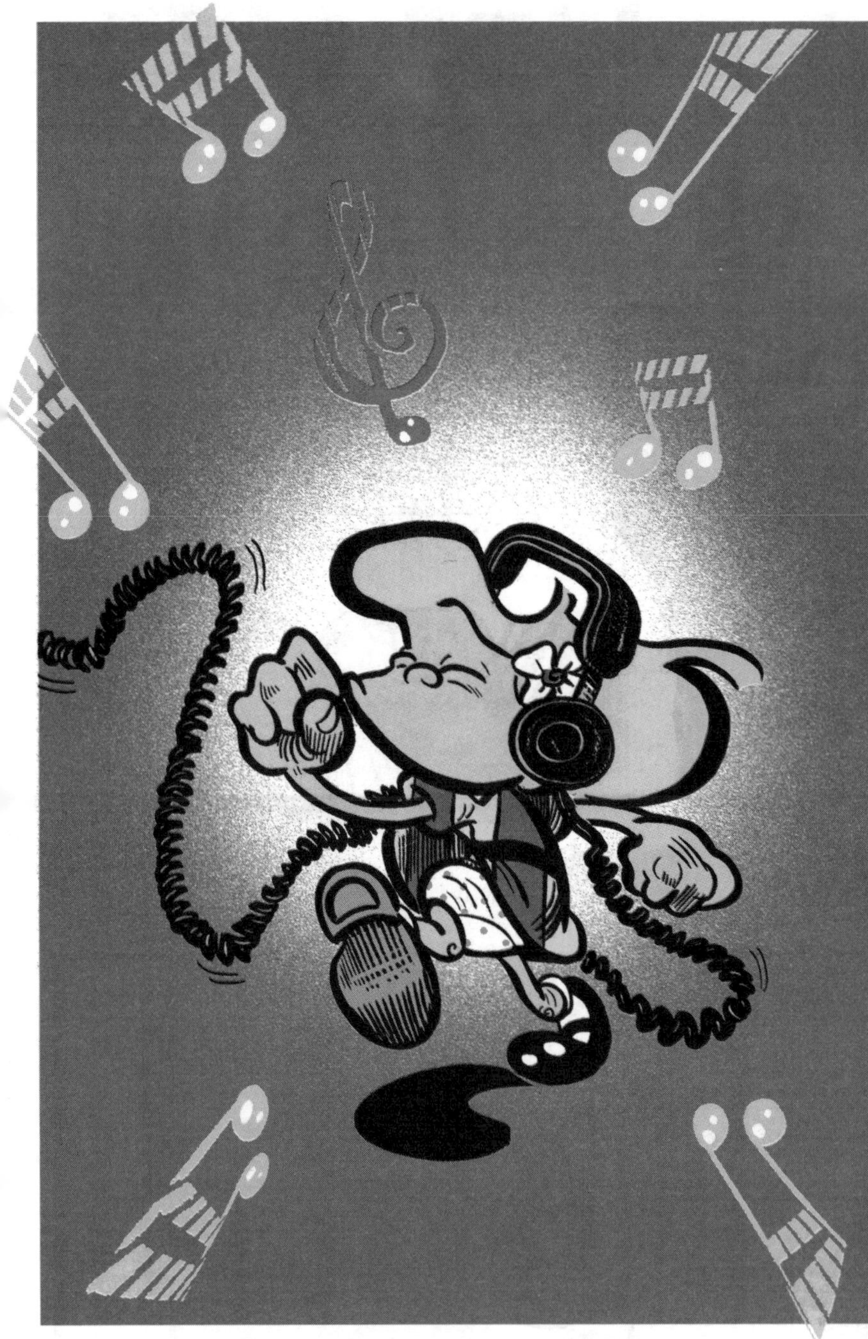

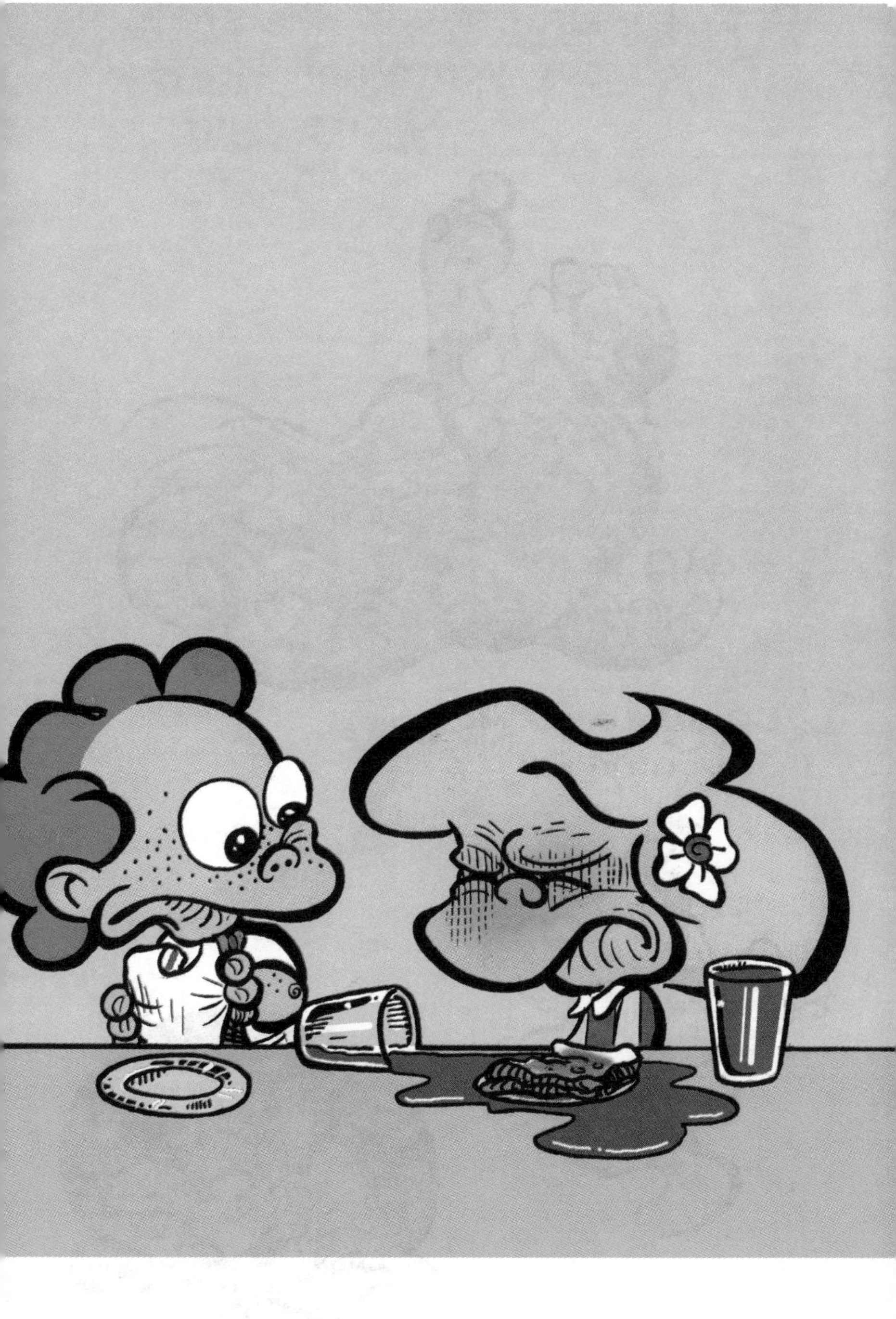

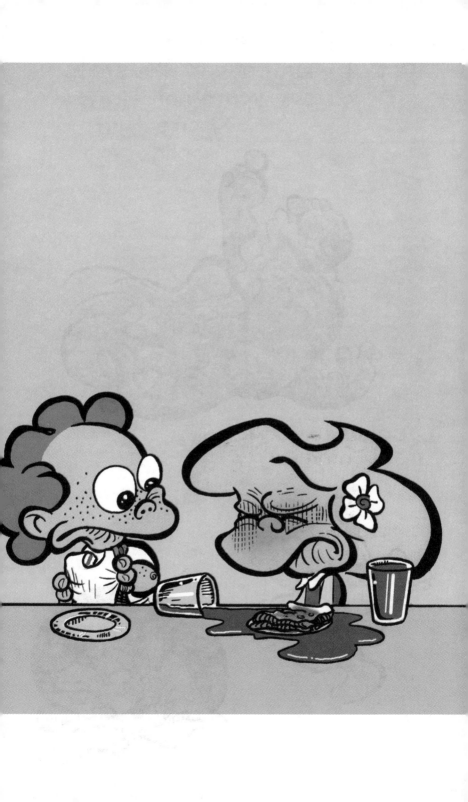

Hey little Sleepy Head-
Put your toys on the shelf.
If you say you're not tired
You're just
fooling yourself.

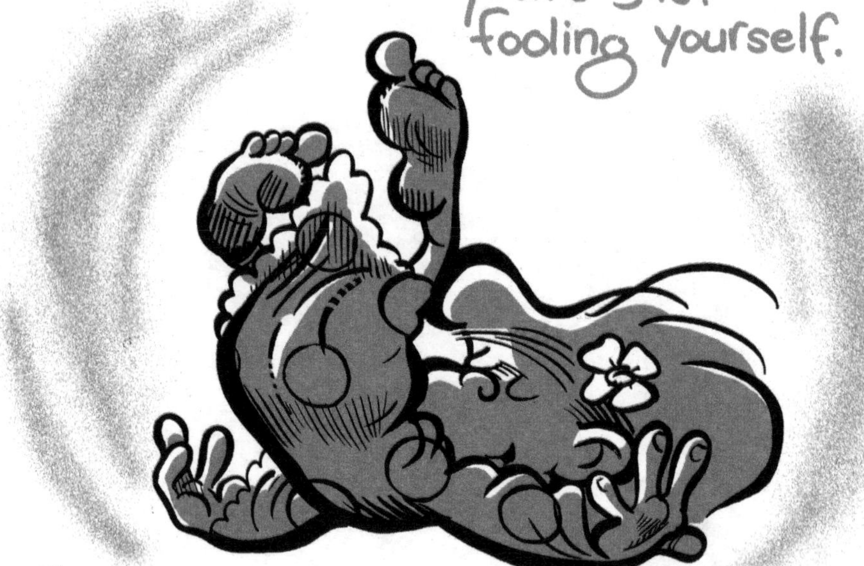

I caught you yawning
and turning away.

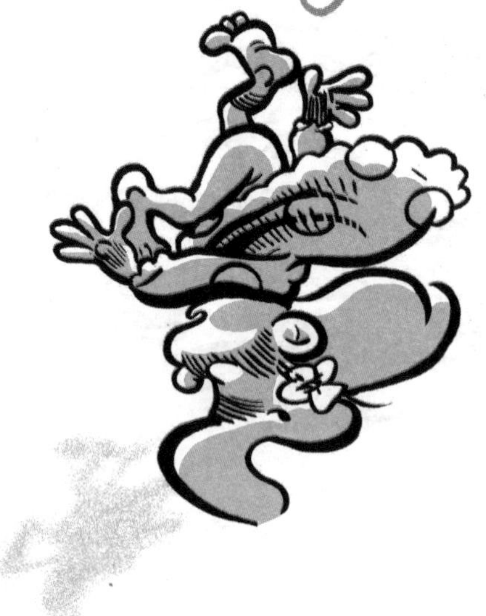

And I know when
you're cranky
It's been a long
day.

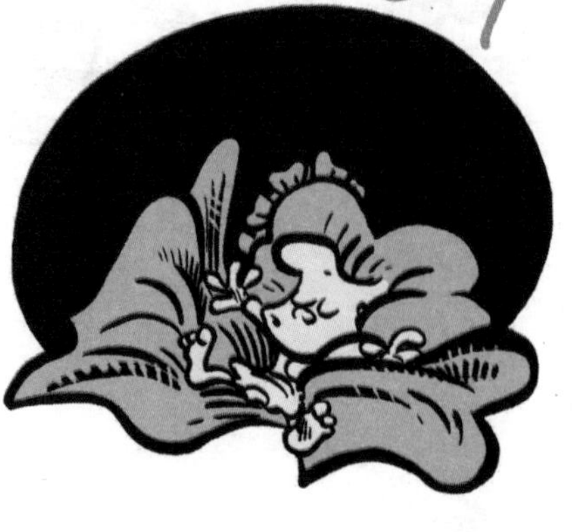

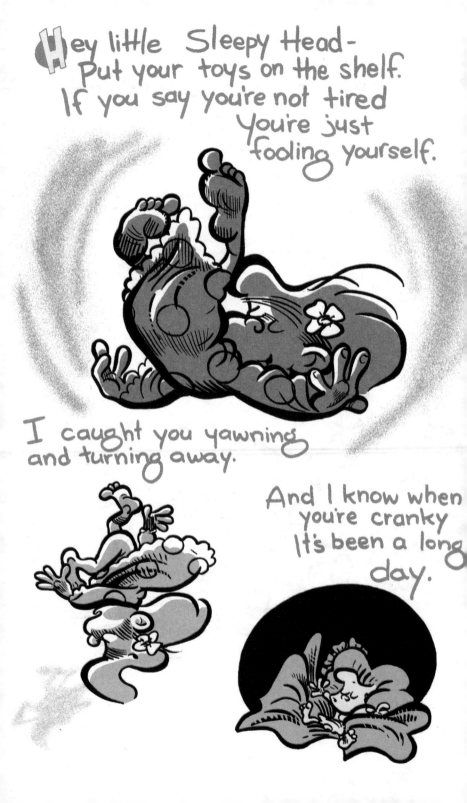

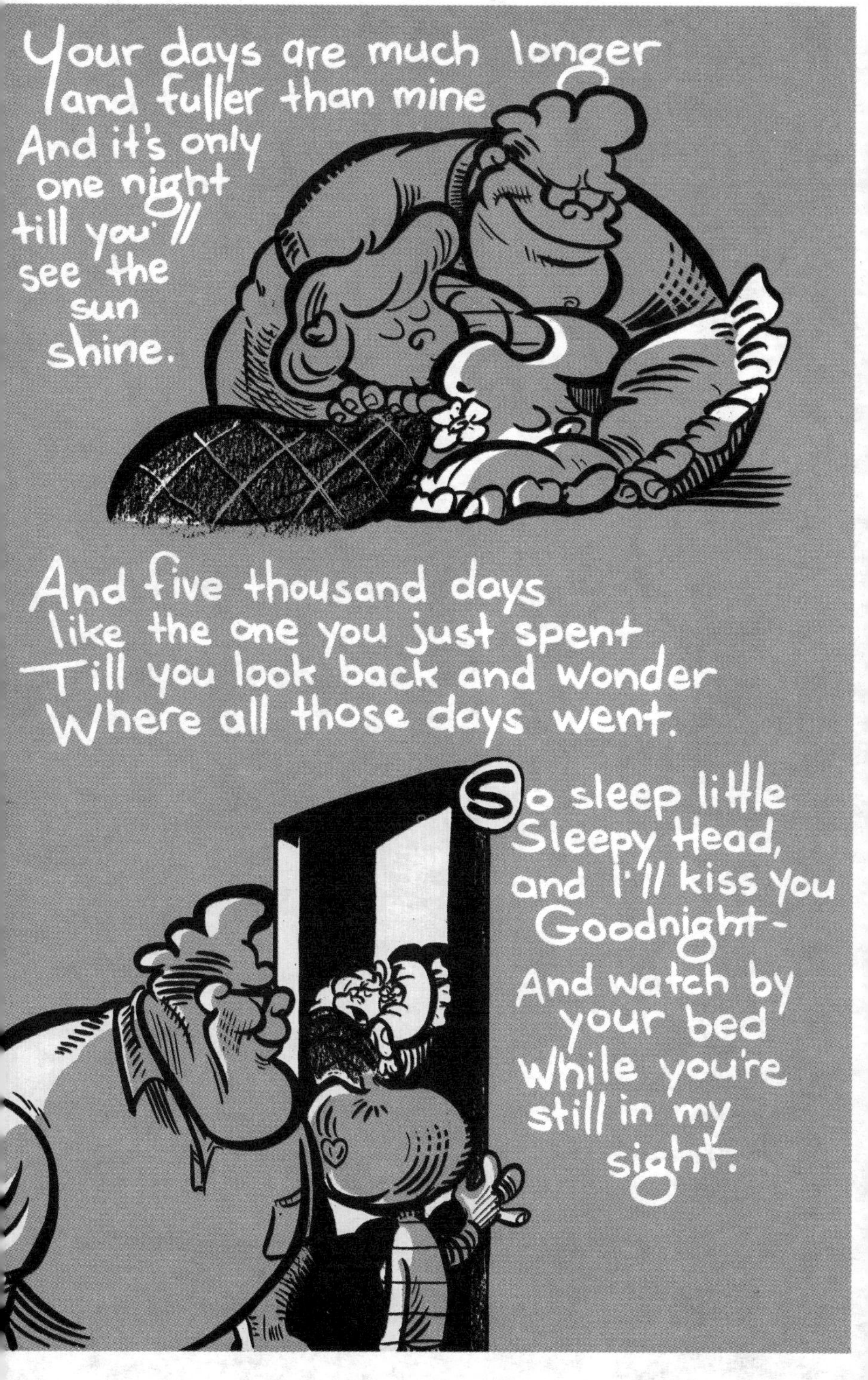
Your days are much longer and fuller than mine
And it's only one night till you'll see the sun shine.
And five thousand days like the one you just spent
Till you look back and wonder Where all those days went.
So sleep little Sleepy Head, and I'll kiss you Goodnight-
And watch by your bed While you're still in my sight.

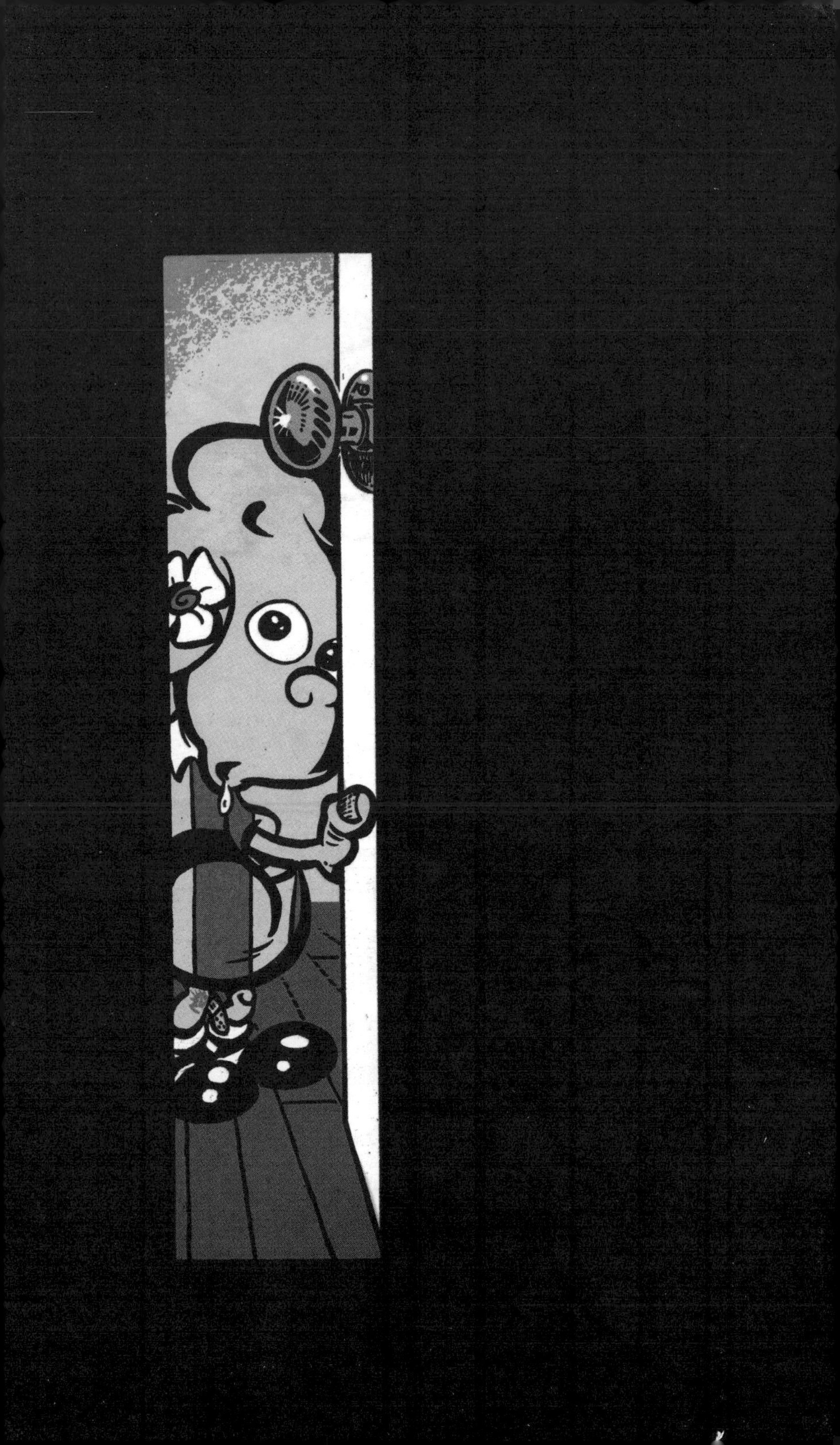